Technology, Education—Connections
The TEC Series

Series Editor: Marcia C. Linn.
Advisory Board: Robert Bjork, Chris Dede, BatSheva Eylon,
Carol Lee, Jim Minstrell, Mitch Resnick.

D0121631

Designing Coherent Science Education

Implications for Curriculum, Instruction, and Policy

EDITED BY

Yael Kali, Marcia C. Linn,
and Jo Ellen Roseman

FOREWORD BY

Robert Tinker

Teachers College, Columbia University
New York and London

This research is based on work supported by the National Science Foundation under grant numbers ESI-0334199 (TELS), ESI-0227557 (CCMS), ESI-0101780 and ESI-0439493 (IQWST), PECASE/CAREER Award REC-0092610 (CASES), ESI-98-19018 (Assessment), ESI-0103678 (Next Generation of Curriculum Materials), ESI-0412537 (Project Pathways), and ESI-0455877 (MODELS). Any opinions, findings, and conclusions or recommendations expressed in this material are those of the authors and do not necessarily reflect the views of the National Science Foundation.

Published by Teachers College Press, 1234 Amsterdam Avenue, New York, NY 10027

Credits and permissions for figures and tables appear on page 240.

Library of Congress Cataloging-in-Publication Data

Designing coherent science education : implications for curriculum, instruction, and policy / Yael Kali, Marcia C. Linn, and Jo Ellen Roseman, editors ; foreword by Robert Tinker.
    p. cm. — (Technology, Education—Connections: The TEC Series)
    Includes bibliographical references and index.
    ISBN 978-0-8077-4913-5 (pbk.)
    1. Science—Study and teaching—United States. 2. Science—Computer network resources. 3. Computer-assisted instruction—United States.
    4. Curriculum planning—United States. I. Kali, Yael. II. Linn, Marcia C.
    III. Roseman, Jo Ellen.

    LB1585.3.D467   2008
    507.1'073—dc22   2008013452

ISBN 978–0-8077-4913-5 (paper)

Printed on acid-free paper
Manufactured in the United States of America

15 14 13 12 11 10 09 08   8 7 6 5 4 3 2 1

Contents

PART III
Synthesis and Policy Implications

Foreword

I T IS OUT OF FASHION these days to focus on learning materials—teaching resources for students and teachers. For a quarter century starting in the mid-1960s, there was unbridled enthusiasm for generating new materials, which was seen as the best way to improve science education. The result was an outpouring of innovative materials for the study of science, starting with high school physics but eventually spreading to every grade and subject from kindergarten through the university. The improvements were almost always in the service of decreasing formalism by focusing on observations and reasoning and substituting vastly greater emphasis on hands-on experiences, vivid media, and discussion.

Viewed from the perspective of current research, many of the materials developed in the 1965–1990 period were excellent. Many attempted to cover less more deeply by focusing on key concepts and their interrelationships. The hands-on materials and discussions helped students develop and refine their own ideas. With some notable exceptions, the materials from that era are now in need of revision and updating to cover new content, take advantage of technology, and incorporate research findings.

In spite of all the enthusiasm and the quality of the materials developed in that earlier period, few were widely adopted and there was no discernible national improvement in student outcomes. As a result, curriculum improvement fell out of favor as a strategy for improving science education. In the late 1980s it became obvious that the value of good materials could be negated by the school environment. One of the most apparent problems was the lack of clarity with regard to what should be taught and assessed. This led to the idea of "systemic change," based on the idea that student performance would improve if only there was an alignment of the topics taught, teacher professional development, and assessments. Enthusiasm for this perspective tended to ignore materials. It was assumed that there was a surfeit of good materials from which well-trained teachers could pick and choose.

Systemic change of precollege science education was a colossal waste of resources, largely because science is only a small part of educational systems that need wholesale change. Trying to change only the science component of education while not addressing larger change is futile. The shift in funding toward systemic initiatives in science, technology, engineering, and mathematics (STEM) put research and development on hold. Even so, the total funding available for STEM represented only roughly 0.1% of the cost of precollege education, and that tiny push did not cause discernible movement.

In the last decade, groups that are trying to improve science education have discounted the value of curricula, and funding agencies have retreated from trying to have any direct impact on science education, through either materials or systemic change. In their place has been increased interest in research. The goal has become to move science education from an art to a science, to document once and for all what works and what doesn't. From the resulting knowledge base, it is assumed that far more effective strategies and materials will evolve, somehow. This would, however, be an empty promise without better materials.

The interest in research is beginning to close the circle by focusing attention once again on learning materials. Classroom research requires reproducibility, and materials provide a way to control some of the natural variability in real schools. Researchers need good materials. Research tends to focus on one improvement at a time—use of an interactive model, employing a particular approach to sharing data, use of debates, or concentrating on evidence and argumentation. Studies of any one of these improvements must take place within a classroom that is using some kind of learning materials. If the materials have fundamental weaknesses, then the improvements being studied may not have any effect. As the Center for Curriculum Materials in Science (CCMS) has shown, most commercial textbooks have serious problems. For these reasons, researchers end up creating new materials to test their theories.

Researchers also need new materials to take advantage of technology. The Technology Enhanced Learning in Science (TELS) Center has shown that technology has much to offer researchers in terms of new instructional affordances and new research techniques. Technology is not essential to improved science education, but to ignore it would be to exclude a valuable resource that will be increasingly important in schools at all levels.

Computational models offer environments that can be explored in exactly the way students can explore a physical system or an open-ended lab. Probeware can extend the range and accuracy of real explorations. But exploration using either of these tools needs to be guided or students will waste time in unproductive dead ends. Technology can assist there, too, by providing scaffolding and help. Because these explorations are done on a computer, software can supply researchers with invaluable data on how students explore, what they learn, and what they miss. The data can be obtained implicitly by watching what choices students make and explicitly by asking questions or posing challenges. Real-time summaries of these same data will also be of great value to teachers.

The new, research-based focus on materials has led to a new appreciation of the importance of the web of knowledge. No discipline is just the sum of isolated facts and observations. Much of the knowledge is in the linkages between facts and observations. Science has unique depth and unity that are seldom accessible to learners in introductory courses. Its web needs to be developed at the lesson level by giving students opportunities to integrate their existing knowledge with new observations and ideas. This is the idea behind "knowledge integration," which is a central theme of the TELS Center. The web that is science knowledge must also be central to the planning of curricula, so that understanding builds coherently between topics and through years. This coherence has been central to the work at CCMS. Together, the two centers have helped focus attention on the importance of learning the web of science knowledge and using technology as appropriate to support this agenda.

This volume is a harbinger for this new approach to improving science education. It is based on the best of that earlier quarter century of curriculum development, improved by designs that are informed by current research, and powered by modern technology. The central theme of the book is that science learning and assessment must emphasize coherence across topics and courses. It provides a roadmap for how this can be done and reports important developments that come from initial traverses of that map. Researchers, materials developers, policy experts, and educators concerned about the state of science education should find hope and ideas in this volume that promise future improvements and innovations that will have lasting impact.

—Robert Tinker

Preface

Yael Kali, Mary Koppal,
Marcia C. Linn, and Jo Ellen Roseman

THIS COLLECTION draws national attention to the need for coherence in science education. Without guidance, students—and adults—often conclude that science has no relevance or utility outside of the science classroom (Linn & Hsi, 2000). Students may learn isolated facts from texts that they cannot connect to experiences outside the schoolroom. For example, some students conclude that objects in motion remain in motion in science class but come to rest on the playground. Students make conjectures based on personal observations, interactions with peers, or media depictions of science. They need curriculum materials that connect diverse examples and guidance to reconcile discrepancies. Students need a commitment to both having a sense of the connectedness of science ideas and having the inclination to link ideas together and apply them to the situation at hand. Knowledge integration includes deliberate efforts to explain observations of phenomena, make decisions about matters involving science and technology, and seek ways to resolve conundrums.

INTEGRATED UNDERSTANDING, KNOWLEDGE INTEGRATION, AND COHERENCE

For the purposes of this book, we use the term *integrated understanding* to describe the desired outcome of student learning, *knowledge integration* to describe the processes used to achieve that understanding, and *curricular coherence* to describe a quality of curriculum materials that can be used to achieve an integrated understanding of science. Students with integrated understanding can make sense of new ideas, identify gaps in their understanding, and engage in the process of improving their ideas throughout their lives. Coherence in science curriculum materials can be fostered within an activity, a unit, or a course, or across an entire curriculum. Coherence can be created through the design of curriculum materials, through teacher interventions, and through the application of media and technology. *Designing Coherent Science Education* focuses attention on the diverse needs of students and how they can be helped to develop an integrated understanding of science over time (see Chapter 2, Roseman, Linn, & Koppal, for more details).

This book considers the factors that enable curricular coherence and development of knowledge integration, along with new opportunities and challenges for curriculum developers that are created by the use of technology and a principled and goals-based design process. Many forces work against curriculum coherence: the pressure to cover every possible topic, the perception (often but not always accurate) that high-stakes testing measures only superficial understanding, the disjointed nature of many texts, the use of abstract representations that can obscure science concepts, and some teachers' own lack of a deep and interconnected knowledge of science. Curriculum materials, whether they are technology enhanced or not, can be a force for, or against, coherence. They can supply an overwhelming torrent of isolated facts and confusing images. They can also provide powerful tools that can be used throughout a curriculum to help students extract the essential ideas and make important connections among them.

THE DECIDE PROJECT

The chapters in this book arise from the Delineating and Evaluating Coherent Instructional Designs for Education (DECIDE) project. The project brings together a multidisciplinary group of researchers who share an interest in the design and use of instructional materials that can help an increasingly diverse range of students to become literate in science. Supported by the National Science Foundation's Centers for Learning and Teaching program to strengthen the leadership and research capacity of K–16 science education, the DECIDE project is a collaboration of the Technology Enhanced Learning in Science (TELS) Center and the Center for Curriculum Materials in Science (CCMS). Involving about 60 scholars and practitioners from more than 25 universities and academic institutions, the DECIDE project aims to synthesize ideas about coherence in science education—focusing especially on curriculum materials and their use—in ways that can inform the work of others.

Both TELS and CCMS conduct research that has documented the lack of coherence in current curriculum materials and the lack of integrated understanding in students' science learning outcomes. TELS approaches coherence through the knowledge integration framework (Linn, 1995; Linn, Davis, & Bell, 2004). TELS is particularly concerned with the design issues encountered when powerful tools and modeling technologies are used in teaching and learning.

CCMS approaches coherence by focusing its materials design research and development efforts on the learning goals articulated in national benchmarks and standards and by adhering to a set of core principles that guide its work (Center for Curriculum Materials in Science, http://www.sciencematerialscenter.org/about_mission.htm; Krajcik, McNeill, & Reiser, 2008). The DECIDE project enabled TELS, CCMS, and other groups concerned with design of science instruction to synthesize research, identify promising research questions, and communicate their findings widely.

This volume provides an opportunity for the two centers to share design principles and issues with a wide audience of education researchers, faculty, students, and policy makers and with the developers and publishers of materials and technologies for science instruction.

THE DECIDE PROCESS: SYNTHESIZING DESIGN KNOWLEDGE

Rather than presenting a collection of independent views held by experts in science curriculum design research, the DECIDE project aimed at synthesis. Through research and practice, TELS and CCMS have built their design knowledge, some of which is unique to each center and some which is common to both centers. Although the centers have emphasized different approaches, the DECIDE project sought to synthesize their design knowledge by identifying the underlying assumptions and guiding principles of each center, negotiating the meanings of terms, specifying methods and procedures, and articulating common ground. As expressed in Chapter 8 (Kali, Fortus, & Ronen-Fuhrmann), "The value of such negotiation is to overcome communication issues that arise from the existence of 'intra-center jargons' in which a great deal of design knowledge is implicitly embedded. These intra-center jargons are useful to each center and facilitate communication regarding the development of coherent materials and research, but they can impede others' access to this design knowledge. By negotiating both centers' design knowledge, we sought to become more aware of intra-center knowledge and to create a more explicit and communicative body of design knowledge" (p. 186).

Guiding Principles, Design Principles, and Pedagogical Criteria

The centers identified three approaches to synthesis. First, both centers had devised *guiding principles* to elucidate their overall commitments. These guiding principles turned out to be very similar. For example, both centers are guided by the idea of focusing materials on science learning goals. These guiding principles could be merged as shown in Chapter 2.

Second, members of both centers have collaborated to characterize *design principles*, which are represented (among others) in the Design Principles Database (http://www.edu-design-principles.org; Kali, 2006; see Chapter 8). Design principles are rules of thumb or guidelines supported by research results that draw attention to similar successful features in distinct instructional approaches. For example, "Enable just-in-time guidance" is a design principle. Discussions leading to the articulation of design principles can strengthen the synthesis of design knowledge (Kali, Spitulnik, & Linn, 2004). Each of the chapters in Part II of this book highlights design principles resulting from the deliberations of the authors and the community.

Third, the CCMS group has benefited from criteria devised for textbook evaluation (Kesidou & Roseman, 2002). The criteria are specific for assessing the degree of coherence that textbooks offer and the support they provide for effective teaching and learning. (For more details, see Chapter 2.)

The DECIDE Process

To foster synthesis, the DECIDE project organized a series of working sessions and conferences. These meetings led to clarification of the meaning of coherence in the context of curriculum materials and in the context of students' understanding (see Chapter 2). To explore the connections across the two centers, we identified five key topics that encompassed the work of the centers. Teams of researchers from both centers synthesized their work on each of the topics and contributed a chapter to the book (the five chapters in Part II). Their syntheses focus on (a) designing learning environments that support students in constructing integrated understandings of science, (b) designing science instruction for diverse learners, (c) supporting teachers in productive adaptation of learning materials, (d) building leadership for scaling science curriculum reform, and (e) assessing integrated understanding of science.

To increase the cohesiveness and breadth of the book, the synergy teams used additional DECIDE working sessions to present their work for discussion by all of the project researchers and chapter authors. In several rounds of internal peer review, each author also provided feedback on at least two other chapters. The culminating activity of the DECIDE project was a 4-day Synergy Conference (http://sites.google.com/a/edu-design-principles.org/decide/) attended by contributors to this book and by invited participants, including leading researchers, educators, and policy makers in science education. Among the invited guests were scholars from a number of institutions and programs. Several guests represented four other National Science Foundation (NSF)–funded Centers for Learning and Teaching: the Center for Informal Learning and Schools (CILS), the Center for Learning and Teaching in Nanoscale Science and Engineering (NCLT), the Learning in Informal and Formal Environments (LIFE) Center, and the Center for the Assessment and Evaluation of Student Learning (CAESL). By providing a venue for sharing our initial syntheses with other researchers and policy makers, the Synergy Conference enabled us to gain a broader perspective on the relevant issues and to find ways to meet the needs of those who make decisions in the field. We expect that the current book, resulting from this synergistic process, will become an important contribution to the literature on science education and curriculum reform.

WHERE WE COME FROM: THE TWO CENTERS

The CCMS Mission

The mission of CCMS is to develop the knowledge and leadership needed to improve curriculum materials for K–12 science education so that all students— whatever their culture, language, gender, interests, or learning styles—can achieve science literacy. This mission derives from widely held beliefs about the potential value of curriculum materials, reported shortcomings of existing materials, and the lack of a coordinated effort focused on improving science curriculum materials since the post-Sputnik era.

Curriculum Materials and Learning. Curriculum materials can powerfully affect what and how science is taught. Technology-based materials as well as traditional textbooks are a primary source of science content, and they promote specific views about the nature of science and about the nature of science teaching and learning. For students, materials can provide engaging activities that explore scientific phenomena, along with helpful analogies, clear explanations, and accurate representations that help students understand the underlying scientific concepts. Materials can also help to contextualize the content that will be learned and to pose questions that will help students make connections among ideas and develop a more sophisticated conceptual framework. For teachers, curriculum materials can provide opportunities to increase their own knowledge of science and of appropriate pedagogy (Schneider, Krajcik, & Marx, 2000). Materials can also alert teachers to students' prior conceptions about specific content, suggest ways to activate students' prior knowledge, and provide suggestions for scaffolding student learning (Lee, Eichinger, Anderson, Berkheimer, & Blakeslee, 1993; Roth, Anderson, & Smith, 1987).

Shortcomings of Existing Materials. Although findings from cognitive science research offer suggestions for the design of effective curriculum materials (Bransford, Brown, & Cocking, 2000), there is a growing concern that on many counts existing materials do not measure up. In its evaluations of middle school and high school science textbooks, Project 2061 of the American Association for the Advancement of Science (AAAS) found that none of the major textbook publishers provided a coherent approach to content or adequate instructional support for teaching and learning (Kesidou & Roseman, 2002). In a separate study sponsored by the David and Lucile Packard Foundation, Hubisz (n.d.) found similar weaknesses in physics textbooks. Most textbooks do not develop science ideas in a systematic manner that will help students build rich understanding of key ideas. Moreover, most curriculum materials do not motivate students to learn science (Yager & Penick, 1986) or to make use of new learning technologies, or nor do they enable teachers to adopt innovative instructional strategies (Krajcik, Blumenfeld, Marx, & Soloway, 2000). Most curriculum materials also fail to provide teachers with resources for continuous assessment of students as they work toward attainment of lesson and topic objectives (Gallagher, 2000).

No Coordinated Effort to Improve Materials. The formation of CCMS was also motivated by the lack of coordinated effort focused on the broad array of issues related to curriculum materials. The knowledge base in this area has been limited, dispersed, and often disconnected from materials development (AAAS, 2005), and there has been an ongoing shortage of leaders able to focus their research and development efforts on K–12 science materials.

CCMS attempts to address these needs directly and, at the same time, to increase the nation's capacity to create high-quality curriculum materials that can help all students achieve science literacy. Drawing on the varied resources of its partner institutions—AAAS Project 2061, Michigan State University, Northwestern University, and the University of Michigan—CCMS engages in research and development activities aimed at improving the quality and use of curriculum materials for K–12 science education.

CCMS Research and Development. The CCMS research agenda focuses on aspects of the design of science curricula that are critical to their quality and effective use. These include the needs to focus on important science learning goals, build pedagogical supports into the materials themselves, take advantage of student investigations to help students understand specific science ideas as well as the nature of science, incorporate learning technologies into materials, serve the needs of diverse science learners, support teachers' implementation and adaptation of materials, and take account of policy implications. With regard to science learning goals, for example, CCMS researchers have found that efforts to unpack and clarify the goals enhance designers' understanding of the goals and lead to curriculum and assessment materials that are better aligned with them (Krajcik et al., 2008; Chapter 2; Chapter 3, Krajcik, Slotta, McNeill, & Reiser; Chapter 7, DeBoer, Lee, & Husic). CCMS researchers are also designing theoretical learning progressions for a variety of topics (AAAS, 2001, 2007; Roseman,

Caldwell, Gogos, & Kurth, 2006), incorporating the notion of learning progressions into the design of multi-year curricula (Krajcik & Reiser, 2006; Shwartz, Weizman, Fortus, Krajcik, & Reiser, in press), and investigating the effectiveness of such sequences in promoting student learning (Duschl, Schweingruber, & Shouse, 2007; Merritt, Schwartz, & Krajcik, 2007).

In addition, CCMS research seeks to identify attributes of curriculum materials that support local adaptation and attend to the learning needs of all students (Chapter 4, Tate, Clark, Gallagher, & McLaughlin; Chapter 5, Davis & Varma). Investigators are particularly interested in how science curriculum materials can incorporate goal-specific pedagogical supports for students and teachers, such as those articulated in Project 2061's textbook analysis criteria (Roseman, Kesidou, & Stern, 1996), Edelson's learning-for-use framework (2001), and Hiebert's framework for problematizing the content to be learned (Hiebert, Carpenter, Fuson, Human, & Wearne, 1996). The curriculum development process itself, teacher learning, and the design of educative curriculum materials are also important areas of CCMS research. Results from CCMS research and reports on ongoing studies are accessible through an online research bibliography on the CCMS Web site (http://www.sciencematerialscenter.org).

The TELS Mission

TELS brings university researchers together with middle school and high school educators to improve instruction in science. TELS includes seven universities, a nonprofit educational research and development organization, and seven school districts. The focus is to investigate how instructional technology can benefit teaching and learning in science. Through this research, participants seek to increase the numbers and diversity of teachers who are using innovative, proven, technology-enhanced science curricula to impart key scientific concepts and methods to their students. TELS participants have identified four research themes for exploring the overall research question: What impact do scientific simulations embedded in inquiry projects have on science learning? The four themes are (a) Curriculum design: Designing and implementing inquiry projects with embedded, high-quality simulations; (b) Teacher learning: Designing and implementing programs for teachers; (c) Assessment: Designing and interpreting assessments; (d) TELS technologies: Designing and implementing open source information technology and building communities of designers.

TELS Curriculum Modules. TELS curricula incorporate interactive software and simulations that guide students' work so that they learn to use scientific inquiry as they examine complex topics in science. These curricula fulfill local and national standards for middle school or high school science classrooms.

TELS projects engage students in scientific inquiry through challenging collaborative activities that emphasize visualization, simulation, and investigation, using information technology.

TELS Curriculum Design Process. Teachers, administrators, and students universally agree that modeling and visualization are essential aspects of scientific literacy (Cullin & Crawford, 2004; Kali, 2002; Shternberg & Yerushalmy, 2003; White & Frederiksen, 1998; Wilensky & Reisman, 2006). Yet students often find simulations and visualizations difficult to understand and epistemologically complex (Tversky, Morrison, & Betrancourt, 2002). To meet this challenge, TELS researchers engaged with teachers and students in partner schools through a process of design, testing, and adaptation of curriculum to develop 12 curriculum units (see Chapter 2).

TELS Technologies. TELS has its roots in the Computer as Learning Partner (CLP) project, which studied the use of data and visualizations in personally relevant contexts (Songer & Linn, 1991). Following CLP, the Knowledge Integration Environment (KIE) project made further progress in developing richly contextualized learning environments (Linn, Bell, & Davis, 2004). The Web-Based Inquiry Science Environment (WISE) project built on KIE to develop a technology framework for scaffolding students and teachers as they performed such inquiry projects. WISE includes an easy-to-use authoring system that allows researchers to rapidly develop the project designs, which also enables rapid cycles of iterative refinement based on observations in the classroom and analysis of student achievement (Slotta, 2004). The resulting projects include a variety of tools and inquiry scaffolds that enable students and teachers to succeed in the complex patterns of collaborative inquiry. Recently, the TELS technology team has created a new Java-based infrastructure for designing, developing, and delivering computer-based curricula that depend on sophisticated applications such as probeware and computational models. A key new technology is the Scalable Architecture for Interactive Learning (SAIL) (see more detail in Chapter 2).

TELS Assessment Activities. The TELS approach to assessment focuses on measuring how successfully students evaluate and change their perceptions about science in light of new information. This approach offers insight into both the overall benefit of TELS projects and the specific impacts of scientific simulations. Consistent with the knowledge integration framework that guides the design of TELS curriculum materials, the TELS assessments ask students to link and connect ideas and give explanations for their conjectures. TELS created six benchmark tests, each composed of comparable research-based and standardized items measuring knowledge integration. The tests cover middle school physical science, life science, and earth science, as well as high school biology, chemistry, and physics (for more detail on the TELS assessment process, see Chapter 7).

Results of TELS Coherent Curriculum Design. Using the benchmark tests described above, the TELS assessment team conducted a cohort comparison study and analyzed pretest and posttest performance. TELS compared students using the typical curriculum with students using the TELS materials taught by the same teachers and found significant advantages for TELS users (Linn, Lee, Tinker, Husic, & Chiu, 2006). Subsequent research investigations have explored the factors that make TELS materials effective.

Pretests, posttests, and embedded assessments provide precise information about student learning at the project level and on a minute-by-minute basis. Many TELS projects embed assessments prior to and following the use of scientific visualizations to gain insight into the impact these visualizations have on student understanding (see the design principle "Embed assessment-for-learning within instruction" in Chapter 8).

TELS Synthesis. TELS has synthesized findings from these and other studies in the Design Principles Database (http://www.edu-design-principles.org; Kali, 2006; Chapter 8). The database includes features from more than 70 innovative curricular projects that have been enhanced with educational technology and lists about 35 design principles contributed and refined by hundreds of researchers.

WHAT'S IN THE BOOK?

Part I sets the stage for this volume's synthesis of curriculum design knowledge. Pea and Collins (Chapter 1) offer a historical perspective, describing four waves of science education reform that have occurred over the past five or six decades. To frame the issues explored in the remainder of the book, we continue with Roseman, Linn, and Koppal's (Chapter 2) characterization of what curriculum coherence and integrated understanding mean. Their chapter describes the approaches of CCMS and TELS to the design of coherent curriculum materials that promote an integrated understanding of science, proposes a common set of criteria for coherent curriculum materials including technology-enhanced materials, and identifies research that would advance the field.

Part II explores five key topics that are central to the work of CCMS and TELS and offers useful syntheses of relevant principles and findings. In Chapter 3, on the design of learning environments, Krajcik, Slotta, McNeill, and Reiser describe six shared design principles that TELS and CCMS use to inform the development of coherent instructional materials and technology tools to create effective learning environments that support students in constructing integrated understandings. Chapter 4 deals with diversity: Tate, Clark, Gallagher, and McLaughlin unpack and illustrate what it means to design science learning materials that respect the diverse ideas and learning practices students bring to science class and that enable all learners to generate, evaluate, and reflect on the links among their ideas. Supporting teachers is the focus of Chapter 5, where Davis and Varma present the two centers' constellations of approaches for supporting teachers in productive adaptation of curriculum material as a facet of enhancing their teaching practices and increasing their knowledge development. In Chapter 6, Bowyer, Gerard, and Marx consider the role of leadership in scaling and sustaining science curriculum reform by examining the successes and challenges of several professional development programs for administrators, principals, and teacher-leaders. Chapter 7 addresses assessment: DeBoer, Lee, and Husic describe various approaches to the development and use of assessments for determining how well students are achieving particular learning goals identified in national, state, and local content standards documents.

Part III offers further synthesis of the five key topics explored in Part II. In Chapter 8, Kali, Fortus, and Ronen-Fuhrmann describe seven design principles that are common to both CCMS and TELS. Finally, in Chapter 9, Linn, Kali, Davis, and Horwitz discuss implications of the issues explored in the DECIDE project for policy makers.

ACKNOWLEDGMENTS

We express our deepest gratitude to the participants in the DECIDE project for engaging in the challenging endeavor of synthesizing design knowledge and crafting the synergetic chapters, which are the heart of this book: Jane Bowyer, Doug Clark, Betsy Davis, George DeBoer, David Fortus, Jim Gallagher, Paul Horwitz, Libby Gerard, Freda Husic, Mary Koppal, Joe Krajcik, Hee-Sun Lee, Ron Marx, David McLaughlin, Kate McNeill, Brian Reiser, Tamar Ronen-Fuhrmann, Jim Slotta, Erika Tate, and Keisha Varma. We especially appreciate the wonderful historical perspective that Roy Pea and Allan Collins conceived to place this work in context. We thank Bob Tinker for sharing his reflections on the DECIDE project in the Foreword.

We are grateful for the enlightening discussions and thoughtful comments by our guest participants at the Synergy Conference in Asilomar (June 2007): Alicia Alonzo, Brigid Barron, Phil Bell, Phyllis Blumenfeld, Joe Campione, Raj Chaudhury, Allan Collins, Rick Duschl, Barry Fishman, John Frederiksen, Paul Horwitz, Sherry Hsi, Doug Kirkpatrick, Ann Novak, Roy Pea, Deborah Peek-Brown, Tony Petrosino, Chris Quintana, Ed Smith, Sean Smith, Iris Tabak, and Michelle Williams. A great contribution to these discussions was also provided by graduate student participants Jenny Chiu, Kristin Gunckel, Cheryl Madeira, Joi Merritt, Vanessa Peters, and Beat Schwendimann.

We extend special thanks to Ji Shen, Libby Gerard, and Jane Bowyer for collecting invaluable information about the type of knowledge policy makers seek from our synthesis, and for conducting the "Listening to the Policy Audience" activity at the Synergy Conference, which helped all of us become more attentive to these voices.

We appreciate the tremendous help and devotion of our project manager, Suki Lechner. The DECIDE working meetings, and especially the Synergy Conference, could not have happened without her thoughtful coordination. We also thank David Crowell for his technical and administrative support in organizing the Synergy Conference. We appreciate the assistance in manuscript preparation from Jonathan Brietbart and Ornit Sagi. We also appreciate our colleagues at CCMS, TELS, and elsewhere for their contributions to the development of this book.

Finally, we especially thank our program officers at the National Science Foundation for their guidance, support, and encouragement. We have benefited from the insights of John "Spud" Bradley, Janice Earle, and Michael Haney.

PART I

Framing
the
Argument

1

Learning How to Do
Science Education:
Four Waves of Reform

Roy D. Pea and Allan Collins

I N THE MODERN ERA of the past half century, we have seen four waves of science education reform activity. Our view is that these waves are building toward cumulative improvement of science education as a learning enterprise. Each wave (a) has been distinguished by a different focus of design, (b) has been led by different primary proponents, and (c) has contributed to new learning about what additional emphases will be necessary to achieve desirable outcomes for science education—and each wave has been followed by a consequent new wave of activity and design. Consideration of these four waves will help contextualize the contributions represented in this volume.

The first wave occurred in the 1950s and 1960s in response to a sense that our schools were not providing the challenging education in science needed to maintain America's edge as a center of scientific research in the post–World War II period. This era of science reform was spawned in significant measure by the creation of the National Science Foundation (NSF) in 1950 and its dramatically accelerated funding following the Soviet Union's 1957 launch of the first man-made space satellite, Sputnik. Scientists in major research universities were leading proponents of new science curricula in this wave, which aimed to introduce students to recent scientific advances and to expose them to use of the scientific method. Teachers' needs to learn this new content, and a focus on all students—not only the elite—were relatively neglected factors, as implementations of these curricula evidenced.

The second wave in the 1970s and 1980s was characterized by cognitive science studies of learners' reasoning in the context of science education. These studies led to careful accounts of differences in expert and novice patterns of thinking and reasoning. As studies were designed to investigate novice and expert reasoning differences, science educators began to consider new ways to diagnose students' developmental levels of understanding in order to foster learning trajectories from novice to expert (e.g., confronting misconceptions, providing bridging analogies). Technologies were developed to enable broader access to learning with simulations and dynamic visualizations of complex scientific concepts and systems. Issues of curriculum standards, teacher development, assessment design, and educational leadership were less central to this wave than in the reform wave that would follow.

The third wave in the late 1980s and 1990s involved the creation of national and state standards to specify what students should know and be able to do at particular grade levels and in specific subject domains (e.g., the *National Science Education Standards*). New learning assessments were also developed in accord with this emphasis on standards, and the needs were recognized to index curricula to specific standards and to align standards, curricula, and assessments. Relatively neglected were the realities of teacher customization of curriculum implementation to serve local needs, the need for fostering coherence of learners' scientific understanding, and the importance of embedded assessments to guide teacher support for improving student learning.

The fourth wave involves the emergence of a systemic approach to designing learning environments for advancing coherent understanding of science subject matter by learners. Science educators and researchers have recognized the need for planful coordination of curriculum design, activities, and tools to support (a) different teaching methods that will foster students' expertise in linking and connecting disparate ideas concerning science, (b) embedded learning assessments to guide instructional practices, and (c) teacher professional development to foster continued learning about how to improve teaching practice. The contributions in this volume represent this fourth wave.

It is important to observe that in any one of these waves of science education reform, there were voices anticipating the emergence of subsequent waves. Our aim is to highlight the dominant central tendencies of American science education reforms during these periods.

THE CURRICULUM REFORM MOVEMENT

Starting in the 1950s there was an outcry against low standards in America's schools that were alleged to have been brought on by the progressive movement in education, which had fostered "life adjustment" education for greater functional relevance to the everyday activities of students. The implication of the life adjustment approach for science education was a focus on application rather than mastery of structured subject matter (DeBoer, 1991; National Society for the Study of Education, 1947). The dissatisfaction with education standards only intensified with the Soviet Union's 1957 launch of the 23-inch-wide, 184-pound Sputnik 1 satellite aboard the world's first intercontinental ballistic missile. Some described this event as a "technological Pearl Harbor" (Halberstam, 1993). Many worried that Soviet scientific prowess had surpassed that of the United States, and Cold War anxieties intensified, with concern that the satellite represented a precursor capability to nuclear attack. Only a month later the USSR launched the far larger 1,120-pound Sputnik 2, spawning fears that missiles were shortly to follow. In response to the Sputnik satellites, within a year the United States government had formed the National Aeronautics and Space Administration (NASA) and the Defense Advanced Research Projects Agency (DARPA), dramatically enhanced NSF research funding, and reformulated science, technology, engineering, and mathematics education policy with the National Defense Education Act (Stine, 2007). This momentum accelerated the efforts—already under way in 1956—of a group of scientists funded by the NSF (as well as the Ford Foundation and the Alfred P. Sloan Foundation) to develop a new curriculum for high school physics that would focus on science as the product of theory and human inquiry through experimentation (Physical Science Study Committee [PSSC]: see Finlay, 1962).

Related efforts followed for high school biology (Biological Sciences Curriculum Study [BSCS]: Glass, 1962), chemistry (Chemical Bond Approach [CBA]: Strong, 1962; CHEM [Chemical Education Material] Study: Merrill & Ridgway, 1969), earth science, and later the social sciences. Jerome Bruner summarizes these views and their grounding in cognitive psychology in his famous 1960 book *The Process of Education*, which was his synthesis from a 10-day-long Woods Hole Conference of scientists and educators convened by the National Academy of Sciences. The curricula these scientists were developing had two goals: (a) to update the content of the materials taught to focus on the latest scientific developments, with a central emphasis on "structure" in terms of fundamental principles and their interrelationships; and (b) to teach scientific inquiry rather than a large array of facts. Students were engaged in hands-on activities designed to teach scientific measurement, hypothesis testing, and data analysis.

These curricula brought together the best ideas of scientists as to how to prepare young people for future careers in science and other occupations that would require systematic thinking and reasoning. In subsequent years, NSF funded introductory physical science courses, as well as elementary school science curricula pursuing the same goals as the high school courses: Science—A Process Approach (SAPA), Elementary Science Study (ESS), and Science Curriculum Improvement Study (SCIS).

How extensively were these curricula used? The new curricula met with initial enthusiasm and were taken up throughout the country by a variety of school districts. By the 1976–1977 school year, 49% of the surveyed school districts were using one of the versions of the BSCS biology materials, 20% were using either

CHEM Study or CBA chemistry materials, and 23% were using either PSSC or Harvard Project physics materials (DeBoer, 1991, pp. 166–167). However, the traditional Holt textbooks were still dominant in the three high school science subjects. And although the biology curriculum met with initial success, there developed a backlash to its emphasis on teaching evolution. The strongest reaction to the new curricula came with "Man: A Course of Study," which was developed to teach social studies to middle school students (Dow, 1991). The course featured comparisons of animal behavior to human behavior, and included videos of Eskimos and the moral decisions they face due to the harsh conditions of living in the Arctic. These topics raised two concerns among conservative Americans: (a) Comparisons of humans with animals seemed to imply that humans were simply animals, which they thought would encourage kids to behave like animals. (b) The Eskimo videos appeared to support *moral relativism*, which violated beliefs in absolute moral standards of behavior. The backlash against the curricula put reauthorization of the National Science Foundation at risk, and led to the end of all curriculum development by the NSF in the early 1980s.

In addition to these salient backlashes, there were many reasons why the curricula were not taken up more widely throughout American schools. Educational faculty were only marginally involved in most of the curriculum development efforts, so unrealistic assumptions were made about the contexts of curriculum implementation. The materials were more sophisticated than most students were accustomed to, and thus their use was concentrated among the strongest science students, who might go on to careers in science. Because the curricula involved scientific inquiry, they required materials that were difficult to manage and that teachers were often unfamiliar with. Hence, the courses were more difficult to teach, which discouraged many teachers from taking them on. Further, the NSF did not invest heavily enough in professional development to support teachers in making the transition to this new approach to science teaching, and often teachers who did adopt the curricula continued to teach in their traditional manner. The approach was in fact so novel, with its emphasis on scientific inquiry, that it is not clear whether most teachers even had the background to master the understanding required to teach the material effectively. And finally, as Hurd (1970) highlighted in reviewing these unprecedented science curriculum reform efforts, the everyday life relevancies of science and the motivations for learning science relating to them were underemphasized. This was an issue not only for the learners but also for the parents, community leaders, teachers, school administrators, and other stakeholders whose support for these reforms was needed.

When the curriculum reform movement faded, the scientists who had been leaders in the attempt to improve K–12 science and mathematics education went back to their laboratories and largely gave up on improving science education. Their movement was followed by a new effort in the cognitive sciences to study the nature of scientific understanding and to develop new tools for fostering student learning.

THE COGNITIVE SCIENCE MOVEMENT

In the 1970s there developed a new approach to studying understanding and learning, inspired in part by the development of the digital computer and attempts to create artificially intelligent programs that could mimic human thinking and learning (Greeno, 1980). The computer provided a kind of lens through which to study how scientific experts do their work and how novices differ from experts in their approach to problems. Cognitive scientists believed that much expert knowledge is tacit, and hence missing from what is taught to students. By studying the contrasting ways that novices and experts think about scientific problems, cognitive scientists believed they could tease out the underlying tacit knowledge that experts use to solve problems. Then they planned to design learning environments that would embed the critical knowledge that learners needed to move through the stages toward expertise (Bruer, 1994; McGilly, 1994).

In carrying out this research agenda, cognitive scientists identified a large number of alternative conceptions about scientific phenomena that are common among novices and that systematically depart from expert knowledge (Smith, diSessa, & Roschelle, 1993/1994). For example, they identified a number of novice ideas about force and motion (e.g., diSessa, 1988; McCloskey, Caramazza, & Green, 1980), about the earth, sun, and moon system (e.g., Sadler, 1987; Vosniadou & Brewer, 1992), about electricity (e.g., Collins & Gentner, 1987), and about biology (e.g., Carey, 1985; Stewart, 1983). Researchers in this tradition have developed techniques for helping students overcome their misconceptions, through approaches such as bridging analogies (Clement, 1993) and identifying different facets of understanding requiring integration (Minstrell, 1991). There was also research directed at identifying and improving the strategies that students use to learn mathematics (Schoenfeld, 1985) and science (Chi, Bassok, Lewis, Reimann, & Glaser, 1989). The goal was to construct learning environments that directly addressed the understandings and misunderstandings that learners brought to learning about science.

A third focus of this work was to design computer-based learning environments that would enhance students' ability to learn science. Over the years cognitive scientists have developed a variety of computer-based environments that teach scientific inquiry and conceptual understanding, such as ThinkerTools (White, 1984), GenScope/Biologica (Hickey, Kindfeld, Horwitz, & Christie, 2003), Galapagos Finches (Reiser et al., 2001), and WISE (Linn & Hsi, 2000). Another goal has been the development of systems for creating scientific models, such as Boxer (diSessa, 2000), Model-It (Jackson, Stratford, Krajcik, & Soloway, 1994), and object-based parallel modeling languages such as StarLogo (Colella, Klopfer, & Resnick, 2001), NetLogo (Resnick & Wilensky, 1998), AgentSheets (Repenning & Sumner, 1995), and World-Maker (Ogborn, 1999). Yet other efforts have provided capacities for students to collect, graph, and analyze scientific data from the environments using sensors and probes (Soloway et al., 1999; Tinker & Krajcik, 2001), and have established scientific data visualization and "collaboratory" project-based inquiry environments for students (Edelson, Gordin, & Pea, 1999; Pea et al., 1997). The development of computer-based systems to foster science learning is still an active research area in the cognitive sciences.

Even as the cognitive science movement had vital influences over thought leaders in science education reform, its practical impact on any significant proportion of the nearly 50 million American K–12 students was minimal. Many of the insights about how to promote individual conceptual change in specific topics in science were derived from small-scale studies in local teaching environments and were not incorporated into curricula that were broadly accessible or implemented. The research-based technologies for engaging learners and teachers in scientific model building, inquiry activities collecting real-world data with sensors and probes, and scientific data visualization and analysis, among other approaches, have been more indicative of leading-edge schools and teachers than of the mainstream. Although part of the issue in the diffusion of these innovations is simply one of funding for technology appropriation on a suitable scale (e.g., Office of Technology Assessment, 1988; Pea, Wulf, Elliot & Darling, 2003; President's Committee of Advisors on Science and Technology, 1997), the scope of cognitive science studies was not inclusive enough to incorporate the issues of alignment with curriculum standards, needed teacher support and professional development activities, assessments for educational accountability, and other facets of the educational system that came to be recognized as essential to promoting learners' scientific understanding in real-world educational settings.

THE STANDARDS MOVEMENT

Following on the heels of *A Nation at Risk: The Imperative for Educational Reform* (National Commission on Excellence in Education, 1983), a new movement to improve science education began to develop national content standards as to what knowledge and skills students should acquire in K–12 education. As DeBoer (2000) makes clear, the timing was propitious, for the science education community was debating "whether science education was primarily about science content or primarily about science-based social issues" (p. 589), following the National Science Teachers Association's (1982) urging that the goal of science education was "to develop scientifically literate individuals who understand how science, technology, and society influence one another and who are able to use this knowledge in their everyday decision-making."

The new standard-setting effort, which worked to reconcile the poles of this debate by integrating them, was led by scientists, science educators, curriculum developers, and assessment experts (Bybee, 1997; Collins, 1998). The first effort along these lines was Project 2061: Science for All Americans, taken up by the

American Association for the Advancement of Science (AAAS: Rutherford & Ahlgren, 1991). Founded in 1985, Project 2061 is a long-term AAAS initiative to help all Americans become literate in science, mathematics, and technology. The work has attempted to specify the important themes in science and the habits of mind critical to science, as well as specifying the critical ideas and skills important to science.

Following the lead of the AAAS, and spurred by the dual events in 1989 of the National Governors' Association calling for "clear national performance goals" as a way to raise standards in education, and the release by the National Council of Teachers of Mathematics (1989) of its *Curriculum and Evaluation Standards for School Mathematics,* the National Research Council (NRC) began in 1992 to work to develop a set of *National Science Education Standards* for K–12 science education (NRC, 1996). These standards outline what students need to know, understand, and be able to do to be scientifically literate at different grade levels. They also develop professional development standards that present a vision for the development of professional knowledge and skill among teachers, as well as specifications for assessments to measure student understanding. Finally, they propose standards for evaluating the quality of science education programs and the support systems to improve science education.

In conjunction with these developments, there has been an effort to develop new assessments to measure how well science education in America is meeting the new standards. The *Benchmarks for Science Literacy* (AAAS, 1993) and the *National Science Education Standards* (NRC, 1996) served as guiding frameworks for each state to develop their science frameworks and their state assessments for science learning. The affiliated science of assessment in this new policy environment is well reviewed in the National Academy of Sciences volume: *Knowing What Students Know* (Pellegrino, Chudowsky, & Glaser, 2001).

The challenges to meeting the formidable standards outlined in these policy documents from AAAS and NRC are evident in reports from the field. As a recent NRC (2007) report argues

> Despite recurrent efforts to improve science education through curriculum reform and standards-based reform, there is still a long way to go. In hindsight, several factors may help to explain the limited impact of these substantial reform efforts. They include the complex political and technical aspects of implementation, insufficient teacher preparation and professional development, discontinuous streams of reform, mismatches between the goals of the initiatives and assessments, and insufficient and inequitable material resources devoted to education and reform (Berliner, 2006; Kozol, 2005; Spillane, 2001). These factors are inevitably part of the education reform problem and constrain how theories of teaching and learning are enacted in school settings. (p. 17)

The policy tensions of enactment of explicit science standards are also a recurrent issue for any science education reform effort. Kirst and Bird (1997; also see Massell, 1994) articulate four primary areas of political tension that help explain the difficulties of establishing supportive coalitions for science content standards in and out of schools: (a) the tension between leadership and political consensus, (b) the tension between flexible and specific standards, (c) the tension between up-to-date dynamic standards and reasonable expectations for change in the system, and (d) the tension between professional leadership and public understanding of what the new standards will entail.

THE SYSTEMIC APPROACH TO COHERENCE IN SCIENCE LEARNING

The contributions in this volume reflect the growing recognition that a systemic approach to designing and assessing science learning environments in schools is essential to the prospects of continuous improvement in science learning outcomes for all students. These efforts highlight the importance of the positive developments in each of the three prior waves of science educational reform. The chapters acknowledge the importance of "structure"—the fundamental principles of science subject matter and their interrelationships—and the contributions of well-designed curricula in promoting student understanding of such structure (first wave). Beyond the contributions of scientists' understanding of content structure, however, the work discussed herein reflects the insights and achievements of the cognitive science and learning science communities in articulating how the development of science expertise is promoted through specific types of learning activities (second wave). The emphasis in this volume on the aim of "coherence" in learner understanding of science content is importantly *generative* in nature, asserting that coherent understanding of science will be evidenced in students' efforts to productively connect science classroom ideas to their observations of the everyday world and to continued science learning throughout their lives.

In addition to the integrative focus on science content structure and on coherence of its generative understanding by learners, the projects reported in this volume are attentive to both the achievements and the shortfalls to date of the standards movement (third wave). In the fourth wave, which we are calling "the systemic approach," we see the emergence of a system-based approach to designing learning environments that are accountable to advancing coherent understanding of science subject matter by all learners. By "coherent understanding of science" the authors refer to a kind of *productive agency in scientific literacy*—"to both having a sense of the connectedness of science ideas and having the inclination to link ideas together and apply them to the situation at hand. Knowledge integration includes deliberate efforts to explain observations of phenomena, make decisions about matters involving science and technology, and seek ways to resolve conundrums" (Kali, Koppal, Linn, & Roseman, Preface, p. xi).

What are the hallmarks of a systemic approach? Most centrally, it is system based in its full recognition of the intercoordinated nature of content *standards,* high-quality *curriculum* current to the science, learning *activities* that foster the development of coherent scientific understanding and literacies, formative *assessments* that can guide instructional support, *teacher development practices* that enhance how practitioners serve the aims of science learning, the roles of *educational leaders* in creating and sustaining science reforms, and the *outcome measures* that provide accountability on improvements in science learning toward meeting the content standards. Secondly, it recognizes the school system and affiliated stakeholder groups as a *learning organization,* in which cycles of adaptation are providing new learning about how to achieve coherent science understanding among learners. For example, these cycles may be about curriculum adaptation, in which teachers modify curricula to serve diagnosed needs among their specific learners; they may be about teacher professional development adaptation, in which educational leaders modify programs for supporting how their teachers learn to promote coherent understanding for all learners; or they may be about assessment adaptation, in that test items developed may better serve their multiple purposes in subsequent iterations once their mettle is tested and revisions developed. The chapters in this volume provide ample evidence illustrating how the efforts of the Technology Enhanced Learning in Science (TELS) Center and the Center for Curriculum Materials in Science (CCMS) to promote coherence can serve as a models for learning organization along such dimensions as these.

THE FUTURE

In retrospect, we can see the beginnings of each new wave of science educational reform in small trends within prior waves. For example, concerns with the issue of development of coherent domain understanding pressed in the contributions in this volume are also expressed in Bruner's (1960) *The Process of Education,* and considerations of the systemic nature of the science educational reform process were expressed in the standards movement wave. Looking toward prospects for future developments, what can we sense of a fifth wave?

In the deliberations during the DECIDE project Synergy Conference, at which chapter authors came together to share perspectives and recommendations on each others' work (see Preface), and in the science educational reform literature more broadly, we see several themes surfacing that may become candidate seeds for the growth of one or more new waves of reform. How these will play out only time will tell.

First, we can imagine an emerging wave in which there is more concentrated effort in addressing the growing issues of better accommodating learner diversity in cultural and language backgrounds, and of systematically bridging informal and formal learning (e.g., Banks et al., 2007; Bransford et al., 2006). To foster coherence in science learning for all Americans, dealing productively with the diversity of informal learning resources available in families, peer networks, communities, and neighborhoods, and among science learning participants from diverse language, cultural, and socioeconomic backgrounds, must become central. Chapter 4 (Tate, Clark, Gallagher, & McLaughlin) foregrounds these issues, and we applaud the efforts of these authors to synthesize design principles for curriculum design and teacher education to make needed progress on encompassing diversity.

We can also see the glimmerings of an expanding science education that better reflects the reshaping of scientific practices to integrally utilize new technologies (e.g., remote instruments such as space telescopes, gene databases, scientific visualization as a tool for data analysis, grid computing for complex multiscale modeling) and new sociotechnical practices for organizing scientific inquiry (e.g., distributed collaboratories). For an extensive list of ways in which cyberinfrastructure is changing how scientific discovery and communication take place, and its implications for education, see the NSF report *Cyberinfrastructure Vision for 21st Century Discovery* (NSF Cyberinfrastructure Council, 2007). Chapter 3 (Krajcik, Slotta, McNeill, & Reiser) serves to illustrate how TELS and CCMS are appropriately employing uses of technology in instruction to help transform the science classroom into an environment in which learners actively construct knowledge: "Learning technologies allow students to extend what they can do in the classroom, using the computer to access real data on the World Wide Web, expand interaction and collaboration with others via networks, use electronic probes to gather data, employ graphing and visualization tools to analyze data, create models of complex systems, and produce multimedia artifacts" (p. 42). Although the challenges of making incorporation of such technologies pervasive for all learners in all classrooms are formidable, it is hard to see how science education can adequately reflect changes in scientific practices and affiliated habits of mind without greater integration of technology into educational activities.

In closing, we observe that the tensions of science education reform described by Kirst and Bird (1997) will not go away under any wave of reform, but are intrinsic to the value-laden nature of the educational enterprise and its complex relationships to the reproduction and continued invention of society. But we can come to recognize these tensions and do everything possible to create innovative systems of design, implementation, assessment, and critical appraisal that will better meet the needs of society for a scientifically literate citizenry. In our view, these four waves of science education reform and the original synthetic contributions of the present volume represent significant progress toward this objective.

Characterizing
Curriculum Coherence

Jo Ellen Roseman, Marcia C. Linn, and
Mary Koppal

INTRODUCTION

THE CENTER for Curriculum Materials in Science (CCMS) and the Technology Enhanced Learning in Science (TELS) Center promote the design of curriculum materials and technology tools that help students develop an understanding of important connections among science ideas and the inclination and ability to use those ideas to make sense of the world. Researchers at both centers analyze the fragmented ideas that students bring to class, identify important connections to be made, and design new materials that enable students to use ideas in a variety of contexts and to regularly improve the connections among their ideas. Both centers distinguish the following:

- *Integrated understanding,* the desired set of connections among scientific ideas that students need as they progress through school. Goals for integrated understanding emerge from careful analysis of science topics and content standards.
- *Knowledge integration,* a lifelong process that involves continuously seeking additional, more valid, and more concise connections among scientific ideas. Identifying knowledge integration processes depends on understanding how students link and connect ideas (where "link" refers to recognition of a relationship between ideas and "connect" indicates the requirement of evidence for the relationship between the ideas). Curriculum materials and technology tools can promote knowledge integration by actively engaging students in making important connections among ideas and applying them to new contexts.

○ *Curricular coherence,* a desired quality of science curriculum materials that involves presenting a complete set of interrelated ideas and making connections among them explicit. Coherent curriculum materials illustrate and model integrated understanding.

This chapter describes how CCMS and TELS have approached the design of coherent curriculum materials to help middle school and high school students move toward an integrated understanding of science. By combining coherent materials and support for knowledge integration processes, instruction can help all students achieve the integrated understanding that is the goal of learning.

Research Context

Both CCMS and TELS build on research on student learning that highlights the importance of helping students make connections among ideas. Bruner (1960, 1995), for example, argues that knowledge of the relationships among ideas and of the fundamental principles that connect the particulars enables learners to integrate new ideas into what they already know. According to Bruner, "the only possible way in which individual knowledge can keep proportional pace with the surge of available knowledge is through a grasp of the relatedness of knowledge" (1995, p. 333). Studies comparing the knowledge and abilities of experts and novices in a discipline describe the advantages of a richly connected understanding (Chi, Feltovich, & Glaser, 1981; Larkin & Reif, 1979; Markham, Mintzes, & Jones, 1994). The integrated knowledge that experts have enables them to use their knowledge in many contexts, including recognizing patterns in observations and explaining them, whereas the fragmented knowledge that students typically bring to science class can stand in the way of even knowing that science is useful for making sense of the world (Grigg, Lauko, & Brockway, 2006; O'Sullivan, Reese, & Mazzeo, 1997; Schmidt, McKnight, & Raizen, 1997). Studies also document the challenge of creating instructional materials with the right degree of coherence for a particular audience; materials representing the richly interconnected understanding of experts may not be the most successful materials for novice learners (Ainsworth & Burcham, 2007; Britton & Gulgoz, 1991; McKeown, Beck, Sinatra, & Loxterman, 1992; McNamara, Kintsch, Songer, & Kintsch, 1996).

CCMS works with the interconnected set of ideas, or learning goals, that both *Benchmarks for Science Literacy* (AAAS, 1993) and the *National Science Education Standards* (*NSES*) (NRC, 1996) have identified as central to science literacy. CCMS designers have articulated an approach to focusing the content of curriculum materials on this set of interrelated ideas, identifying important connections among the ideas in the set, and helping students to make connections among the ideas and use them to explain phenomena (Krajcik et al., 2008). In so doing, they seek to meet the criteria that served as the basis for the science

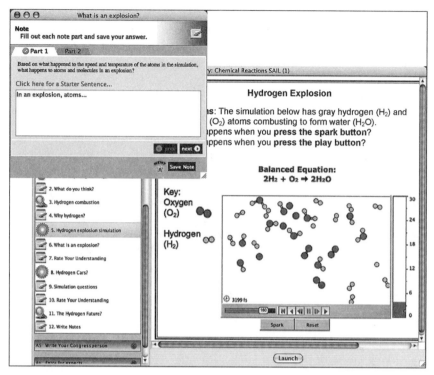

FIGURE 2.1 TELS inquiry learning environment, illustrating dynamic visualization of a hydrogen explosion and a note tool.

textbook evaluation studies of AAAS Project 2061 (Kesidou & Roseman, 2002; Stern & Roseman, 2004). As CCMS designers investigate the impact of their materials on students and teachers, the focus on learning goals guides those efforts as well (Chapter 3, Krajcik, Slotta, McNeill, & Reiser; Chapter 7, DeBoer, Lee, & Husic).

TELS builds on design principles that grew out of longitudinal research (Linn & Hsi, 2000), design studies (Linn, Davis, & Bell, 2004), and a series of workshops and conferences leading to a database of features, research evidence, and principles (the Design Principles Database, http://www.edu-design-principles.org; Kali, 2006). These principles are reflected in the knowledge integration framework (Linn, 1995, 2006; Linn, Lee, et al., 2006). TELS researchers take advantage of the Web-Based Inquiry Science Environment (WISE) and technological innovations from the Concord Consortium (see Figure 2.1) to create and study how curricular materials can promote knowledge integration. The curricular materials developed by TELS address science topics that teachers identify as (a) difficult for students, (b) required by standards, and (c) likely to benefit from technology enhancement. TELS has refined and tested the modules in classroom studies and shown that they improve knowledge integration (Linn, Lee, et al., 2006; Linn & Slotta, 2006).

Design Context

In attempting to design coherent materials that promote knowledge integration, both CCMS and TELS have developed and applied specific principles and criteria. CCMS design draws on criteria used in Project 2061's evaluations of science textbooks and on findings of those studies, which shed light on the coherence of available textbooks and the quality of their instructional design (Kesidou & Roseman, 2002; Roseman, Stern, & Koppal, 2008; Stern & Roseman, 2004). TELS design draws on its own principles for knowledge integration (Kali, 2006; Linn, Davis, & Bell, 2004). To synthesize their work, the centers identified a single set of research-based guiding principles that provide the basis for both research programs. The guiding principles include

- Focusing materials on science learning goals
- Building pedagogical supports into materials
- Incorporating learning technologies into materials
- Promoting the use of student investigations as learning activities
- Serving the needs of diverse science learners
- Supporting teacher learning
- Taking account of policy contexts

This chapter and Chapter 3 describe how the two centers address the first three guiding principles. The remaining principles are the focus of other chapters in this volume.

THE CCMS APPROACH TO CURRICULUM COHERENCE

This section speaks to the role of curriculum materials in illustrating and modeling an integrated understanding and in promoting knowledge integration. It highlights Project 2061's study of the coherence of high school textbooks and describes criteria for analyzing their coherence and the quality of their support for teaching and learning.

Analyzing Textbook Coherence

CCMS argues that the content of curriculum materials is coherent when it focuses on an important set of interrelated ideas and makes various kinds of connections explicit. CCMS researchers have used these characteristics of coherent content to evaluate the content of existing curriculum materials and to design new ones.

Alignment with a Coherent Set of Ideas. The starting point in any discussion of coherence is the relationships among the specific ideas that students are expected to learn. CCMS focuses its work on science learning goals that are derived from *Science for All Americans* (AAAS, 1989), which recommends a set of knowledge and skills in science, mathematics, and technology that characterizes science literacy for high school graduates. Instead of presenting a list of topic headings and terms, *Science for All Americans* provides a scientific account of the world that includes some of the most important ideas and connections among them. For example, in characterizing knowledge about matter and energy transformations in ecosystems, *Science for All Americans* articulates connections between life science and physical science that all high school graduates should know:

> However complex the workings of living organisms, they share with all other natural systems the same physical principles of the conservation and transformation of matter and energy. Over long spans of time, matter and energy are transformed among living things, and between them and the physical environment. In these grand-scale cycles, the total amount of matter and energy remains constant, even though their form and location undergo continual change. (p. 66)

The authors of *Science for All Americans* then present examples of matter and energy transformations to illustrate relationships between living systems and physical systems at several levels of biological organization—molecule, organism, ecosystem.

To allow time for students to develop a deep understanding of these ideas and their interconnections, *Science for All Americans* limits the total number of ideas to be learned to a central core of the most important ideas. Hence, in life science (as in physical science, social science, mathematics, and technology), the authors left out several topics that are typically included in textbooks. For example, details of plant anatomy and the metabolic steps of photosynthesis and respiration were not considered essential for making sense of everyday phenomena or for making social and personal decisions about matters involving science, mathematics, and technology. Decisions about what to include and what to exclude from the science curriculum carry through to *Benchmarks for Science Literacy* (AAAS, 1993), a companion volume to *Science for All Americans,* which specifies what students should know and be able to do at the end of Grades 2, 5, 8, and 12. To achieve the vision of science literacy described in *Science for All Americans,* the learning goals in *Benchmarks* convey key concepts while including selected supporting details, are specific enough to be informative but avoid fragmentation, and are comprehensible by students at each grade and developmental level. To emphasize the interconnectedness of this core knowledge, the two-volume *Atlas of Science Literacy* (AAAS, 2001, 2007) displays K–12 connections among ideas for nearly 100 topics.

Figure 2.2 shows a progression of ideas (included in both *Benchmarks* and *NSES*) from primary school through middle school that contributes to an understanding of matter and energy transformations in ecosystems. The progression has been adapted from several related *Atlas* maps and can be used to serve the needs of both curriculum and assessment design. The map shows that by the end of Grades K–2, students should be able to view food as a *need* of organisms, which requires students to connect observations of particular plants and animals around them to that general principle. By the end of elementary school, students are expected to have a more functional definition of food—food provides material for body repair and growth—and to associate growth with an increase in body weight (mass). In middle school, students are expected to link the growth of organisms to the synthesis of new molecules in chemical reactions. With these foundational ideas in place, students in high school are then able to connect the synthesis and breakdown of molecules in organisms to the cycling of atoms in ecosystems and to recognize that the workings of all living organisms are governed by physical principles of transformation and conservation. Thus, at each grade level students are expected to relate their new knowledge to what they already know and to make more sophisticated links among ideas.

In thinking through what would constitute an appropriate story about matter and energy transformations in middle school, the developers of *Benchmarks* considered the benefits and costs of helping students understand the underlying molecular mechanisms for each. Students who understood the underlying mechanisms would benefit by being able to tie together seemingly unrelated phenomena. By learning about matter transformation and the rearrangement of atoms during chemical reactions in physical systems (where matter transformations are more directly observable), students are better able to understand the same mechanism at work in biological systems (where changes in matter are not easily observed). Costs would arise from the need to first help students understand that the properties of substances and mixtures of substances are determined by the molecules they are made of, that changing the molecules changes the properties, and that changes in molecules in chemical reactions involve changing the arrangements of atoms making up the molecules (but not the atoms themselves). Given the documented difficulties students have with these ideas and the experiences of other curriculum developers on this and related topics, the CCMS researchers working on the middle school science curriculum "Investigating and Questioning Our World Through Science and Technology" (IQWST), a 3-year

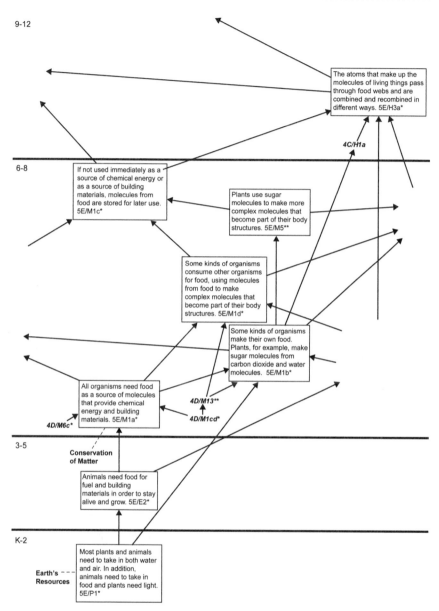

9-12

The atoms that make up the molecules of living things pass through food webs and are combined and recombined in different ways. 5E/H3a*

4C/H1a

6-8

If not used immediately as a source of chemical energy or as a source of building materials, molecules from food are stored for later use. 5E/M1c*

Plants use sugar molecules to make more complex molecules that become part of their body structures. 5E/M5**

Some kinds of organisms consume other organisms for food, using molecules from food to make complex molecules that become part of their body structures. 5E/M1d*

Some kinds of organisms make their own food. Plants, for example, make sugar molecules from carbon dioxide and water molecules. 5E/M1b*

All organisms need food as a source of molecules that provide chemical energy and building materials. 5E/M1a*

4D/M13**

4D/M1cd*

4D/M6c*

3-5

Conservation of Matter

Animals need food for fuel and building materials in order to stay alive and grow. 5E/E2*

K-2

Earth's Resources

Most plants and animals need to take in both water and air. In addition, animals need to take in food and plants need light. 5E/P1*

FIGURE 2.2 Map developed by AAAS Project 2061 showing a sequence of ideas from kindergarten through 12th grade that contribute to students' integrated understanding of the flow of matter and energy in living systems.

middle school science curriculum, estimated that it would take between 8 and 16 weeks to provide students with the chemical foundation they would need. Despite this significant investment of instructional time, the researchers decided that the potential benefits for students' understanding justified the costs of targeting these ideas in their middle school curriculum.

In contrast, the IQWST developers decided that including a molecular level mechanism for energy transformation in middle school could not be justified. Including a mechanism for energy transformations in chemical reactions such as photosynthesis and cellular respiration would require knowledge of the link between molecular structures and chemical energy, why changes in molecular structure are accompanied by changes in chemical energy, and how energy from the sun is transformed into chemical energy. Providing the necessary foundation for this learning in the available time would overburden students struggling to understand and apply the mechanism of matter transformation. In the end, IQWST researchers concurred with the decisions reflected in *Benchmarks for Science Literacy* (AAAS, 1993, p. 85) and the *Atlas of Science Literacy* (AAAS, 2007, p. 25) to limit the energy story at the middle school level to patterns in observable energy transformations.

Connections Between the Ideas of Science and Phenomena in the Natural World. For students to appreciate the explanatory power of science ideas, they need to have a sense of the range of phenomena that the ideas can explain. Appropriate phenomena help students to view scientific concepts as plausible and enhance students' sense of the usefulness of scientific concepts (Anderson & Smith, 1987; Champagne, Gunstone, & Klopfer, 1985; Strike & Posner, 1985). To understand how matter is transformed within ecosystems, it is important that students appreciate various transformations at the molecular level not only within organisms but also between organisms in ecosystems and the abiotic environment. Curriculum materials need to provide a range of observable phenomena involving matter transformations within organisms and relate the phenomena to underlying molecular explanations. For example, materials could show students that as the egg yolk and egg white decrease in mass during the development of a chick embryo, the body of the chick increases in mass; that as a weight-lifter "bulks up," the increase in muscle mass looks quite different from the milk, eggs, and cheese consumed; or that plants grown in air enriched in carbon dioxide produce more sugar and starch and grow faster than plants grown in normal air.

Connections to Prerequisite and Other Related Ideas. Coherence also includes making connections between new ideas and prior knowledge explicit (Bishop & Anderson, 1990; Eaton, Anderson, & Smith, 1984; Lee et al., 1993; McDermott, 1984).

As shown in Figure 2.3, the idea that "carbon and hydrogen are common elements of living matter" provides necessary, though not sufficient, information to understand a few simple transformations of matter in organisms, starting with the idea that "plants make sugar molecules from carbon dioxide (in the air) and water" (Idea a_1 in Figure 2.3). Curriculum materials could make a connection between these two ideas by explaining that carbon dioxide and water molecules contain atoms of the elements carbon and hydrogen (and also oxygen) and that photosynthesis by plants begins the process of incorporating these atoms into larger molecules, which can then lead to their incorporation into the much larger molecules that make up body structures (parts of Ideas b_1 and c_1 in Figure 2.3).

Connections are particularly important when new ideas and their prerequisite ideas are presented in different chapters of a text. For example, a textbook's chapter on cells should make a link between the elements that make up cells (particularly carbon), the ability of carbon atoms to form large and complex molecules (which might be presented in an introductory chemistry chapter), and chemical reactions in cells that link carbon atoms to form sugars (Idea a_1 in Figure 2.3) and then use those sugars to make more complex molecules of body structures (Ideas b_1 and c_1 in Figure 2.3). A connection could be made by reminding students that living things don't violate basic chemical principles:

> *Carbon atoms can easily bond to several other carbon atoms in chains and rings to form large and complex molecules. And in fact they do. Plants take simple molecules of carbon dioxide and water and put them together to form rings and put the rings together to form more complex structures. All of this is possible because carbon can bond to other carbon atoms in rings or chains.*

Similarly, the idea that "within cells are specialized parts for the capture and release of energy" (typically presented in a chapter on cells) should be linked to key ideas about the release of that energy by plants and animals (Ideas b_2 and c_2 in Figure 2.4). Curriculum materials might make such a connection by pointing out that cells with high energy needs tend to have more of the specialized parts for releasing energy than do cells with lower energy needs. Curriculum materials can connect these ideas to relevant phenomena, such as by pointing out that cells located on the upper surface of leaves—where there is more direct access to light energy—have more of the parts used to capture the sun's energy than do cells located on the undersurface of leaves.

There are also opportunities for curriculum materials to make connections between ideas taught in life science and underlying principles typically taught in chemistry. As noted earlier in this chapter, *Science for All Americans* suggests that students learn that "However complex the workings of living organisms, they

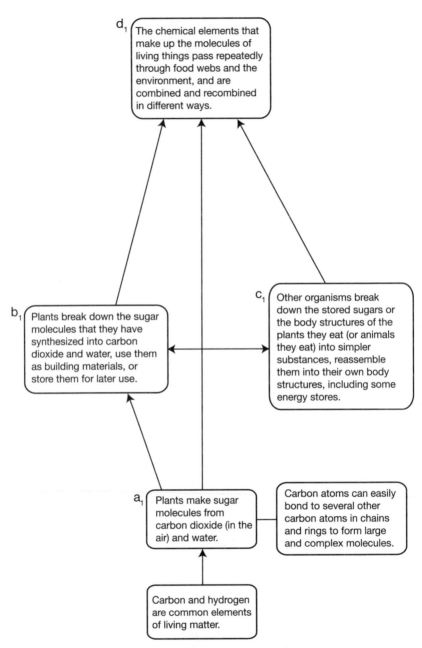

FIGURE 2.3 Detail from a map showing relationships among ideas about matter transformations that were the focus of AAAS Project 2061's review of biology textbooks (AAAS, 2005).

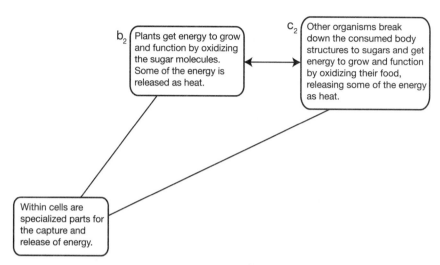

FIGURE 2.4 Detail from a map showing relationships among ideas about matter and energy transformations that were the focus of AAAS Project 2061's review of biology textbooks (AAAS, 2005).

share with all other natural systems the same physical principles of the conservation and transformation of matter and energy" (AAAS, 1989, p. 66). Textbooks often present individual ideas in separate chapters—photosynthesis and cellular respiration in a chapter on cells, food breakdown in a chapter on the human digestive system, nutrient cycles and energy pyramids in a chapter on ecosystems—and never convey the idea that these processes are instances of matter and energy conservation and transformation (which students typically encounter in physical science courses). To support the interconnectedness of ideas from the life sciences and the physical sciences, matter transformations in living systems can be described in terms of atoms combining and recombining in cells, organisms, and ecosystems.

Connections to Evidence Supporting the Ideas. Coherence also comes from connections between scientific ideas and the enterprise that produced them. Curriculum materials can help students appreciate ideas about the nature of science by providing evidence-based arguments for the scientific ideas presented. Using logical arguments to link evidence to conclusions can also give students a sense of why particular ideas are believable and why scientists believe them. In attempting to build a case for science ideas, it is important that materials present a case that is valid (e.g., by making legitimate inferences from observations and presenting sufficient evidence to support arguments). It is also important that the case be comprehensible to students (e.g., by presenting evidence at an appropriate level of sophistication and presenting the argument and links to evidence in manageable steps). Textbooks typically assert ideas without evidence. When they do provide evidence, it is not adequately linked to the idea it supports. For example, on the topic "Matter and Energy Transformations" biology textbooks rarely present Priestley's experiment (which showed that plants produce oxygen) or Ingenhousz's experiment (which showed that oxygen is only produced in the presence of light). When textbooks do present these experiments, they fail to link them to the equation for photosynthesis or to students' own observations that plants grown in the presence of light produce sugars, whereas plants kept away from light do not.

Avoidance of Nonessential Information. It is also important that curriculum materials pay attention to the relevance and comprehensibility of what is included. Curriculum materials can reduce coherence by including distracting technical detail that goes beyond what is needed to understand the essential ideas and their connections. For example, on the topic "Matter and Energy Transformations" textbooks often include details of metabolism, such as the reactions of Photosystems I and II and the Calvin cycle, which make it difficult for students to extract the main story about photosynthesis. Or materials may include abbreviated diagrams of the Krebs cycle and formulas for molecules such as NADH, NAD^+, ATP, and ADP, which have no meaning for students who do not yet have an understanding of organic chemistry.

Subtle forms of content inaccuracy can also detract from coherence. One form consists of the juxtaposition of statements that may lead students astray even though neither is factually wrong. Diagrams, rather than clarifying ideas, may reinforce common student misconceptions (Tversky et al., 2002). For example, diagrams of nutrient cycles in biological systems, such as the carbon–oxygen cycle or the nitrogen cycle, often misrepresent the transformation of matter by showing atoms of carbon for one organism represented in the diagram but not for others. By failing to show atoms of a particular element throughout the cycle, a text can reinforce the misconception that matter can disappear in one place and reappear in another, as opposed to simply changing forms (by combining with different atoms to make new molecules). Similarly, diagrams of energy pyramids that indicate decreases in energy (without indicating that energy is given off as heat) can reinforce students' misconception that energy is not conserved.

To summarize, for students to understand how matter is transformed within living systems, it is important that they appreciate various transformations at the molecular level not only within organisms but also between organisms in ecosystems. It is particularly important that curriculum materials make it clear that matter transformations in an ecosystem are a consequence of transformations of matter in the organisms that make up the ecosystem, and that the recycling of elements in an ecosystem results from repeated cycles of synthesis, storage, and breakdown in the organisms and involves movement of matter between organisms and the abiotic environment. When textbooks treat only part of the story or fail to make important connections among different parts of the story, students are likely to be left with fragmented knowledge. They are also less likely to appreciate what they are taught when the ideas are not linked to practical applications such as explaining the growth of organisms or considering claims about the effects of global climate change on ecosystems.

Designing Coherent Materials That Promote Knowledge Integration

Both the criteria used to evaluate the coherence of textbooks' presentation of content and the criteria used to evaluate the quality of their instructional support for knowledge integration have been adapted for use by materials designers. Chapter 3 describes the role of these criteria in the design of IQWST materials, and Project 2061 uses them as a basis for formative feedback provided to IQWST and other development teams (Heller, 2001; Krajcik et al., 2008).

Learning-Goals-Driven Design. CCMS researchers believe that the detailed content analysis illustrated above is a crucial part of the design process and must be done for virtually every topic; only general design guidelines are applicable across topics. Such careful thinking about ideas, connections, and sequences has been part of the development process being used by CCMS researchers working on IQWST. Describing their approach as a "learning-goals-driven design model," the IQWST developers begin their work by first identifying in *Benchmarks* and *NSES* the content to be targeted in their curriculum units. To ensure a close alignment of the ideas addressed in the curriculum with those specified in the standards, the IQWST developers then "unpack" each standard to consider "the science concepts articulated ... in depth and how they link to other science ideas" (Krajcik et al., 2008, p. 7). The science content is then "mapped" beginning first with the relevant maps from the *Atlas of Science Literacy* followed by construction of more detailed maps for each sequence of ideas. According to the developers, mapping has enabled them to "identify clusters of standards that interrelate, determine what are the big ideas ... and build an instructional sequence to foster more complex understandings over time" (Krajcik et al., 2008, p. 6).

As a result of this learning-goals-driven design approach, the IQWST developers have designed a coherent sequence of units that contrasts sharply with the model that is typical of most middle school science curricula. Sequencing is especially critical for the IQWST curriculum because it relates ideas across life, earth, and physical sciences. For example, IQWST developers have sequenced their units to ensure that students understand chemical reactions in physical systems (where the inputs and outputs of these reactions are observable) *before* the students encounter chemical reactions in living systems (where the inputs and outputs are more difficult to observe). For similar reasons, IQWST first targets ideas about conservation of energy in physical systems, using examples that involve readily detectable forms of energy. This gives students a sense that, like matter, energy does not disappear or appear from nowhere. IQWST then builds on students' emerging ideas about energy conservation to introduce the idea of chemical energy as a new type to account for changes in the energy types they are already familiar with. Once students accept the existence of chemical energy, they are then able to use it to explain phenomena in which energy seems to have disappeared. Ideas about both matter and energy transformation are tied together in IQWST's eighth-grade unit on the synthesis of sugars by plants and its subsequent oxidation to extract energy. Chapter 3 describes in more detail the IQWST design process and its contribution to students' integrated understanding.

Pedagogical Supports. Focusing on learning goals and thinking through the kinds of connections that must be made explicit and sensible to students are essential first steps. However, these are not sufficient to help students achieve the knowledge integration needed for lifelong science learning. Curriculum materials should do more than present content to students; they should also support the teaching and learning process. For that reason, CCMS contends that science curriculum materials should include goals-specific pedagogical supports for students and teachers that are based on empirically tested theories of learning. For its evaluation of biology textbooks, AAAS Project 2061 developed a set of criteria to consider the extent to which textbooks incorporated these pedagogical supports (AAAS, 2005).

By pedagogical supports we mean the text, activities, and assessments used by curriculum materials to motivate and help students to learn, along with the background information, suggestions, diagnostic questions, and remedial strategies used to help teachers monitor and promote that learning. Pedagogical supports can be incorporated directly into students' materials as well as materials intended specifically for the teacher, such as teacher editions of textbooks. To help all students gain important and lasting science knowledge and skills, curriculum materials must provide a wide array of supports that enable students and teachers to meet the following challenges:

- Taking account of prerequisite knowledge and student misconceptions to enable students to construct new understanding that builds on their prior understanding
- Helping students appreciate the purpose of classroom activities and the content they are learning to provide an adequate level of motivation to learn
- Using phenomena and representations to clarify the meaning of abstract ideas and to make the ideas plausible to students
- Helping students interpret phenomena and representations in light of the ideas

- Promoting student reflection and application of their developing understanding
- Using continuous assessment and student feedback to inform instruction
- Enhancing the learning environment to enable students with different abilities and levels of preparation to experience success

The demands of teaching for understanding are significant, especially in today's classrooms that serve students with widely diverse backgrounds, abilities, and interests. Teachers certainly cannot be expected to design their own research-based pedagogical supports for an entire curriculum. Therefore, CCMS researchers have incorporated these supports as an integral part of their IQWST student and teacher materials. The supports are based on empirically tested theories of learning that have been described by Edelson (2001) and Kesidou and Roseman (2002).

Through attention to the research-based content and pedagogical criteria used in Project 2061's textbook evaluations, CCMS developers are mindful of the kinds of difficulties many students are likely to have and of the kinds of supports that are likely to help. Chapter 3 and Chapter 8 (Kali, Fortus, & Ronen-Fuhrmann) describe and illustrate the application of these criteria to the design of IQWST student materials, and Chapter 5 (Davis & Varma) describes their application to the design of educative materials for teachers.

THE TELS APPROACH

The goal of TELS is to spur design of technology-enhanced materials that lead to knowledge integration and support a lifelong tendency to seek connections among ideas. TELS approaches this by designing and testing inquiry learning environments that incorporate educational software and simulations of scientific phenomena to promote an integrated understanding of science in students. To help future designers, TELS incorporates guiding principles and contributes to the Design Principles Database (http://www.edu-design-principles.org; Kali, 2006; Kali & Linn, 2007; see also Chapter 8). TELS extracts design processes and patterns from successful instructional materials to highlight ways to stimulate knowledge integration (Linn, 2006; Linn & Eylon, 2006). Research from TELS also strengthens the WISE learning environment (see Figure 2.1), creates effective professional development (Chapter 5), builds a community of school leaders (Chapter 6, Bowyer, Gerard, & Marx), and stimulates an open source community of developers (see Chapter 3).

Knowledge Integration Processes and Patterns

TELS has identified four reasoning processes that, taken together, are used to construct pedagogical patterns (sequences of activities) that can promote knowledge integration (Linn & Eylon, 2006). The pedagogical patterns incorporate prior research on technology-enhanced learning (Bell, Davis, & Linn, 1995; Buckley et al., 2004; Horwitz & Christie, 1999; Linn, Lee, et al., 2006; Slotta & Linn, 2000; Songer & Linn, 1992). The pedagogical patterns feature four interrelated processes of knowledge integration in combinations that contribute to integrated understanding. These processes are (a) elicit current ideas, (b) add new ideas, (c) develop criteria for evaluating ideas, and (d) sort out ideas. Materials can interleave the four processes, revisiting some and visiting others only once. In TELS research, the patterns are combined to form curriculum materials tailored to specific disciplinary characteristics. This section describes the four knowledge integration processes and illustrates them with examples from research on the successful Japanese Ikatura method for science inquiry learning (Hatano & Inagaki, 1991). The next section ("The TELS Design Process") discusses how the patterns inform design of the TELS modules.

Elicit Current Ideas. As documented in research on student reasoning, students develop a repertoire of ideas about any phenomenon (Clark & Linn, 2003; diSessa, 1988). TELS research suggests that students need to articulate their varied ideas as part of the process of building a more integrated view of a topic. When instructional materials present a single view without encouraging students to consider their own views, the new view is typically added to the repertoire rather than integrated (Bransford, Brown, & Cocking, 1999). Eliciting ideas in multiple contexts ensures that they are considered in forming a view of a scientific topic. Studies of contextualized learning show that when students study science in abstract contexts, for example, they fail to connect the instruction to their everyday ideas, often even claiming that science in school differs from science in everyday life (e.g., Bell & Linn, 2002; Gilbert & Boulter, 2000). For example, students often remark that cold flows on a snowy day but only heat flows in the classroom. Chapters 3 and 8 describe how instruction can support contextualization.

Eliciting ideas is the first step in the Ikatura method. When using this method, Japanese instructors first pose a dilemma and elicit student ideas. They list all of the student ideas on a whiteboard. They then ask students to select one perspective or another, in essence making predictions about the outcome of the demonstration. In one example, students explore adding either a wood or a metal object of similar mass to a beaker filled with water. They predict whether the mass of the beaker with the wood object floating on the water or with the metal object sinking in the water will be the same. That is, students compare the mass of the water plus the floating object with the mass of the water plus the sinking object. By eliciting predictions, teachers engage their students in the experiment and also learn about the ideas held by their students.

Add New Ideas. As shown in the analysis of CCMS curriculum materials, adding new, normative ideas is an essential part of science instruction. Historically, science instruction has introduced new ideas in lectures or text accounts of a phenomenon, in a manner that is often consistent with a model of the learner as an absorber of information (Thorndike, 1963). Recently, however, research has demonstrated the benefit of careful design of the ideas that are added to the mix held by students. Researchers have studied bridging analogies (Clement, 1993), benchmark lessons (diSessa & Minstrell, 1998), didactic objects (Thompson, 2002), prototypes (Songer & Linn, 1992), and pivotal cases (Linn, 2005). For example, Clement (1993) describes bridging analogies, such as comparing the behavior of a book on a spring, pillow, and table to help students understand the forces between the book and the table.

Adding these types of ideas motivates learners to examine their own repertoire of ideas. For example, the phenomenon of thermal equilibrium can be illustrated through two pivotal cases. In one case, to help explain why objects feel different even though they are the same temperature, students use an interactive animation to explore the rate of heat flow in different materials, such as metal and wood, learning that heat flows faster in metal than in wood. Students use this pivotal case to make sense of their sensory observations that metals feel colder than wood, even when both are the same temperature. In another case, to help disentangle ideas about materials and their temperature, students recall personal experiences to compare the feel of wood and metal at room temperature with the feel of these materials at the beach on a sunny day. Students use this pivotal case to sort out ideas about insulation and conduction. Both cases stimulate learners to reconsider their existing ideas (Linn & Hsi, 2000). Research suggests criteria for successful pivotal cases, including (a) make a compelling, scientifically valid comparison between two situations; (b) draw on accessible, culturally relevant contexts, such as everyday experiences; (c) provide feedback that supports students' efforts to develop criteria and monitor their progress; and (d) encourage students to create narrative accounts of their ideas using precise vocabulary so they can discuss them with others (Linn, 2005; Linn & Hsi, 2000).

To further its goal of designing and testing powerful interactive, dynamic visualizations as pivotal cases for central topics in middle school and high school science, TELS takes advantage of the visualization software designed by the Concord Consortium (http://www.concord.org) and also creates new visualizations using NetLogo and other resources (see Figure 2.1). Although TELS has found that most students claim that they are visual learners, many research studies suggest that visualizations either lack value or interfere with learning, which is consistent with CCMS findings about textbook diagrams (e.g., Stern & Roseman, 2004; Tversky et al., 2002). TELS has identified design principles to help designers find effective ways to use interactive visualizations. TELS has evidence that the interactive visualizations are key to the success of the TELS modules (Casperson & Linn, 2006; Liu, Lee, Hofstetter, & Linn, 2008).

In the Ikatura method, after eliciting ideas teachers use experiments or demonstrations to add new ideas. In the study of mass mentioned above, students conduct a valid comparison of the mass of the beaker with a floating object (wood) or a submerged object (metal), analyze the feedback from the experiment, connect the experiment to their own ideas about things like the floating and sinking of boats, and create narratives to summarize their work.

Develop Criteria for Evaluating Ideas. To help them develop coherent ways to evaluate the scientific ideas they encounter, students need to have criteria for selecting among views. Students often accept questionable scientific information, such as advertisements for new drugs, persuasive accounts of research findings, and compelling personal anecdotes. They rarely explore the controversies that led to scientific advances or learn that research methods have limitations (Bell & Linn, 2000; Roseman et al., 2008). Often, the scientific method is exalted rather than explained as a social construct open to negotiation (Keller, 1983; Longino, 1994). Students may accept bogus results—encountered on the Internet or in quasi-scientific publications—because they are cloaked in scientific jargon. Alternatively, students may discredit all of science when they learn that new advances discredit previously established ideas about medical treatments or nutritional practices. Successful instruction helps students develop sound ideas about criteria for evaluating scientific information. Ultimately, students need to understand the fallibility of experimental investigations, the epistemology of methods in varied disciplines (such as earthquake prediction, cloning, design of new drugs, and environmental conservation), and the nature of scientific advancement. Although science standards help determine the level of sophistication appropriate for specific grade levels, empirical research is needed to be sure that the recommendations in the standards are feasible and that they enable students to reason effectively about practical problems.

To help students develop criteria for distinguishing among ideas, teachers in the Ikatura method ask students to align evidence from their experiments with their ideas, to revise their ideas based on the experiments, and to use the evidence to convince peers who have alternative ideas. Students discuss the validity of the evidence, make further predictions, and conduct more experiments to resolve differences of opinion.

Sort Out Ideas. To help them sort out new and current ideas, students need opportunities to apply their criteria to the ideas in their repertoire, distinguish ideas, and weigh evidence. Students benefit from applying their criteria to evidence, sorting out potential contradictions, and identifying situations where more information is needed (Bagno, Eylon, & Ganiel, 2000; Bransford et al., 1999; Collins, Brown, & Holum, 1988; Linn & Hsi, 2000; Scardamalia & Bereiter, 1999). To succeed, students need to allocate their limited energy to the most central confusions, to evaluate their progress, and to seek clarification when necessary (Bielaczyc, Pirolli, & Brown, 1995; Lin & Schwartz, 2003). Instead, many students respond to the barrage of information in science courses by memorizing information they expect on tests (Songer & Linn, 1992) and then forgetting what they memorized (Bjork, 1994).

In the Ikatura method, teachers help students sort out ideas by encouraging small groups to discuss their ideas and reach joint conclusions. When groups of four cannot reconcile their views, the whole class listens to the alternative ideas and contributes criteria as well as evidence. This approach to helping students develop coherent understanding has proven successful in many studies of Japanese instruction (e.g., Lewis, 1995; Lewis & Tsuchida, 1998) and in studies inspired by the method (e.g., Clark & Sampson, 2007).

TELS CREATES pedagogical patterns by using the four processes described above. An instructional *pattern* is a sequence of activities followed by teachers and students in a classroom that features all four processes: elicit current ideas, add new ideas, develop criteria for evaluating ideas, and sort out ideas. Activities such as experimentation often fail to promote knowledge integration when used in isolation. As the Ikatura method illustrates, experimentation can succeed when implemented as part of a pattern where learners articulate their ideas before experimenting and sort out alternative interpretations afterward. Similarly, pedagogical patterns can improve collaborative learning by ensuring that students contribute their own ideas before they hear the ideas of others, adding multimedia examples that serve participants as pivotal cases, guiding learners to agree on criteria for critiquing evidence, and motivating learners to reconcile alternatives (Brown & Campione, 1994; Linn & Hsi, 2000; Scardamalia & Bereiter, 1999). Linn and Eylon (2006) identified 10 instructional patterns that incorporate all four of the knowledge integration processes and apply to common classroom activities such as experimentation, collaboration, and critique.

The TELS Design Process

To create curriculum modules, TELS forms partnerships that include individuals with expertise in classroom teaching, the science discipline, technology, student learning, curriculum, and professional development. The partnerships use the WISE learning environment to design instruction (see Figure 2.1) and the partnership process to develop the design (Linn & Holmes, 2006). TELS design partnerships use guiding principles, design principles, and pedagogical patterns to create the modules. Modules feature pivotal cases of scientific phenomena often designed by the Concord Consortium (http://www.concord.org). For example, one module on natural selection implements a series of patterns including explore a visualization, debate, reflect, discuss, and reflect again. In this module, students generate ideas about natural selection in the context of plants, fish, and dinosaurs (Teruel, 2006). They then explore a visualization that uses a pivotal case in the form of an interactive Flash animation to compare learning within a generation versus survival across generations. Next they reflect on the difference between natural selection and developing expertise. They compare fish that learn when to swim fast with fish that survive because they are faster swimmers. Using a debate pattern, students research alternative accounts of the impact of habitat change on fish populations, develop arguments, formulate criteria, and participate in a class debate in which they need to use their criteria to evaluate the ideas of their peers. A discussion pattern allows students to articulate their ideas more accurately. Finally, students use the reflection pattern to develop a report summarizing their ideas.

Kali and Linn (in press) illustrate how design principles can help materials developers create effective modules. Whereas patterns assist designers in determining sequences of activities, design principles guide the design of each activity. For example, in implementing the discussion pattern, designers draw on two design principles: "Scaffold the process of generating explanations" and "Enable multiple ways to participate in online discussions."

The WISE environment supports extensive student guidance (Linn, Clark, & Slotta, 2003). Recently, the TELS technology team has created a new Java-based infrastructure for designing, developing, and delivering computer-based curricula that extends the capabilities of WISE. The Scalable Architecture for Interactive Learning (SAIL) manages persistence in a network environment (allowing student work and software versions to be stored and retrievable over time). The technology offers powerful authoring, logging, and experimentation capabilities that enable rapid design and refinement of instruction.

TELS Classroom Research

TELS has conducted longitudinal studies and comparison studies to identify effective ways to teach science. For example, to study how best to design a molecular workbench visualization, the learning environment can deliver alternative treatments within the same class (when alternatives are similar) or in different classes taught by the same teacher.

In the first year, TELS created and tested 10 modules and assessments aligned with those modules to measure knowledge integration (Chapter 7). In addition, TELS designed a principal network to support teachers (Chapter 6) and professional development to rapidly prepare users (Chapter 5).

In a cohort comparison study involving 50 teachers (Linn, Lee, et al., 2006), TELS found that studying with the module instead of the regular lesson resulted in student gains of about one third of a standard deviation in integrated understanding. TELS is now in the process of sorting out the factors that jointly result in the success of the modules, including guided inquiry; pivotal cases based on interactive visualizations, models, and probeware; eliciting ideas in relevant contexts that interest students; ample time for reflection; a focus on integrating prior experiences with new observations; and support for student collaboration.

The modules were extensively revised based on classroom trials, and modules showing positive impact on student learning were placed in the TELS Library (see http://www.wise.berkeley.edu). These modules are free for use by researchers and teachers. By spring 2007, over 100 TELS teachers had used the modules with over 14,000 students in more than 30 schools in five states.

Studies of the modules, teachers, professional developers, and science students have improved instruction. Results have led to revision of design principles and pedagogical patterns (Ronen-Fuhrmann, Kali, & Hoadley, 2008). Results of this research resonate with the findings from CCMS and suggest next steps for increasing the emphasis on coherence in science courses.

SUMMARY AND CONCLUSIONS

The work of both CCMS and TELS points to the importance of careful planning, analysis, and iterative refinement in the early stages of curriculum development to ensure that (a) materials present a coherent and explicitly related set of important and useful ideas and (b) students have the pedagogical support necessary to help them integrate their knowledge in the classroom and beyond. It also makes clear the need for policies throughout the education system that can promote the development of high-quality curriculum materials and sustain their effective implementation in schools. Taken together, these research programs offer some proven guiding principles, design principles, and pedagogical criteria that can be applied by those who evaluate and design science curriculum materials and by those who articulate and carry out policies to guide science education.

Implications for Research and Curriculum Design

The idea maps from the *Atlas of Science Literacy* (AAAS, 2001, 2007) offer researchers a starting point for considering the coherence of a topic both within and across grade bands. *Atlas* maps also provide a rationale for the design and sequencing of phenomena-based activities that can be tested by empirical studies of student learning. Project 2061's textbook evaluation criteria can guide the design and testing of student experiences with phenomena and representations, and the TELS instructional design patterns and principles can provide similar guidance in the design and assessment of technology-based instructional materials. By taking advantage of these analytical tools and resources in the early stages of development, curriculum designers will have a more thoughtfully designed draft and a more informed set of questions to investigate in the classroom. To benefit from this work, designers should (a) consider the learning trajectories depicted in the *Atlas* maps, (b) ensure that materials have face validity according to Project 2061's textbook coherence criteria, (c) adhere to the instructional design criteria used by CCMS, (d) employ the TELS design principles and patterns, and (e) engage in iterative rounds of evidence-based refinements *before* investing in large-scale empirical studies.

Studies on learning are only just beginning to examine what it would take to develop students' understanding of a well-defined set of interrelated ideas in key topics and across several grades. At CCMS, for example, researchers are drawing on the K–12 progressions of understanding suggested in Project 2061's *Atlas* maps to develop, refine, and test more detailed instructional sequences for the topics addressed in their IQWST curriculum. At TELS, researchers are exploring the impact of using the same visualizations for common topics in middle school and high school science. More study is needed to extend the work of both centers to additional topics, different learners, varied instructional contexts (e.g., self-guided technology-based modules as well as print-based units), and the design process itself.

Future research should investigate the processes by which students develop an integrated understanding of science, their motivations for continuing to link ideas together, and the factors that support this process across the lifespan. (See, for example, CCMS's draft national research agenda available at http://www .sciencematerialscenter.org/research_agenda.htm.) In addition, research on more targeted questions—such as identifying features of curriculum materials that make a difference in students' learning—deserve attention.

Implications for Policy

CCMS and TELS both acknowledge that well-aligned and coherent curriculum and assessment materials are insufficient on their own to accomplish the kinds of changes that are needed in science teaching and learning. The goals targeted must be feasible for learners. Teachers need the knowledge and skills to make effective use of materials, which requires changes in how teachers are prepared and in the environments in which they work. School leaders need knowledge and opportunity to guide teachers and students. The curricular issues raised in this chapter point to a few modest recommendations for federal and state education policies that can make a difference.

National Science Benchmarks and Standards. Ideally, all science curriculum materials would be based on high-quality learning goals, and there would be adequate instructional time available for students to achieve those goals. In reality, however, the materials being used in most of the nation's classrooms are based on 50 different sets of state science standards, and most of these materials have been judged to be lacking in coherence as well as accuracy and specificity (Roseman et al., 2008). Time allotted for science instruction continues to shrink in response to the emphasis on reading and mathematics in the current era of No Child Left Behind. Both the *Benchmarks for Science Literacy* (AAAS, 1993) and the *National Science Education Standards* (NRC, 1996), while imperfect, offer educators and curriculum developers and publishers a starting point for addressing the incoherence resulting from state standards. Some debate has focused on the idea of national standards and their benefit if carefully designed (Olson & Hoff, 2006). The framework for the 2009 National Assessment of Educational Progress (NAEP) in science, which draws extensively on *Benchmarks* and *NSES*, offers one possibility for building national consensus on science learning goals. How many topics and ideas can be targeted in ways that foster students' integrated understanding of science depends on the nature of the learner (including prior experiences), the time available, and the quality of the curriculum materials themselves. Ultimately, what is needed are well-designed science standards that are both coherent and feasible for students to achieve in the time available. Empirical tests to identify more precisely what, how, and when students are able to learn important science ideas are crucial.

Textbook and Technology Adoption. States and school districts need to offer more flexibility in textbook and technology adoption policies and in assessment practices so that schools can take advantage of the innovative, research-based curriculum materials now being developed. Allowing schools to adopt textbooks and technologies that are aligned with national standards and benchmarks, as well as with the relevant state standards, would be a good first step.

Investment in Curriculum Research and Development. Little improvement in science learning can be accomplished without better and more uniform data on what works, why, and with whom. Those involved in designing and carrying out research on the effectiveness of curriculum know the enormous complexities involved in conducting the kinds of research that are needed and in interpreting the results, yet it is essential to have high-quality data to inform the many decisions in which curriculum plays a role.

Whatever approach is taken, it is important that all involved be realistic about the time and resources needed to produce high-quality materials and to evaluate their effectiveness. It will require significant and more consistent funding over the long term from federal government agencies such as the National Science Foundation and the Department of Education, from private foundations and professional organizations, and from state agencies. Research on the effectiveness of curriculum materials should be viewed as an essential step in the development of standards, assessments, and curriculum. Budgets and timelines for development projects should reflect this reality.

Research programs need to include more studies that have a broader focus. Many learning studies provide insight into what can be accomplished under carefully defined conditions, using precisely focused instruction, working with a small number of students, and dealing with a small number of ideas and skills. Broader contexts must now be studied to fully understand the role that powerful curriculum materials could play as more and more users participate. Funding for TELS, for example, has enabled study of the effects of scaling up its interventions to over 150 teachers in entire school districts in six states. At the same time, studies are needed to guide customization of instruction for specific learners and teachers.

PART II

Perspectives on Integrated Understanding and Coherence

3

Designing Learning Environments to Support Students' Integrated Understanding

Joseph S. Krajcik, James D. Slotta,
Katherine L. McNeill, and Brian J. Reiser

A S ROSEMAN, LINN, AND KOPPAL (Chapter 2) argue, current instructional materials, textbooks, and learning technologies often fail to apply what is known about teaching and learning in their effort to help support effective science learning environments. A learning environment encompasses the characteristics and interactions in the classroom context that are influenced by the teacher, the students, the physical environment, and resources, including instructional materials and technology tools. In this chapter, we focus on design principles used to inform the development of coherent instructional materials and technology tools that will create effective learning environments that support students in constructing integrated understanding. We discuss the current need for innovative and coherent science instructional materials, describe the shared design principles that the Technology Enhanced Learning in Science (TELS) Center and the Center for Curriculum Materials in Science (CCMS) employ to develop such materials, then illustrate those design principles through a discussion of examples. We close by discussing some challenges and implications for designers of new instructional materials as well as for policy makers.

Major breakthroughs in science will require students to learn science content in greater depth and to gain the habits of mind that will allow them to use such knowledge in new situations they encounter throughout their lives. Various policy documents (Duschl et al., 2007; Wilson & Berenthal, 2006) stress that all students, including those with a diversity of backgrounds and prior knowledge, need to develop a deeper understanding of a few big ideas through carefully sequenced instructional materials. The *National Science Education Standards* (NRC, 1996) espouse this same point of view by arguing that "less is more."

Focusing on big ideas allows learners to explain a range of phenomena and sets the stage for further learning, as these ideas provide meaningful structures that students can apply in other contexts. The big ideas of science include both conceptual ideas and scientific practices, and during the last 20 years educational scientists have uncovered ways to promote such learning in classrooms (Bransford et al., 2000). Several existing research projects point to the viability of learning environments geared toward elucidating the big ideas (Linn & Hsi, 2000; Quintana et al., 2004). Yet, schools in the United States still continue to slip back into coverage of randomly selected and unconnected ideas that teachers and school administrators presume will be on high-stakes tests. TELS and CCMS have responded to the call for reform of science education by developing instructional materials for teachers and students that engage learners in developing integrated understanding of key concepts.

SHARED DESIGN PRINCIPLES

CCMS and TELS share a commitment to project-based science, wherein students actively pursue new science topics to develop a personally relevant understanding. Project-based science has the potential to help students develop a deep understanding of science as they explore important and meaningful questions through a process of investigation and collaboration. Project-based science incorporates explicit design principles that encourage active engagement of students to promote learning (Krajcik & Blumenfeld, 2006). Design principles are guidelines that have the potential to productively bridge theory and practice (Kali, 2006). To promote engagement and integrated understanding, CCMS and TELS make use of the following common design principles:

1. Align materials and assessments with learning goals
2. Contextualize the learning of key ideas in real-world problems
3. Engage students in scientific practices that foster the use of key ideas
4. Use technology as a tool to explore problems and to provide scaffolding
5. Engage students and teachers in collaborative environments
6. Support teachers in adopting and carrying out inquiry-based projects

Align Materials and Assessments with Learning Goals

This design principle reflects a commitment to the creation of learning environments that address well-specified learning goals. National and state standards (AAAS, 1993; NRC, 1996) have the potential to provide guidelines for the science content and scientific inquiry skills that schools and teachers must focus on, yet the usefulness of this guidance depends on the quality of the standards. As argued in Chapter 2, the development of standards that are coherent and feasible is a significant issue in itself. Ideally, standards will provide clear learning goals for a curriculum. Science education reform efforts advocate alignment of instructional materials and assessments with local, state, or national science standards (Knapp, 1997; Wilson & Berenthal, 2006). Teachers and school districts rightly demand such alignment, in order to understand for themselves what portions of the curriculum standards are being covered by project-based activities. Thus, creating instructional and assessment materials that help students focus on the big ideas of science (Chapter 2; Chapter 7, DeBoer, Lee & Husic), as well as specific standards for content and inquiry skills, is central to the design of learning environments within CCMS and TELS.

Contextualize the Learning of Key Ideas in Real-World Problems

Contextualizing instruction to connect with students' everyday experiences is an important consideration in designing science instruction for diverse learners (Chapter 4, Tate, Clark, Gallagher, & McLaughlin). To implement this design principle, researchers from CCMS and TELS design learning environments in which students are engaged in meaningful problem-solving activities. One way to accomplish this is through the use of driving questions. Driving questions are a hallmark of project-based science in that they anchor instruction to a real-world problem that learners find meaningful and important (Blumenfeld et al., 1991; Krajcik & Czerniak, 2007). In this way, driving questions help to contextualize what students will learn, engage a variety of learners, and connect learning goals throughout a unit. An example of a driving question that has proven highly engaging to middle school students is "Can good friends make me sick?" (Hug, Krajcik, & Marx, 2005). Hug et al. have used a project built around this question for a number of years, and it has sustained the interest of students from urban and suburban areas, and those with a variety of different backgrounds and interests, as they worked toward important learning goals related to body systems and the spread of communicable diseases.

It is important to select the driving question carefully so that it will steer students toward an important set of ideas and the connections among them. The driving question serves to organize and direct activities of the project and provides a context in which important science ideas and practices can be used and explored. Driving questions hold designers accountable for ensuring that the need for science ideas and practices is evident to and appreciated by students.

Engage Students in Scientific Practices That Foster the Use of Key Ideas

In addition to targeting an important set of science ideas, learning environments should engage students in complex tasks that require them to use those ideas through a variety of scientific practices. TELS and CCMS employ a variety of scientific practices within their designs in ways that highlight the importance of knowledge in use, meaning that students are able to apply the relevant content knowledge to investigate, represent, and explain phenomena. The various scientific practices that are addressed in project-based activities include constructing scientific explanations and arguments, constructing models, collecting and using data as evidence, finding and evaluating information, designing and conducting investigations, and collaborating with peers in design or debate.

To support students in such scientific practices, both TELS and CCMS have designed learning environments that make use of scaffolds. In this context, scaffolds are defined as temporary supports that allow students to take part in complex tasks that they otherwise would not be able to accomplish independently. The purpose of scaffolding is to provide support to extend student competencies according to what students know (Bransford et al., 2000; Wood, Bruner, & Ross, 1976). Kali (2006) and Quintana et al. (2004) have suggested guidelines that developers can use to design scaffolds to support students as they engage in complex tasks.

Use Technology as a Tool to Explore Problems and to Provide Scaffolding

Technology can help transform the science classroom into an environment in which learners actively construct knowledge (Linn, 1997; Metcalf-Jackson, Krajcik, & Soloway, 2000; Novak & Krajcik, 2004). TELS and CCMS use technology both as a learning tool and as a means of providing scaffolding for students and teachers, referring collectively to these systems as *learning technologies*. Learning technologies can be powerful cognitive tools that help teachers foster inquiry and student learning. Learning technologies allow students to extend what they can do in the classroom, using the computer to access real data on the World Wide Web, expand interaction and collaboration with others via networks, use electronic probes to gather data, employ graphing and visualization tools to analyze data, create models of complex systems, and produce multimedia artifacts.

Engage Students and Teachers in Collaborative Environments

CCMS and TELS have developed their materials in partnership with teachers, knowing that classrooms are integral communities and that any curriculum innovation must fit within the ecology of each classroom in which it hopes to succeed (Chapter 5, Davis & Varma). These learning environments promote learning within a social context. The aim is to allow the science classroom to become a community of learners (Lave & Wenger, 1991) wherein students collaborate with their peers and their teachers to ask questions, form conclusions, make sense of information, discuss data, and present findings. Collaboration helps students build shared understanding of scientific ideas and of the nature of the scientific enterprise as they engage in discourse with their classmates and with adults outside the classroom.

Support Teachers in Adopting and Carrying Out Inquiry-Based Projects

Enacting reform-based instructional programs, such as project-based science, raises challenges for teachers who may be unfamiliar with the pedagogical techniques required to successfully implement the new approach (Davis & Krajcik, 2005; Chapter 5). Moreover, when adopting materials developed by researchers, teachers may also lack important content knowledge (Magnusson, Krajcik, & Borko, 1999; Shulman, 1986). Thus, if teachers find themselves short on content or pedagogical background, it will be particularly taxing for them to adopt a new project-based method in which they are expected to help students develop in-depth understanding of science content and scientific practices as they conduct project activities. To assist teachers in meeting the high expectations of enacting projects that engage learners in complex tasks, TELS provides teachers with professional development opportunities and technology supports, whereas CCMS designs instructional materials to be educative for teachers, so that by promoting teachers' learning they can expand teachers' comfort zones and ultimately benefit students (Ball & Cohen, 1996; Davis & Krajcik, 2005). In addition, because teachers work in unique environments, TELS and CCMS materials must accommodate adaptation and customization by teachers to provide a good match to individual classroom situations.

ILLUSTRATING DESIGN PRINCIPLES

In the next section, the six design principles are illustrated using examples from TELS and CCMS researchers as they designed learning environments for project-based science.

Align Materials and Assessments with Learning Goals

To ensure that students learn the most important ideas of science, TELS and CCMS researchers design learning environments to meet key learning content and practice goals. In selecting these learning goals, researchers from both centers choose goals that will provide the most leverage in helping students reach broad scientific literacy. Complex inquiry projects typically require considerable curriculum time in order to enable students to focus on ideas, revisit those ideas, collaborate with peers, apply concepts in a fertile context, and develop deep understanding. Teachers must feel confident that the investment of that much time is warranted in terms of meeting required state and local science standards.

Although alignment of instructional materials, assessments, and standards is currently a national goal, few if any instructional materials actually succeed in meeting it. By designing curriculum and assessment materials to align with key learning goals that target the big ideas of science content and practices, TELS and CCMS researchers simultaneously help students meet established standards and prepare them for their future studies.

Aligning Instructional Materials with Content Standards. All TELS materials and assessments prioritize the needs of teachers, schools, and school districts with respect to identifying learning goals. TELS performs a standards mapping for all projects to help teachers readjust their own curriculum plans and document content coverage for purposes of school and district accountability. This standards map includes a special emphasis on the inquiry component of state and national science standards—a component that is often not adequately addressed by teachers, who typically give priority to the coverage of content standards.

TELS has also been very deliberate in choosing project topics that are directly aligned with science standards and that appeal to teachers. The initial matrix of TELS curriculum topics was determined through a focus group method that involved teachers from middle school earth, life, and physical sciences and from high school chemistry, biology, and physics (Linn, Husic, Slotta, & Tinker, 2006). The result of those focus group studies was a set of 12 topics that represented the most important and most challenging science topics from the six science course areas addressed by TELS.

Content and inquiry standards are used as important design references in the development of TELS curricula. For example, one major topic to be addressed for high school chemistry was balancing chemical equations. The TELS "Chemistry Science Investigators" (CSI) project therefore had to address this learning goal in addition to the important inquiry objective of linking different kinds of representations in chemistry (e.g., molecular diagrams with chemical equations). TELS designers chose the context of global climate change, and employed a variety of inquiry activities relating to the chemical reactions that result in the buildup of greenhouse gases. In developing the specific sequence of activities for this project, TELS researchers consulted content standards related to the topic of chemical reactions and made sure that these standards were directly addressed or that teachers were given specific suggestions about how to build connections to the standards through preliminary or subsequent instruction.

One of the major principles of CCMS is the importance of meeting key learning goals. Designers of CCMS's "Investigating and Questioning Our World Through Science and Technology" (IQWST) middle school curriculum ensure that materials will meet key learning goals by applying a three-step process. These steps, which are described in detail below, are (a) select big ideas that link to

TABLE 3.1   Example of an Unpacked Standard

Content Standard	Unpacked Standard
A substance has characteristic properties, such as density, a boiling point, and solubility, all of which are independent of the amount of the sample.*	Substances have distinct properties that can be used to distinguish and separate one substance from another. Properties such as density, melting point, and solubility describe the unique characteristics of substances. Density is the mass contained within a unit volume. Melting point is the temperature at which a solid changes to a liquid. Solubility is the ability of a solid to dissolve in a liquid.

National Science Education Standards (NRC, 1996, p. 154).

standards, (b) unpack the standards, and (c) develop learning performances that express the desired cognitive tasks and that align with the curriculum and assessments (Krajcik et al., 2008).

IQWST designers select big ideas by two primary methods. First, the big idea must have explanatory power in that it is necessary for understanding a variety of phenomena. Second, the big idea must be necessary for future learning in the sense that it is generative or is needed to understand related topics. The particle nature of matter is one such idea. The particle nature of matter helps explain a host of phenomena from how water evaporates to why mass is conserved in chemical reactions. Moreover, understanding the particle nature of matter gives an individual the ability to understand related advanced topics such as molecular genetics. It is also generative in that learners can use the particle model to explain other related phenomena, such as why a sealed can explodes when thrown into a fire. The particle nature of matter also links to national standards. In fact, the *Atlas of Science Literacy* (AAAS, 2001) has an entire strand map dedicated to it.

Once the designers have identified a big idea and the corresponding standards, IQWST researchers unpack the standards. The process of unpacking involves breaking apart and expanding the various concepts in a standard to elaborate on the intended science content. When IQWST researchers unpack a standard, they also determine whether the content is suitable for middle school students by considering common student difficulties, prior conceptions that pose challenges, as well as what prior science knowledge the students may or may not have. Unpacking allows designers to develop a much deeper understanding of what the content and inquiry standards mean, and of the essential aspects of standards that need to be considered in curriculum design (Krajcik et al., 2008). Table 3.1 shows an example of an unpacked standard from the IQWST seventh-grade chemistry unit "How Can I Make New Stuff from Old Stuff?" The left column shows the standard in its original form, and the right column shows the unpacked version.

Designing Learning Performances. Developing a deep understanding of the content standards is a critical step in the IQWST design process. However, science standards are declarative statements of scientific ideas, and as such they do not specify the type of reasoning students need to engage in with the ideas. Consequently, once IQWST designers have identified and unpacked the key science standards, they begin work on developing learning performances (Krajcik et al., 2008). The learning performances concept builds on the "understanding performances" of Perkins, Crismond, Simmons, and Unger (1995). Learning performances specify the cognitive tasks that students must accomplish. To develop learning performances, IQWST researchers focus on the scientific practices described by the Habits of Mind Standards of AAAS (1993) and on the scientific inquiry portions of the *National Science Education Standards* (NRC, 1996). IQWST researchers have identified a variety of practices students should engage in, such as designing investigations and creating models (Krajcik et al., 2008). Through learning performances, IQWST researchers translate science content ideas into cognitive tasks, allowing them to carefully specify reasoning activities that will require students to actually use the content they are learning. Thus, creation of learning performance tasks allows designers to move beyond mere superficial links to standards and into the reasoning students need to apply to use that knowledge.

Table 3.2 illustrates how IQWST designers develop learning performances by crossing a content standard with a practice. In this example, students must use their understanding of the characteristic properties of a substance to write a scientific explanation about whether the material in one sample is the same as the material in another sample. Development of learning performances is an essential part of the design of both the learning tasks within the curriculum and the assessment tasks used to evaluate student learning, because the learning performances provide clear and explicit goals for the designers (Krajcik et al., 2008).

Aligning Assessments. TELS has designed and implemented a series of benchmark, pre-, post-, and embedded assessments. The goal is to assure teachers, school and district administrators, and policy makers that TELS materials are aligned with a carefully articulated set of learning goals that can be measured for the effectiveness of their impact (see Chapter 7). Each year, TELS has conducted a comprehensive benchmark assessment in all participating schools, testing some students who use the TELS curriculum materials and some who do not. The following year, the same benchmark assessment is performed again, also with some students who used TELS curriculum materials the previous year and some who did not. Over a sequence of years, TELS has been able to compare the impact of its curriculum approach on cohorts of students who have worked with the technology-enhanced projects for 1, 2, 3, or 4 years. Moreover, for all students who conducted a TELS project, pre- and postassessments were performed, along with embedded assessments. This elaborate assessment program helps TELS develop-

TABLE 3.2   Developing Learning Performances

Content Standard ×	Practice (Scientific Inquiry Standard)	= Learning Performance
A substance has characteristic properties, such as density, a boiling point, and solubility, all of which are independent of the amount of the sample.*	Develop ... explanations ... using evidence.† Think critically and logically to make the relationships between evidence and explanation.‡	Students construct scientific explanations (a) stating a claim whether a sample is the same as another sample, (b) using evidence in the form of properties, and (c) reasoning that a substance has characteristic properties, all of which are independent of the amount of the sample.

*National Science Education Standards (NRC, 1996, p. 154).

†National Science Education Standards (NRC, 1996, p. 145, Content Standard A: 1/4, 5–8).

‡National Science Education Standards (NRC, 1996, p. 145, Content Standard A: 1/5, 5–8).

ers and educators understand how these carefully aligned curriculum projects directly address student understanding of content and inquiry standards.

The key lesson learned through the IQWST approach is that the unpacking of content standards followed by development of learning performances allows designers to create materials that have well-aligned instructional and assessment components (Krajcik et al., 2008). The National Research Council (Wilson & Berenthal, 2006) has recently argued for the importance of aligning learning goals with instruction and assessment. The IQWST process provides a concrete model that allows curriculum designers to operationalize alignment of standards with instructional tasks and assessments. Chapter 7 discusses the IQWST assessment process in greater detail.

Contextualize the Learning of Key Ideas in Real-World Problems

Coherent science instruction should have students exploring solutions to questions (NRC, 1996, 2000b) that they find meaningful and relevant to their lives. Both TELS and CCMS researchers strive to design learning environments that contextualize learning with meaningful questions, problems, and phenomena that students find of value and that can sustain their interest over time. One of the major challenges developers face is creating relevant and engaging contexts that also meet important learning goals.

Creating Richly Contextualized Inquiry Projects. TELS researchers have developed a successful approach to creating richly contextualized inquiry projects. First, they articulate a suitable context that allows relevant connections to the targeted science learning goals (e.g., design projects such as "Houses in the Desert" or debate projects such as the "Deformed Frog" debate or the "Genetically Modified Food" debate). Next, they carefully author the sequence of project activities and technology scaffolds to help students apply science content to the project context through inquiry practices (e.g., critique of evidence, argumentation, and design). In "Houses in the Desert," students apply science principles and make use of evidence gathered from their own Web searches to design a house that is suitable for desert dwelling (Cuthbert & Slotta, 2004). Such projects provide a fertile context in a contemporary controversy (e.g., the design of houses to be energy efficient) and engage students with relevant science content as they conduct inquiry activities relating to the context.

Technology scaffolds for learning activities may include interactive models or simulations developed by the Concord Consortium (e.g., Genscope, Dynamica, or Molecular Workbench: see http://www.concord.org). For example, for the high school physics topic of "relative velocities," the TELS designers chose the context of automotive airbags. The challenge to students was to determine why airbags sometimes kill shorter drivers or babies in car seats, and to think about the design of "smarter" airbag systems. Students made progress in this project by exploring a model (using Concord's Dynamica system) of a driver and an airbag that moved from opposite directions toward one another (see Figure 3.1).

Each TELS project is carefully designed in this way to help students apply inquiry practices to develop their own ideas about science content in the context of the project. A project typically includes between five and eight activities, each of which takes students approximately 1 day to complete. An activity consists of steps that are followed by students (e.g., Web pages to visit, notes to take, or online discussions) within the Web-Based Science Inquiry Environment (WISE), a technology framework designed to help learners stay on course through complex inquiry projects and to help teachers monitor their progress. (A more complete description of WISE follows, in the discussion of the use of technology as a tool to provide scaffolding.)

Using Driving Questions. CCMS and TELS curriculum units motivate inquiry through creating meaningful contexts to engage diverse students in learning science. The units are structured around driving questions and phenomena that are motivating and personally relevant to students. In pursuit of answers to the driving questions or explanations of the phenomena, students are required to apply science concepts and strategies to investigate a complex set of data.

The context for the inquiry is created through the use of a driving question, an open-ended question that connects with authentic interests and curiosities all students have about the world (Blumenfeld et al., 1991; Singer, Marx, Krajcik, &

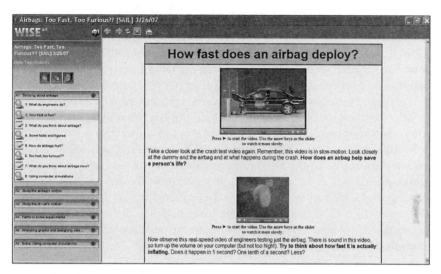

FIGURE 3.1   Screen shot from "Airbags: Too Fast, Too Furious??"
This TELS inquiry project addresses the content learning goal of "relative velocities" through the context of automotive airbags and risk of injury.

Chambers, 2000). Driving questions must meet the four criteria outlined by Krajcik et al. (2002): Is it worthwhile in that it focuses on key scientific ideas? Is it feasible? Is it real world? Is it meaningful? And, to create a unit that is broadly applicable, designers must add a fifth concern: Will students from a variety of backgrounds and experiences will find the question engaging?

For the seventh-grade IQWST chemistry unit, designers selected the driving question, "How can I make new stuff from old stuff?" Although this question at first might not seem motivating to middle school students, this unit has been in use for the last 5 years, and it has held the interest of students from urban and suburban settings and with a variety of different backgrounds and interests (Krajcik et al., 2008; McNeill & Krajcik, 2008c). However, IQWST designers have learned that a driving question in itself will not sustain student engagement and motivation. Driving questions need to be tied to anchoring events (Cognition and Technology Group at Vanderbilt, 1990) that help students see the value of the driving question. Anchoring events provide students with key phenomena that will stimulate their interest in pursuing the driving question (Krajcik & Blumenfeld, 2006). For instance, students explore "How can I make new stuff from old stuff?" by making soap from fat (lard) and sodium hydroxide. They begin by investigating the properties of fat and soap. Many students are surprised that the slimy and greasy material of fat (the "old stuff") can be changed into a common household product used every day, soap (the "new stuff").

Motivating with Phenomena. In addition to the driving question and the anchoring event, the "Stuff" unit is filled with motivating phenomena in the form of real-world examples of the importance of new stuff formed from old stuff. For instance, students explore why the Statue of Liberty is green and what happens in fireworks. Throughout the unit, IQWST designers use students' everyday experiences and interests with fat and soap, as well as other phenomena, to help them see that chemical reactions do not happen only in science classrooms and science laboratories, but rather they are constantly occurring in the everyday world and are critical in our lives (Krajcik et al., 2008). Besides experiencing phenomena in the classroom, students are provided with a variety of vicarious experiences through reading materials that take into consideration the developmental level and experiences of the learners (Textual Tools Study Group at the University of Michigan, 2006). For instance, students read about how baking a cake or cookies, a common experience for most students, is an everyday example of a chemical reaction.

Contextualizing Learning Goals. In creating curriculum units, IQWST designers carefully think through the desired learning goals to ensure that the driving questions and contexts are worthwhile—that is, that they will engage and move students along a path to understanding additional important learning goals. The driving question for the "Stuff" unit was designated as "How can I make new stuff from old stuff?" because that question could encompass learning goals for the unit: ideas about substances and their properties, chemical reactions, and conservation of mass. The driving question for the unit allowed designers to focus on meeting learning goals associated with these important ideas. For instance, in order to understand *that* new stuff was made from old stuff, students must understand that the bulk properties of the products are different from those of the starting materials, and in order to understand *how* new stuff is different from old stuff, students must understand that the atoms that made up the molecules of the old stuff combined in new ways to create the new stuff.

It is critical for designers to realize that developing driving questions that align with learning goals is challenging. Development of IQWST units starts with learning goals—the main ideas students need to learn. Only after the learning goals of a unit are selected and understood do IQWST researchers wrestle with developing a driving question that is meaningful and is part of the real world of the students. This process helps ensure that each of the units in IQWST will allow students to learn important ideas.

In contrast, Center for Learning Technologies in Urban Schools (LeTUS) units were designed by starting with fertile contexts and a driving question and then seeing what science concepts and principles were needed to answer the driving question. Starting with a contextualized setting allows for the development of richly motivating environments. However, this approach does not necessarily allow designers to systematically meet learning goals that link to standards or to build coherent curriculum units. In this context, the definition of coherence is similar to that used in Chapter 2, in that the materials help students link their scientific understandings to make sense of experiences and observations and explain new situations. Often, integrated understanding develops over time as students grapple with the deeper meanings of ideas.

The two approaches of IQWST and LeTUS require different trade-offs. Starting with important learning goals allows designers to build curricula that ensure learning goals linked to standards will be met, but designers must struggle to find contexts that will simultaneously engage learners and sustain their interest in meeting those goals. In contrast, designers can begin with richly contextualized environments that will motivate learners, but then they will face a challenge in finding important learning goals that can be systematically developed in the unit.

Engage Students in Scientific Practices That Foster the Use of Key Ideas

Engaging students in scientific practices such as constructing explanations and designing investigations serves as a central design principle in creating learning environments that capture the interest of learners and foster inquiry. In CCMS and TELS projects, students operate in complex contexts in which they try to answer the driving question through a series of investigations and explorations. During this process, students employ a variety of scientific inquiry practices, such as asking questions, designing investigations, using data as evidence, constructing scientific explanations and arguments, and developing and testing models. Although engaging in these types of activities is essential, middle school students often struggle because the practices are new to them (Krajcik et al., 1998).

Using Models and Visualizations. To encourage students to build their own understanding, TELS projects frequently prompt learners to reflect about the topics (e.g., an opening prompt to start the investigation of airbags asks students, "Why do you think that airbags deploy so quickly in an accident? Do you think an airbag could injure you?"). TELS projects also emphasize authentic lifelong science practices, such as critiquing evidence and designing arguments. These are practices that will help students succeed throughout their lives when they encounter scientific evidence (e.g., new evidence about global climate change, or findings from the U.S. Food and Drug Administration) or scientific debates (e.g., debates about stem cell research).

TELS curriculum projects were designed to engage students deeply in scientific practices related to the use of models and visualizations. In the airbags study, the model is carefully presented to students one element at a time: first the airbag, so that students can systematically manipulate its movement, including a linked graph of position versus time; next, the driver's head, which students can adjust for as many trials as they wish. Finally, when presented with the combined model of the driver and the airbag, students are asked to specify their goal for each trial of the model, thereby making their goals and rationale more explicit for themselves, their group partner, and their teacher.

The IQWST sixth-grade physics and chemistry units support students in constructing scientific models (Shwartz et al., in press). In the sixth-grade unit "Seeing the Light: Can I Believe My Eyes?" students develop models of how light interacts with matter. The key idea is for students to create a model that can explain various phenomena related to how humans see.

In addition to modeling and visualization, TELS tries to include in its curricula other scientific practices, such as collection of data from hands-on experiments with electronic sensing devices, data table creation, graph manipulation, evidence critique, and argumentation. All of these student actions are captured by the WISE technology environment, providing teachers with easy access to details of students' activities for purposes of assessment and feedback. For example, the SenseMaker software has been used within the WISE environment to engage students in argumentation around topics such as light propagation. In the discussion of the use of technology as a tool to provide scaffolding, we will provide more detailed examples of technology tools that support students in these scientific practices.

Constructing Scientific Explanations. At CCMS, one of the ways that IQWST designers support students in scientific practices is through task decomposition (Quintana et al., 2004). For example, IQWST designers developed an instructional framework for scientific explanation that breaks down the complex practice into three components: claim, evidence, and reasoning (McNeill, Lizotte, Krajcik, & Marx, 2006; Moje et al., 2004). Science is fundamentally about explaining natural phenomena (Nagel, 1961), and justifying claims is part of the social construction of knowledge in a scientific community (Driver, Newton, & Osborne, 2000). To support students in this complex practice, IQWST designers developed an instructional framework to make the normally implicit structure of scientific explanation explicit by reducing the complexity and focusing the learner's attention on the relevant features of the practice (Pea, 2004). Like many science educators, IQWST designers use an adapted form of Toulmin's (1958) model of argumentation. The *claim* (similar to Toulmin's claim) is an assertion or conclusion that answers the original question or problem. The *evidence* (similar to Toulmin's data) is appropriate and sufficient scientific data that are used to support the claim. Finally, the *reasoning* (a combination of Toulmin's warrant and backing) is justification that articulates why the data count as evidence to support the claim by using scientific principles.

During the first pilot of the "Stuff" chemistry unit for seventh-graders, IQWST designers did not explicitly integrate the instructional framework for scientific explanation into the instructional materials. Analysis of student artifacts, pretests and posttests, and classroom discourse revealed that students struggled with justifying their claims with appropriate evidence and reasoning (Harris, McNeill, Lizotte, Marx, & Krajcik, 2006; Krajcik et al., 2008). In particular, students struggled with the reasoning component and were not able to provide a justification for why their evidence supported their claim. Consequently, IQWST designers revised the curriculum by integrating the instructional framework of claim, evidence, and reasoning into the materials and providing both the teacher and the students with a variety of supports (Krajcik et al., 2008). For example, a lesson was added to the unit that introduced scientific explanations, and curricular scaffolds were integrated throughout the student materials (McNeill et al., 2006). In the next enactment of the curriculum, students had much greater success in writing scientific explanations, especially in terms of their inclusion of appropriate evidence and reasoning (Krajcik et al., 2008).

Although the students had much greater success with the revised curriculum, IQWST designers were also interested in finding the most effective design of the curricular scaffolds for scientific explanations. Consequently, IQWST designers investigated whether the curricular supports were more effective if they remained constant throughout the 8-week unit, or if the language in the supports decreased or faded over time (McNeill et al., 2006). IQWST investigators found that fading written prompts for scientific explanations better prepared students to write scientific explanations when they were not provided with support, particularly for the reasoning component, which the students had struggled with the most (McNeill et al., 2006). This suggests that fading support might also be an appropriate technique for other complex scientific practices, such as designing investigations and developing and testing models.

Use Technology as a Tool to Explore Problems and to Provide Scaffolding

Science education should help students become lifelong technology learners. Technology should not be used simply as a means of delivering traditional content (e.g., multiple-choice assessments or text materials) or to add visual or audio media to traditional instructional materials. Rather, technology should serve as a cognitive partner for students and teachers (Linn & Hsi, 2000; Salomon, Perkins, & Globerson, 1991), helping them explore questions, design their own solutions, and construct an integrated understanding of science topics. Technology tools that serve as cognitive partners have the potential to extend the range of what students can do in the classroom, at home, or on the playground.

For example, visualizations or simulations of science topics can provide opportunities for students to visualize and explore phenomena and test conjectures in ways that would not otherwise be possible. New opportunities for learning can also be presented through real-time display of data from electronic sensing devices, through collaboration environments that encourage students to critique and expand upon one another's ideas, or through creativity tools that allow students to quickly design artifacts or arguments. Below, we outline some of the ways in which CCMS and TELS use learning technologies to support students in developing integrated understanding.

Scaffolding Student Work in Projects. TELS designed the WISE technology environment to help learners stay on track throughout the course of complex inquiry projects, which can require between 3 and 10 class periods (45 minutes per period) to complete (for more information about WISE, see the Preface). An inquiry map guides students as they conduct project activities. This frees teachers to interact deeply with students in the class who might be having difficulty. Numerous learning technologies have been developed as part of WISE to scaffold different learning processes. For example, the SenseMaker application helps students sort their evidence from the Web into common "claims" within an overarching argument, enabling them to use diverse kinds of evidence in developing and supporting their point of view within a debate project. The WISE drawing tool provides students with a background image that is relevant to the curriculum (e.g., a map of the United States) and several functions they can perform with that background (e.g., rubber stamps of an invasive species) to represent their ideas visually. These examples illustrate how computer-based environments can support students in various scientific practices.

The WISE environment, which is used for all TELS curricula, scaffolds students in a wide range of activities where they work individually, in pairs, and as a whole class. Students search the World Wide Web for relevant information to support their arguments or designs. They observe simulations and manipulate models, create concept maps, and graph data. They collaborate online, using peer-review software that allows one group of students to prepare a presentation for critical review by peers, and then review other groups' presentations.

In addition to serving students, WISE can scaffold teachers as they integrate complex inquiry projects into curricula. Technology tools and environments can support new kinds of interactions between students and teachers. Teachers are freed to move about the classroom, observing the contents of students' work and learning about their ideas. Teachers can have small-group discussions with students as they work on project activities, leading to timely discussions with the whole class. In addition, the same technology environments can facilitate assessments and student feedback by providing management tools through which teachers can access all student work.

Helping Students Visualize Concepts and Test Their Ideas. Technology tools can extend and enhance the observations students can make in classrooms. For instance, in the CCMS unit "Seeing the Light: Can I Believe My Eyes?" students explore the transmission of light through different materials by using electronic light sensors (probes). Next, they compare what they perceive with their eyes to what they measure with the sensors to reinforce the value of using measuring devices. Electronic sensors attached to computers allow students to digitally record and graph data, thus providing the students with scientific laboratory tools that can extend their observations. Using probes to collect scientific data, of course, is not a new idea. What *is* new, however, is the development of more user-friendly and sophisticated interfaces and software for data collection and graphing, as well as the explicit integration of such technologies into the middle school curriculum. What hasn't changed is that these tools can serve as partners to aid students in observing and making sense of phenomena.

TELS also allows students to investigate ideas by using models and simulations, declaring hypotheses, then setting up tests and performing multiple trials with different settings. In a module on asthma and urban environments (for more details, see Chapter 4), students work with real data from the Web concerning the possible sources of pollutants in their neighborhood. In this way, technology resources (e.g., the Web), interactive applications (e.g., simulations), and learning tools such as data tables and graphs are placed in service to project-based inquiry.

Helping Students Find and Explore Trends in Data. CCMS researchers make use of technology tools to support students in finding trends and making sense of data. Middle school students typically have difficulty making sense of large and dispersed data sets, such as weather and climate data. This is not surprising, because many skilled adults have the same problem. In fact, researchers in these fields often use visualization techniques to make sense of data (Edelson, 2001). For instance, in the IQWST seventh-grade earth science unit called "How Is Weather Predictable?" students use visualization software (Edelson & Reiser, 2006) to find trends in weather and climate data. Visualization software supports students in identifying patterns in the data that would be difficult to recognize without the supports. Visualizations can include diagrams, maps, charts, and graphs. For instance, it is difficult for students to see how temperature fluctuates across a large region just by observing average temperatures for the region. However, software that converts numerical data to visual patterns allows students to see trends in the data (Edelson & Reiser, 2006). By visualizing numerical data in this fashion, the technology tools once again support and serve as an intellectual partners for students.

Simulating Events Not Possible in the Classroom. Learning technologies also allow students to explore what it might be like to manipulate variables in ways that would otherwise be just too difficult, unethical, or impossible without the technologies. For instance, in the LeTUS project, researchers designed a tool called Cooties™ for the Palm Pilot (http://www.goknow.com/) that allows students to explore the spread of disease (Hug et al., 2005). Students meet and possibly "infect" each other by beaming between Palm devices. The Cooties program tracks which students have met and will tell students if their program has become a carrier of the disease. After the wave of meeting and infection, students can work together to determine who were the initial carriers of the disease and trace its transmission path. Cooties allows students to explore how disease can spread through a community, an activity that would be prohibited without the tool.

In the current IQWST work, researchers make use of learning technologies to help students engage in explorations of complex relationships among variables. In a sixth-grade biology unit called "Where Have All the Creatures Gone?" students explore population dynamics using a simulation model developed in the NetLogo environment (Wilensky, 1999). The program allows students to explore the ebb and flow of predators and prey, explorations that students would not be able to conduct without the technology. In the sixth-grade chemistry unit called "How Can I Smell Things from Across the Room?" students use molecular animations available through the Concord Consortium (http://www.concord .org) to explore the behavior of gases. In this case, learners examine a model that corresponds to the scientifically normative view of the behavior of gases. The students view and manipulate animations of the particles that make up a gas— manipulations and visualizations that were not possible before the use of technology tools in the classroom. Such technologies are used widely in the materials developed by both TELS and CCMS, providing new opportunities for exploration that can help students form deep and connected understanding of ideas (Linn, 2006).

Creating Dynamic Models. Powerful technology tools can help students build dynamic models, which is an essential inquiry practice. Creating models also supports students in developing integrated understanding (Novak & Krajcik, 2004). In developing models, students begin by specifying the components and rules that govern a phenomenon. Researchers from the University of Michigan developed a program called Model-It (Metcalf-Jackson et al., 2000). This software helps students plan models, supports them in building dynamic models using qualitative relationships, and aids them in testing and evaluating their models (Novak & Krajcik, 2004; Zhang, Liu, & Krajcik, 2006). Thus, Model-It supports students in an essential component of constructing models that previously was extremely difficult if not impossible to accomplish with middle school students. With Model-It, students represent, interpret, and refine their thinking so that they develop more robust understanding. By building models, students also make their thinking visible. Researchers at LeTUS have made use of Model-It in several curriculum units. For instance, in the LeTUS unit called "What Is the Quality of Water in My River?" students build dynamic models of the factors that can affect water quality.

Promoting Valuable and Equitable Exchanges Through Online Discussions. Online discussions enable *all* students to share ideas within a class discussion, in contrast to the typical situation in which only a few students reply to a teacher's questions, and any individual student only rarely receives a reply from his or her peers. Technology tools can open up new opportunities to support peer exchange, in the form of online discussions as well as more elaborate forms of peer collaboration (Linn & Slotta, 2006). The rapid explosion of social networking software and multiuser environments suggests an increasingly important role for such technology in the classroom, as students and teachers alike will come to expect this functionality. TELS has taken some early strides in employing useful collaborative design environments, such as the WISE Collaborative Search Page, where students share resources they found on the Internet (Cuthbert & Slotta, 2004), and the WISE Show-and-Tell environment, where students exchange their work with peers and provide critical feedback. In addition, online discussions are used in nearly all TELS inquiry projects in order to promote equitable and universal participation, as well as a richer array of connections between peers regarding their ideas in science. These applications are discussed in greater detail in the next section.

Engage Students and Teachers in Collaborative Environments

Learning collaboratively with peers is an important lifelong learning skill, and it should be a primary goal of education in science as well as other disciplines. Moreover, substantial research has demonstrated the advantages that can be gained from collaborative learning (e.g., Anderson et al., 2001; Brown & Campione, 1994; Palincsar & Brown, 1984; Scardamalia & Bereiter, 1994). Science educators should therefore investigate how peer interactions and exchanges can lead to greater levels of engagement, more meaningful participation, deeper understanding of science topics, and new roles for teachers. A focus on collaborative inquiry can help transform the thread-worn patterns of lecture and laboratory work too often found in classrooms today (diSessa, 2000; Tyack & Cuban, 1995). Both TELS and CCMS have a rich history of research into the value of collaborative inquiry, resulting in its selection as a common design principle for the centers (discussed by Kali, Fortus, & Ronen-Fuhrmann, Chapter 8, as "Promote productive interactions"). Some of the key findings from both centers related to this principle will be reviewed below.

Promoting Scientific Patterns of Discourse in the Classroom. Traditionally, science classrooms have been dominated by authoritative discourse in which the classroom interactions consist mainly of the teacher initiating a question, a student responding, and the teacher evaluating the response (Lemke, 1990). TELS and CCMS researchers have developed curriculum approaches that move classroom discourse away from this traditional pattern, supporting teachers and students in sharing and building on each other's ideas. For example, CCMS researchers Kuhn and Reiser (2006) transformed typical classroom discourse by requiring students to debate claims and support those claims with evidence. They developed three instructional supports to encourage students to debate one another's ideas during classroom discussions: first, create a need for students to use evidence in the classroom context by requiring students to go beyond regurgitating facts or data and instead to apply evidence to solve a problem; second, create a need for students to argue, through the use of an argument jigsaw and a whole-class debate; and third, make the epistemic criteria explicit by introducing students to an instructional framework for constructing and defending arguments. This framework included a list of questions such as "Why should I believe that your evidence is not an opinion?" and "How is your evidence connected to your claim?" which help students understand the scientific thinking typically included in argumentation.

Scaffolding Student Interactions with Peers and Instructors. Early studies by TELS investigators demonstrated a dramatic increase in the equity of participation in technology-assisted threaded discussions (Linn & Hsi, 2000). Girls, often intimidated in question-and-answer discussions led by teachers, participated equally with boys. In fact, these studies documented nearly universal participation by students. Even more important was that students replied to their peers' ideas, and did so respectfully. It would be very difficult indeed for a teacher to achieve universal participation in a class discussion without technology—particularly if the goal is to get students to reply constructively to their peers' comments and not just to the teacher's questions.

TELS has explored the use of technology scaffolds to transform the classroom into an environment of collaboration and critical reflection. Technology-enhanced inquiry projects can do just that, if they have been carefully designed to allow students opportunities to interact with peers and teachers in meaningful ways. If designed poorly, technology-enhanced instruction can serve to isolate students from peers, and replace the teacher with computer-based instruction. Rather, technology should connect students with peers and guide their interactions, providing helpful information and timely prompts for reflection. TELS has designed technology scaffolds that guide students in preparing for classroom debates, that help them critically review the designs or arguments of their peers, and that enable productive online discussions. Interactions between students and the teacher, typically unspecified by curriculum designers, can also be guided by technology environments. Teachers can be prompted to interact with students, and the technology environment can even reveal student ideas that can inform teacher–student interactions (see Chapter 5).

In studying students' online discussions about malaria control, Slotta (2004) observed that a single classroom could generate nearly 1,000 lines of written text in a single 45-minute session, with most students replying to other students' ideas rather than just the seed topic. This is considerable impact for one class period of activity, given that these students were debating one another's perspectives concerning the control of malaria (i.e., advocating social programs, vaccine research, pesticides, or some combination). Cuthbert and Slotta (2004) explored a more elaborate collaborative scheme, in which students working on the WISE "Houses in the Desert" project were each given a design specialization (roofs, windows, or walls). These students developed a deep understanding of the functions and design applications of their specialization, and then they collaborated with peers from other specialization groups to design their desert houses.

TELS curricula build on this prior research to design collaborative opportunities for students and teachers within the flow of inquiry activities that comprise a project. Online discussions are used in most TELS projects as a means to help students exchange ideas about topics or to help them prepare for a classroom debate. Peer review, using the WISE Show-and-Tell technology tool, is also used to help students exchange ideas and receive feedback in preparation for a final design or debate activity. Perhaps most important, students never work alone in any TELS project. They are always placed by their teacher in a group—typically pairs but sometimes groups of three. The technology environment tracks which students are working together and helps coordinate individual contributions within the group. A new generation of technology environments developed by TELS (for more details, see the Preface) will enable researchers to investigate even more complex designs for peer collaboration, including new ways for teachers to be included in online exchanges with students. Such exchanges— even when they occur between people who are physically in the same room—can be used constructively for purposes of targeted feedback and communication that focuses on the ideas developed by students within a project.

Improving Scientific Discourse in the Classroom. Recent work by CCMS researchers in the IQWST project has also developed supports for teachers and students to engage in a variety of classroom discussions, including argumentative discourse. Whether online or face-to-face, discussions can help students build a more sophisticated understanding by supporting them in making connections between ideas, making sense of concepts, and learning from other students.

However, fostering effective discussions in project-based classrooms can be extremely challenging (Krajcik, Blumenfeld, Marx, & Soloway, 1994). Research shows that students' discussions can improve through scaffolding (Songer, 1996). Quintana et al. (2004) suggest that providing learners with reminders and guidance can facilitate articulation during sense making.

IQWST materials make use of this scaffolding strategy to facilitate sense making and conversations between students by providing teachers with a list of prompts to facilitate and guide discussions. Moreover, the IQWST materials are very explicit in the types of conversations that students and teachers are encouraged to take part in. IQWST researchers have identified three primary types of discussion used across IQWST units in order to help teachers incorporate these types of discussion in their classrooms. Table 3.3, modified from the frontmatter of the IQWST materials (Sutherland & Shwartz, 2007), describes the various discussion types and provides example prompts used in the IQWST materials.

Typical discourse in the classroom would include a variety of these different discussion types. For example, a teacher might use both brainstorming questions and probes for understanding. The conversation types can also become intermingled. For example, when summarizing what happened during an investigation, students might make different claims from the results of their work. This can lead easily into a discussion that incorporates argumentative discourse in which students debate different conclusions and provide evidence for their conclusions. Current research is still examining whether and how these discussion prompts are taken up in classroom enactments of the curriculum and how they impact classroom discourse and student learning.

Support Teachers in Adopting and Carrying Out Inquiry-Based Projects

Teachers play a critical role in supporting students in scientific inquiry (NRC, 1996). In inquiry-oriented learning environments, teachers act as facilitators and learning partners for students. Fulfilling these roles requires a nuanced craft knowledge that teachers can only gain with considerable practice and reflection. Instructional materials need to be designed not only to support student learning but also to be educative in promoting teacher learning and practice (Ball & Cohen, 1996; Davis & Krajcik, 2005). In addition, because the materials designed by researchers will never be perfect for every teacher's classroom, some customization will have to occur, as the teacher tailors the materials to fit within his or her specific context. Customization may also be necessary or at least helpful to match curricula to local student populations or geographic variables. Chapter 5 discusses the role of the teacher and teacher learning in more detail, but support of teachers will be discussed briefly here as well, because it is a critical design principle for CCMS and TELS curriculum development.

TABLE 3.3   Types of Discussion*

Type of Discussion	Definition	Example Prompts
Brainstorming	Students share ideas without evaluating their validity or worth.	What have you observed or experienced? What else is on your group's list?
Synthesizing	Students put ideas together in ways that include generalizing from specific activities to wider applications.	How does ... help us think about other times when ...? How can we put these four ideas together into one process that we might call "the water cycle"? What happens first, second, ...?
Pressing for understanding	Students figure things out or make sense of readings and activities. Pressing for understanding pushes students to make deeper connections between ideas.	How does X compare with Y? How can ...? How might ...? How do you know? What does it mean to say ...?

* Modified from Sutherland and Shwartz (2007).

Supporting Teachers in Customizing Curriculum. The initial version of any TELS curriculum project is always designed in close partnership with the teacher who will be first to enact that curriculum. However, researchers cannot restrict the use of their materials to the small group of teachers who were members of the design team, and eventually they must extend their innovations to the broader population of teachers. These teachers may be talented and eager to adopt new approaches, but at the outset they will be unfamiliar with the ideas and rationales that went into the design of a new curriculum. TELS has found that these adopting teachers require some professional development in which they can acquaint themselves with the curriculum and adapt it to their own courses and student populations (see Chapter 5).

Further, the TELS technology environments can help scaffold teachers as they conduct their early enactments. Slotta (2004) compared two teachers who were enacting the same WISE project called "Cycles of Malaria," wherein students compare and critique three different strategies for controlling malaria worldwide. The two teachers worked at the same school and taught different sections of the same seventh-grade life science class. Based on preliminary interviews and observations, the teachers differed considerably in their experience with technology and in their patterns of interaction with students. However, despite the fact that their practices diverged from the ideal enactment of the project, the technology environment was able to accommodate the distinct approaches, scaffolding each of the two in a somewhat different fashion. Thus, although it is important to include teachers deeply in the design of innovations, and to provide them with several successive opportunities for planning and reflection, it is also noteworthy that the innovations themselves can help to scaffold teachers' adoption of new pedagogical techniques.

Providing New Opportunities to Design Formative Assessments. The TELS technology environment also provides teachers with new opportunities for formative assessment, revealing details about students' understanding in a timely fashion. TELS investigators are currently designing new technology scaffolds that will help teachers to survey all students in a class and target those who appear to be most in need of intervention. TELS is also conducting an ongoing program of professional development research (see Chapter 5), with mentored planning activities for teachers and a summer retreat each year. A portion of any improvement seen on the annual benchmark assessment should be due to teachers' improved prowess at using the inquiry and technology methods. This factor of professional growth is being included in analyses of assessment data.

Supporting Teachers Through Educative Curriculum. To illustrate how CCMS supports teachers, we return to the example of the incorporation of an instructional framework for scientific explanation into the IQWST "How Can I Make New Stuff from Old Stuff?" unit. As mentioned earlier, this framework integrated instruction in claim, evidence, and reasoning through curricular supports (McNeill et al., 2006). In the first two enactments of the "Stuff" unit, IQWST designers noticed variation in how teachers used the instructional materials in their classroom, specifically in terms of supporting students in constructing scientific explanations. Consequently, the instructional materials were revised to have a more explicit focus on supporting the *teacher* in adopting and using the portions of the curriculum related to scientific explanation.

IQWST designers included a number of educative features in the instruction materials for scientific explanation. These features include discussing why scientific explanation is important, describing what a scientific explanation is, providing general strategies as well as concrete examples of supporting students with scientific explanations, and providing examples of both strong and weak student explanations. For example, in the introductory materials for the unit, the rationale for why scientific explanation was incorporated in the unit was discussed, as were instructional practices the teachers could use to help support their students.

During the 2003–2004 school year, McNeill and Krajcik (2008c) conducted a study that examined enactment of the "Stuff" materials by 13 teachers with 1,197 students. McNeill and Krajcik examined the teachers' engagement in four different instructional practices: defining scientific explanation, making the rationale for studying scientific explanation explicit, modeling scientific explanation, and connecting scientific explanation to everyday explanation. They were interested in how the teachers used these different practices and whether or not their use of the practices influenced student learning in terms of the students' ability to write scientific explanations. With this information, McNeill and Krajcik hoped to develop a better sense of how the teachers were adapting the materials and what features needed to be revised or added to the curriculum to provide teachers with better support.

Not surprisingly, McNeill and Krajcik (2008c) found quite a bit of variation in the teachers' use of the four instructional practices. For example, the majority of the teachers engaged in both defining and modeling scientific explanation, and they tended to provide the least support for students' reasoning. Yet, reasoning was the most difficult aspect for students, suggesting that curriculum developers needed to provide teachers with more support in how to help students develop appropriate reasoning for their claims. There was a significant interaction between the effects of the four different instructional practices. With teachers who provided a rationale for studying scientific explanation and accurately defined its components, students had the greatest learning in terms of their ability to write scientific explanations. The study also revealed that a number of the teachers did not provide any rationale for why a student would even want to construct a scientific explanation. This finding suggested that curriculum designers needed to incorporate greater supports in the curriculum for the teachers in terms of having them provide their students with a rationale for constructing scientific explanations. Studies of this sort underline the importance of integrating educative support for teachers into curriculum design, because no matter how innovative the materials, teachers will continue to play a pivotal role in supporting students in scientific inquiry.

CHALLENGES AND IMPLICATIONS FOR RESEARCH, CURRICULUM DESIGN, AND POLICY

Although the instructional materials designed by TELS and CCMS engage diverse learners in complex tasks, they bring new challenges to designers, teachers, students, and professional development professionals. As discussed in Chapter 2, current science instructional materials often look very different from those designed by CCMS and TELS. For example, the CCMS and TELS materials provide greater focus on scientific inquiry practices and on developing collaborative environments in the classroom. The long-term, coherent instructional materials developed in IQWST pose additional challenges for teachers because often teachers are not accustomed to helping students build ideas over time.

Currently, teachers face pressure to meet the demands of the No Child Left Behind legislation. In such a political environment, teachers and administrators need to be concerned about whether all students are accomplishing key science learning goals. Unfortunately, some state standards do not focus on core ideas of science (Knapp, 1997; Wilson & Berenthal, 2006), and the pressure to meet standards could prevent the adoption of innovative materials such as the ones created by CCMS and TELS researchers. However, recent documents such as *Rising Above the Gathering Storm: Energizing and Employing America for a Brighter Economic Future* (Committee on Prospering in the Global Economy of the 21st Century, 2006) and *Taking Science to School* (Duschl et al., 2007) argue for the importance of moving away from traditional science curricula that focus on unconnected and trivial topics and toward curricula that engage all students in complex scientific practices and big ideas. These types of curricula can help students develop integrated understanding of key science ideas.

Because of the innovative nature of the new materials, more research must be conducted in a variety of contexts and with a variety of students to develop a richer understanding of the characteristics of the materials that promote greater student learning. Another area in need of further study is scaling innovative curricula, which can provide unique challenges. And, of course, scaling of innovative materials cannot occur unless there is sustained professional development (Fishman, Marx, Blumenfeld, Krajcik, & Soloway, 2004). Thus, future policy initiatives need to include funding for further development and research in all of these critical areas.

4

Designing Science Instruction for Diverse Learners

Erika D. Tate, Douglas B. Clark,
James J. Gallagher, and David McLaughlin

I N THIS DISCUSSION of coherence in science education, we strive to unpack and illustrate what it means to design science learning materials that (a) respect the diverse ideas and learning practices students bring to science class and (b) enable all learners to generate, evaluate, and reflect on the links among their ideas. To begin, we acknowledge the elusive nature of the term *diverse*. Many researchers, practitioners, and policy makers work tirelessly on issues of diversity, yet they address it from varied perspectives. Through the lens of curriculum design, we describe how the Technology Enhanced Learning in Science (TELS) Center and the Center for Curriculum Materials in Science (CCMS) use coherent science learning materials to address diversity. Both centers use *general* and *targeted* curricular design strategies to promote an integrated understanding of science among diverse groups of learners. A general approach considers diversity as any differences among students, such as prior knowledge, academic achievement, learning disabilities, or personal interests. When employing a general design approach, the centers seek to create high-quality curricula that can engage and support *all* students. Such materials often include design features, such as driving questions and interactive visualizations, that allow teachers and students to adapt the content and activities to various academic levels and interests.

Although a general approach to design recognizes and values differences among students, it does not necessarily politicize them or take into account the historical and cultural factors that influence them. In contrast, a targeted approach considers the racial, linguistic, cultural, and gendered identities and experiences that students bring to the classroom, and attempts to remedy the inequitable distribution of resources and opportunities that has led to disparate learning experiences for certain groups of students (Atwater, 1996; Eisenhart, Finkel, Behm, Lawrence, & Tonso, 1996; Ladson-Billings, 1998; LIFE Center, 2007; McGinn & Roth, 1998; Zacharia & Calabrese Barton, 2004). When working from a targeted design approach, TELS and CCMS seek to create high-quality curricula with specific objectives that support students in making connections between science and their personal and political lives. Exemplar targeted design features include language supports and contextualization of science ideas within culturally relevant topics. Both centers believe that coherent curriculum materials designed to engage and support students who have been underserved have the potential to benefit *all* learners.

TELS and CCMS do not consider general and targeted design approaches to be in competition. Rather, they advocate use of both approaches as complementary and context-dependent strategies for addressing diversity. To this end, we argue that in order to develop coherent science curricula for diverse learners, instructional designers must create materials that value, harness, and build on students' prior ideas, experiences, and interests. In addition, designers must situate science topics in contexts that offer multiple entry points for connection to the content. These entry points may include meaningful activities that illustrate the relevance of science to students' present or future lives or that afford students the opportunity to apply their prior knowledge. Finally, designers need to create materials that enable teachers to monitor students' learning and plan instruction that appropriately scaffolds students' integrated understanding of science.

To make the case, we first characterize the challenges facing diverse students. After providing this backdrop, we then review the ways that the National Science Foundation's Centers for Learning and Teaching (CCMS and TELS in particular) are working to develop better approaches for serving all students in terms of three core themes: (a) connections to students' communities, interests, and prior knowledge, (b) language use and support, and (c) instructional supports for teachers. We present action scenarios from CCMS and TELS to elaborate each theme. The chapter concludes with a synthesis of design principles and features from these high-level themes and action scenarios for teachers, policy makers, curriculum designers, and teacher educators.

DIVERSE STUDENTS IN THE UNITED STATES

To set the stage for our discussion of pedagogy and curricula to better support all students, we first consider some of the challenges facing urban and rural schools with respect to issues of diversity of race, ethnicity, culture, and social class. We then discuss issues related to the prevalent linguistic diversity among school-age children in the United States (García, 2001). Finally, we present an overview of general educational trends that affect diverse students in the United States, and consider the challenges and importance of reforming K–12 science education to better support all students. These discussions provide core context and background for thinking about the range of ideas and experiences that diverse students bring to the classroom, as well as the specific challenges and shortcomings of the current system and traditional curricula. An appreciation of this background will serve as the foundation for our subsequent examination of strategies under development by CCMS and TELS to improve K–12 science education for all students.

Urban Schools

Urban schools reflect the increasing diversity in the United States. According to a report by Standard & Poor's (2005), urban districts are likely to enroll more students of color and more English language learners than the national average. Although these students bring rich cultural and linguistic resources to the classroom, they often bring experiences marred by racial and economic discrimination. Students in urban schools are more likely to be economically disadvantaged and to have greater exposure to poverty, crime, and substance abuse. Their families may experience high rates of mobility and excessive stress levels, and they may possess inadequate health insurance (LIFE Center, 2007; Standard & Poor's, 2005). These realities limit students' educational opportunities.

Many urban schools are labeled as sites of underachievement because learning—as measured by standardized tests, rates of high school graduation, and college attendance—trails that of White students in nonurban settings. This achievement gap persists because of failed education policies and what Rodriguez (1998) calls the meritocracy myth. This myth insists that all students who work hard receive the expected rewards, but it fails to acknowledge the inequity that has been institutionalized in the U.S. educational system. Several studies have shown correlations between income level and quality of preparation for school (Polakow, 2000) or between zip code and school achievement (Wing, 2004). These studies reveal the inequities of schooling and their adverse effects on students of color and those who are economically disadvantaged.

Rural Schools

Today, rural America includes a widely scattered, highly diverse segment of our nation's population. Immigration and migration from urban to rural communities have been powerful forces contributing to rural growth (Isserman, 2001). As a result, rural communities and their schools have become more diverse over time, and projections suggest that this trend will continue (Castania, 1992). Similar to urban America, the population of rural America varies in socioeconomic status, cultural background, religion, and values. Further, a larger percentage of families in rural areas live at the poverty level and may experience a greater scarcity of resources than in urban areas (Maleki, 2001).

Geographic constraints also contribute to challenges facing rural schools. Unlike urban areas, where residences, businesses, and schools are located near each other, rural communities are spatially dispersed. Often schools in the same district are located far from each other. This makes communication among schools difficult and frequently leads to feelings of isolation among school administrators, teachers, and students (Kusmin, 2006). In addition, these long distances may result in limited Internet access for both students and their teachers, which restricts access to potentially valuable learning resources.

Linguistic Diversity

In addition to racial, cultural, and geographic diversity, linguistic diversity also figures prominently in education and curriculum development in the United States. English language learners (ELLs) are the fastest growing population of students in schools today. As the national population of 5–17-year-olds grew 17% from 1990 to 2000, the national ELL population grew 46%. Spanish speakers alone grew by 57% from 1990 to 2000 (U.S. Department of Education, 2002). During the 2001–2002 school year, total K–12 enrollment increased by 12% over the 1991–1992 school year, whereas limited English proficient student (LEP) enrollment increased by 95% (U.S. Department of Education, 2002). This growing linguistic diversity increases the critical importance of promoting educational equity in our classrooms (NRC, 1999).

Many linguistically diverse students have had unsuccessful schooling experiences because their strengths and needs were not adequately addressed (García, 2002). In 1992, 15% of U.S. teachers were estimated to have at least one ELL in their respective classrooms; 10 years later, in 2002, the percentage had increased to 43% (Abedi, 2003). The U.S. Department of Education (2002) reports that fewer than 3% of teachers with LEP students have a degree in bilingual education.

Although learning a language other than English is generally considered prestigious for native English speakers, schooling in the United States rarely considers the native language abilities of ELLs as assets. Instead, schooling tends to systematically (a) exclude their histories, languages, and experiences from the curriculum, (b) impose a "tracking system" that restricts their entry into high-level courses, and (c) limit access to developmentally appropriate learning configurations (García, 2002; García & Lee, 2008; LIFE Center, 2007). This short-sighted hypocrisy overlooks the important advantages of bilingualism. Significant research suggests that the intellectual experience of acquiring two languages contributes to advantageous mental flexibility, superior concept formation, and a generally diversified set of mental abilities and metalinguistic awareness (e.g.,

Galambos & Hakuta, 1988; García, 2001; Goncz & Kodzepeljic, 1991; Kessler & Quinn, 1987; Peal & Lambert, 1962; Swain & Lapkin, 1991).

Challenges and Importance of Reforming K–12 Science Education

Recent science education reform efforts advocate increasing scientific literacy for all citizens (AAAS, 1989; NRC, 1996). Among the objectives of these efforts is producing individuals who can be competent participants in "scientific labora-tories, activist movements, the judicial system, or other locations/communities where science is created and used" (McGinn & Roth, 1999, p. 14). As the science education community works toward scientific literacy among the U.S. public at large, people of color, children from low-income families, and women are con-sistently underrepresented in advanced high school science courses, college majors, and professional careers (National Science Foundation, 2004). This has led to their marginal participation in the science and technical career workforce and in critical decision making regarding their community environments and personal health. To ensure that all students have meaningful opportunities to develop science understanding, science educators must be prepared to engage a student body that is increasingly diverse culturally, economically, and linguisti-cally (National Center for Education Statistics, 2006).

Several factors contribute to the many challenges diverse students face as they learn science. High-stakes testing focused on math and literacy deemphasizes the importance of science in the school curriculum and has relegated science in recent years to the status of a noncritical school subject (although this is begin-ning to change in several states). In addition, state science standards require teachers to provide instruction on numerous science topics during the school year. This limits the time teachers can spend teaching any particular area of the mandated science content, and results in students memorizing and quickly for-getting disjointed, decontextualized, superficial science "facts."

Given these constraints on school science instruction, traditional approaches often present science as an isolated and "culture-free" enterprise that endorses only objective, value-free inquiry. This fosters learning environments that often discourage women, rural students, and people of color from participating in science in the classroom and beyond (Lee & Fradd, 1998; LIFE Center, 2007; Peterson & Barnes, 1996; Roth & Lee, 2004; Warren, Ballenger, Ogonowski, Rose-bery, & Hudicourt-Barnes, 2001; Wellesley College Center for Research on Women, 1992). Science instruction often emphasizes ways of knowing and prac-ticing science that privilege White, middle-class, and male standpoints and inter-action patterns (Eisenhart et al., 1996; Rodriguez, 1998; Roth & Lee, 2004; Tobin, Seiler, & Walls, 1999). For example, teachers often engage in whole-class instruc-tion, use the textbook as the main artifact for teaching and learning, and dole out uniform assignments despite the rich diversity among students. These practices foster a classroom culture that positions teachers and textbooks as the main source of knowledge and centers instruction on content that may be inaccessible and irrelevant to many students' lives (Bouillion & Gomez, 2001; Calabrese Barton, 1998).

School science instruction often provides learning opportunities that have little connection to students' diverse home, cultural, or linguistic experiences. Bouillion and Gomez (2001) report that "teaching and learning are often disconnected from the day-to-day life of the community, and students don't see how the skills they acquire in school have currency in business, at home, and in other communities beyond school" (p. 878). Findings from a study by Atwater and Wiggins (1995) illustrate students' separation of school science from their future aspirations. Researchers found that even though the majority of urban African American students hold favorable attitudes toward science careers, only 25% hold favorable attitudes toward school science (Atwater & Wiggins, 1995). In failing to link school science to students' personal lives, educators miss the opportunity to help students form an integrated understanding of science. Instead, students are encouraged to isolate their science understanding from their worldview. More importantly, instruction fails to demonstrate the importance and utility of science in their personal experiences and decision making.

Often, this school/home disconnect persists because school science instruction does not recognize or value the knowledge and experiences students bring to the classroom. Teachers who maintain racial, ethnic, or cultural biases and stereotypes demonstrate negative attitudes toward their non-White students. They often view students from culturally diverse backgrounds as less capable (Gay, 2000). As a result, they hold these students to lower academic standards, provide them with less encouragement to excel, and neglect the individual and cultural resources they bring to school (Bryan & Atwater, 2002; Ladson-Billings, 1994; Villegas & Lucas, 2002).

Beyond biases in attitudes, teachers' own educational preparation often impacts science learning among diverse learners. Students enrolled in schools with a large number of students of color, ELL students, or students from low-income households have a higher probability of learning from a science teacher without appropriate teaching credentials (Glenn, 2000). Teachers with inadequate science content or pedagogical preparation usually select less optimal instructional materials or enact innovative curriculum materials ineffectively. As a result, "diverse learners are most apt to be at the mercy of poorly written texts and curriculum materials, and their teachers are least able to compensate for these weak materials due to lack of content knowledge and pedagogical skills" (Lynch, Kuipers, Pyke, & Szesze, 2005, p. 914).

Even teachers who are qualified according to traditional standards require ongoing professional development and support to successfully teach diverse learners. In schools where administrators and parents pressure teachers to "teach to the test"—a mandate that obscures the complexity of teachers' work—both teacher effectiveness and student learning are constrained. These environments often discourage teachers from seeking innovative science curricula and more effective methods of teaching. Furthermore, teachers may experience difficulty acquiring support—such as release time to attend professional development programs and allocation of funding for resources—to implement and sustain innovative science instruction that has the potential to benefit wide-ranging groups of students (Duke, 1993).

The challenges of providing a quality education for all students regardless of their personal and cultural histories are clear. Although the challenges may be daunting, overcoming them provides science educators with plentiful opportunities to improve instructional methods and materials. To design instructional materials that make a difference, we must carefully consider the resources and support necessary for *all* students and teachers rather only than a chosen few (Fradd, Lee, Sutman, & Saxton, 2001).

DEVELOPING CURRICULA TO SUPPORT ALL STUDENTS: ACTION SCENARIOS FROM CCMS AND TELS

With these challenges in mind, many Centers for Learning and Teaching (CLTs) across the nation have worked to improve the education of diverse students in science or mathematics. Some centers explicitly address the needs of specific student populations, whereas others maintain a general commitment to serve all students. In an interview study conducted by Gallagher and McLaughlin (2007), leaders and staff members of nine CLTs were interviewed about what they have learned from their research efforts regarding effective approaches to teaching, assessment, curriculum design, and teacher staff development. The inquiry focused on CLT staff members' work with diverse students and their recommendations for the design of science curriculum materials and teacher education. Although several themes emerged from the study—such as valuing science for all and enhancing teacher professional development—we limit our discussion here to the three themes most directly focused on diverse students. (Refer to Gallagher and McLaughlin [2007] for a discussion of the full list of themes, including relevant quotes from CLT leaders.)

Specifically, we address three diversity-related themes that the CLT Principal Investigators and staff members considered critical for supporting diverse learners studying science: (a) connections to students' communities, interests, and prior knowledge, (b) language use and support, and (c) instructional supports for teachers. For each theme, we provide an overview of the issues and then describe an action scenario from CCMS or TELS that demonstrates an approach for addressing each one. These scenarios are intended not as strict recipes but rather as illustrations of how science educators can translate the themes into coherent curriculum materials.

Connections to Students' Communities, Interests, and Prior Knowledge: The TELS "Asthma" Action Scenario

The CLT leaders repeatedly emphasized that, to engage learners in school, teachers need to be able to relate to their lives outside of school (Gallagher & McLaughlin, 2007). They need to not only understand the ideas, values, goals, and interests students bring into the classroom, but also make science personally relevant to the students. This means generating real connections with students' lives that extend beyond dressing up conventional science activities with superficially engaging stories. When students see authentic relationships between their own lives and the ideas they investigate in science class, they are more likely to construct an integrated understanding of science (Gallagher & McLaughlin, 2007).

Even though the CLT leaders viewed curriculum materials as pivotal in promoting students' interest and understanding in science, they acknowledged that creating learning contexts for curricula that are appropriate and highly motivating for a wide variety of learners is difficult for many reasons. For example, designers cannot anticipate all of the different experiences and prior knowledge of learners, especially when designing a curriculum for a national audience instead of a local one.

Community-based science curriculum materials, such as the TELS "Improving Your Community's Asthma Problem" module, have the potential to enhance the science experiences of diverse groups of students and help educators establish authentic connections between school science and students' lives outside of school. The "Asthma" module targets students in underserved communities and aims to minimize the gap between students' home life and school science. The following action scenario highlights design decisions that provided students the opportunity to do and learn science in ways that are meaningful to them. It explains how the designers selected the context for learning, engaged in a community partnership to develop the learning materials, and created activities that elicited and used students' prior knowledge about health and their community.

Curriculum and Technology Design. The "Asthma" module approaches asthma as a community-based science problem. Learning goals include developing an understanding of the physiology and the social implications related to asthma. In addition, students learn how to use evidence and consider trade-offs when making decisions about community-based science problems. As students investigate their local asthma problem, they seek to answer the driving question, "Which program works better to improve the asthma problem in your commu-

TABLE 4.1   Activity Flow for TELS "Asthma" Module

Activity	Description
Your Asthma Problem	Evidence pages and an interactive map introduce (a) the asthma problem in students' community, (b) the driving question, and (c) the diesel reduction and asthma clinic interventions.
How Does Asthma Affect the Body?	Dynamic visualizations explain the physiology of breathing and asthma.
What Causes an Asthma Attack?	Static visualizations explain asthma triggers and the physiology of an allergic immune response.
How Does Diesel Exhaust Impact Your Community's Asthma Problem?	Multiple pieces of evidence provide explanations about how diesel pollution impacts asthma and general health.
How Do People Manage Their Asthma?	Multiple pieces of evidence provide explanations about how asthma management and health care can affect asthma-related hospitalization rates.
Improving Your Community's Asthma Problem	Students debate proposed solutions and generate new solutions.

nity?" Students decide between two viable interventions: (a) a diesel reduction program that provides local businesses with funds to retrofit or replace vehicles with highly polluting diesel engines, and (b) an asthma clinic that provides comprehensive medical care for asthmatics who do not have health insurance. Students are expected to integrate evidence related to physiology, diesel pollution, asthma management, and their community to make an informed decision about which intervention to implement.

Table 4.1 provides an overview of the "Asthma" module. The designers generated six activities that strategically integrate evidence involving static and dynamic visualizations, environmental and clinical reports, area maps, and community data charts. Consistent with the design principle "Embed assessment-for-learning within instruction" (see Chapter 8, Kali, Fortus, & Ronen-Fuhrmann, for a discussion of the major design principles common to TELS and CCMS), designers included assessment activities, such as questions that required interpretation of evidence or activities that encouraged critique of decision justifications. These embedded assessments were intended to reveal students' thinking and provide teachers with opportunities to give ongoing feedback as students add, sort, and connect evidence to inform and support their decision making (Chapter 5, Davis & Varma). The "Asthma" module also includes several offline activities, including student investigations of their indoor and outdoor air quality, a debate about the proposed solutions, and a poster activity that allows students to propose solutions they think will work best for their community.

Selecting Authentic Contexts for Learning Science. To make science accessible, the "Asthma" project centered its inquiry on an authentic science problem in students' neighborhoods. Designers selected asthma as the community-based problem because of (a) its rising prevalence among school-age children, (b) the sociopolitical factors that contribute to disparity in disease management, (c) the diverse opportunities for scientific inquiry, and (d) the existing community mobilization around asthma-related issues. The community frame of reference was intended to help students realize how science can intersect with their lives and the needs of the community (Bell, 2004; Bouillion & Gomez, 2001; Calabrese Barton, 1998; Fusco & Calabrese Barton, 2001; LIFE Center, 2007). This perspective allowed the designers to present asthma as a multifaceted problem, increasing the number of ways students could engage with the topic. For example, students may regard the asthma problem as relevant because they have asthma, are concerned with social justice issues, or simply are interested in neighborhood happenings. By creating multiple opportunities for students to participate in science, the designers increased the potential for students to generate links between school science and their personal lives.

In addition, the designers aimed to promote lifelong learning by demonstrating the relevance and importance of science to students' lives. Situating the asthma problem in a community context allowed the designers to make explicit some of the social factors impacting the asthma problem. This design decision was intended to enable students to perceive science as a socially constructed entity, decreasing its abstractness and enhancing its relevance to their lives. Through an intentional approach to inquiry, including reconsidering scientific ideas, making sense of interdisciplinary data, and seeking a meaningful understanding of their local community, the "Asthma" project demonstrated science as a "source of agency" (Bouillion & Gomez, 2001, p. 893) and a force that allows people to "challenge the existing social conditions in which they lived" (Calabrese Barton, 1998, p. 390).

Community Partnerships. Designing a community-based science curriculum required not only identifying a real-world problem but also transforming it into effective learning materials. To ensure the accurate representation of the asthma problem from a community perspective, the designers applied a partnership model that included teachers, researchers, and scientists (Linn, Eylon, & Davis, 2004; see also Preface). Although all TELS modules make use of partnerships, the "Asthma" module benefited from inclusion of the expertise of health workers and community residents. In addition, one member of the design team actively participated in a local community asthma coalition throughout the design process. These partnerships and experiences directly influenced how the designers presented asthma throughout the module. For example, the driving question mentioned earlier ("Which program works better …?") was based on actual interventions that have been implemented in communities locally and nationally.

The community partnership also provided insight into how the people and institutions involved in exacerbating or improving the asthma problem understand sociopolitical issues (such as disparities related to land use and access to medical care) in relation to the underlying science. These insights informed the design of learning activities aimed at promoting an understanding of asthma as a community science problem. For example, in the activity "How Do People Manage Their Asthma?" students learn about strategies for managing asthma, including drug therapies and avoidance of triggers. In addition, the module provides a range of evidence highlighting the differences in medical treatment based on health insurance coverage, and the percentages of people in their county with and without health insurance.

Designing Learning Activities That Use Student Knowledge. In selecting a community problem that requires interdisciplinary knowledge and expertise from all members of the community, the designers sought to realize the design principle "Connect to personally relevant contexts" (Chapter 8) and foster a learning environment that recognized students' prior ideas and experiences as resources for science learning. (Refer to Chapter 2, Roseman, Linn, & Koppal, for further discussion of how integrated understanding can be promoted by eliciting students' prior ideas.) The designers embedded local asthma data, such as a table that displayed the number of asthma cases for children, teenagers, and adults in the students' county of residence, as an initial point of engagement for students. Seeking to move beyond simply supplying additional ideas about the students' neighborhood to their repertoire, the designers included embedded assessments that would afford students the opportunity to bring their own community knowledge into the module. For example, one assessment involves use of the Google map tool, which geographically organizes local information such as the locations of residences, highways, schools, parks, and bodies of water. This activity asks students to map their social, economic, and environmental understanding—such as knowledge of which neighborhoods are poor, industrialized, or heavily polluted—onto this geographic representation (see Figure 4.1). This integration of curricular and student ideas positions learners to become co-constructors of their understanding of their local asthma problem.

By broadening the notion of "doing science," students are given the opportunity to apply their wide-ranging prior knowledge to science inquiry (Bouillion & Gomez, 2001; Calabrese Barton, 1998). This was encouraged through the design of learning activities that center on the community decision-making

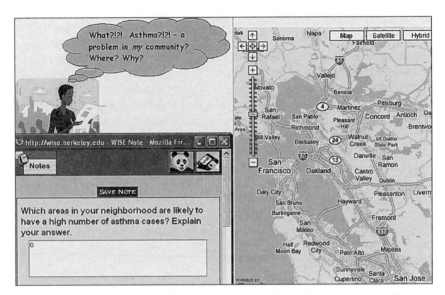

FIGURE 4.1 Interactive Google map and embedded assessment from the TELS "Asthma" module, a community-based curriculum designed to connect school science with students' everyday lives.

task—choosing between the asthma clinic and the diesel reduction program. Several times throughout the module, students must select one of the proposed interventions and construct an evidence-based argument to support their position. To promote students' use of physiological, community, environmental, and clinical evidence, the designers included "Making the Best Decision" mini-lessons (see Figure 4.2). These lessons cover evidence collection within and outside the module, argument construction, and evidence critique. In addition, students used evidence organizers to collect, critique, and sort the evidence presented in the module. Finally, the designers repeated embedded decision-making assessments throughout the module to encourage students to base their decision making between the asthma clinic and diesel exhaust reduction interventions on evidence of their community's needs.

Determining the Effectiveness of Community-Based Science Curricula. In the spirit of community-based science curricula, the "Asthma" module designers integrated goals for both school science and community participation. Researchers have used multiple methods to assess the impact of the module on students' integrated understanding of asthma as a community problem. Tate's (2008) investigation across eight classrooms and four stages of design sought to determine how the module improved students' integrated understanding of the sci-

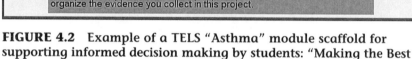

Making the Best Decision

Collecting Evidence

As you work through this project, you will collect *evidence* -- information that supports your decision. Evidence can include:

Information you learn in this project
Reports or visualizations (e.g. graphs, models)
Observations or investigations
Comments by your classmates or teacher

Information you learn outside this project
Past science lessons or lessons from other subjects
Your experiences related to asthma
Television commercials or web sites

Ask your teacher for the worksheet, *Evidence Organizer.* It will help you organize the evidence you collect in this project.

FIGURE 4.2 Example of a TELS "Asthma" module scaffold for supporting informed decision making by students: "Making the Best Decision" mini-lesson on collecting evidence.

ence of asthma. She found that students in all classrooms significantly increased their ability to explain the physiology of breathing, asthma attacks, and asthma as an allergic immune response. During development of the module, Tate applied the knowledge integration (KI) framework to score student responses to formative and embedded assessments (see Chapter 7, DeBoer, Lee, & Husic). Table 4.2 provides examples of representative differences in students' explanations before and after completion of the module.

As educators work to make science more inclusive for all students, designers and researchers must investigate students' science participation beyond cognitive goals. To understand how students do science, Tate (2007, 2008) characterized students' decision making as it related to their repertoire of ideas, use of evidence, and consideration of trade-offs. Throughout the "Asthma" module, responses to embedded assessments provided evidence that students possessed a diverse repertoire of ideas about asthma, clinical management, environmental factors, and social implications. In their responses, students also included ideas localized to their community. In addition, most student answers demonstrated partially or fully integrated understanding, meaning that they either mentioned a claim or piece of evidence (partial integration) or linked evidence to a claim (full integration). Finally, Tate's studies reported that students considered trade-offs, such as which program benefits more people or how each program prevents or treats the

TABLE 4.2   Selected Student Responses to Specific Assessment Items
Embedded in the TELS "Asthma" Module*

Assessment Item	Less Integrated Response	More Integrated Response
O₂ Inhalation	In the drawing, you can see that air comes in from the outside, then it goes down the trachea into the lungs, enabling the person to breathe. —KI† score 3	Oxygen enters through the mouth/nose, travels into the lungs, goes through air passageways, and comes to little sacs at the end of each passage, alveoli. Inside the sacs, oxygen is transferred to red blood cells in the capillaries to be transported to the rest of your body. —KI score 5
Allergen/Irritant Difference	Allergens clog your airways and irritants just irritate them. —KI score 2	Allergens activate antibodies which trigger the asthma attacks. Irritants directly cause the attacks by attaching to the wall of the bronchi. —KI score 5
Allergic Immune Response	The pollen clogs the nose so Juan doesn't get enough air. —KI score 2	When pollen comes into Juan's body, Juan's antibodies attack and produce histamines as a product. Histamines cause the reaction that leads to asthma attacks. —KI score 5

*Tate (2008).

†KI = knowledge integration.

asthma problem. The exemplary response below illustrates how an integrated understanding can support community decision making:

> *The Diesel reduction program will have a long-lasting effect as it helps everyone. Clinics only help patients with asthma who visits the facility. It is a treatment whereas the Diesel Reduction Program is more of a preventative measure and a relief. With less gasses in the air, asthmatic patients will suffer fewer attacks as there will be less particulate matter in the air stimulating symptoms....*

In conclusion, the "Asthma" module is one example of how curriculum materials can address some of the challenges facing diverse learners in science. Aiming to minimize the gap between students' home life and school science, the designers situated asthma-related science in students' communities. The community context was intended to make science accessible by providing students with multiple opportunities to engage with the curriculum. Students could have recognized the relevance of the asthma problem because of personal experience with asthma, concern for social justice, or interest in neighborhood issues. Design features such as incorporation of local data and demonstration of community decision-making processes promoted lifelong learning by encouraging students to use their community knowledge as a lens for understanding science. In the end, the designers of the "Asthma" module sought to establish a perception that science is a critical tool for transforming the lives of students, their families, and their communities.

Multilingual, Multimodal Language Supports: The TELS "Wolves" Action Scenario

All students face language demands in science classes. Specialized vocabulary and patterns of interaction frequently differ significantly from what children are exposed to at home, in the media, and during conversations with peers. There is a danger that English language learners and many other students may have difficulty acquiring the specific and technical discourse patterns that are traditionally valued in science classes. Several leaders of CLTs have addressed language issues and relating curriculum to students' prior knowledge and experience (Gallagher & McLaughlin, 2007).

Expectations for academic performance need to take into consideration language demands placed on students for whom English is not a first language. CLT leaders identified tensions in determining the appropriate method for reducing language demands on students. Although it may be possible to minimize the number of new technical terms, any reduction of the "richness" of the language may negatively impact the process of developing content knowledge and initiating students into the shared vocabulary of science.

The TELS "Wolves" action scenario demonstrates how technology can help ELLs develop an integrated understanding of complex science while supporting their understanding of the surrounding academic English. Science curricula that include technology-based language supports, such as the "Wolves" module, can potentially create a learning environment that affords students the opportunity to build on their natural linguistic practices. To realize this project, TELS partnered with the Technology Opening Diverse Opportunities for Science (TODOS) research group at Arizona State University. Much of the technology for the "Wolves" module, including the modeling components and some of the original source material, draws on the work of the TELS grant from the National Science Foundation and its predecessors (for more information about the TELS modeling components, see the Preface, Kali, Koppal, Linn, & Roseman; and Chapter 3, Krajcik, Slotta, McNeill, & Reiser). The TODOS group developed its multilingual, multimodal supports within the module and has investigated how the technology-based language supports within the online science learning environment enhance learning amid the linguistic diversity of urban classrooms. Like the designers of the "Asthma" module, the "Wolves" designers worked to *make science accessible* and *promote autonomous learning,* but with a unique focus on supporting the language use and language development of ELLs.

Curriculum and Technology Design. The "Wolves" module, intended for middle school, seeks to help students (a) consider the perspectives of various participants in the wolf management controversy, (b) investigate the basic biology of wolves, food chains, and predator–prey relationships, (c) compare wolf management options and strategies that have been implemented by different states, and (d) create, present, and defend a plan of their own that they believe best serves the needs of wolves, humans, and the environment.

The TODOS language tools help students to harness their understanding of both spoken and written Spanish and English to bootstrap their understanding of both the science content and the language presented. As part of this process, students choose and freely switch the language in which the paragraph text is displayed, which is referred to as the "paragraph language." As illustrated in Figure 4.3, when students move the mouse cursor over a word or phrase in the paragraph text, a small text box pops up immediately above it with the same word or phrase in the "support language" the student has chosen. In addition, an audio file of the same text can be played in the support language. Like the text supports, students choose and freely switch the support language of the audio supports. The support language can be different from, or the same as, the paragraph language. This allows students to hear pronunciations of the paragraph text or translations of it. Finally, when students click the mouse on a word or short phrase in the paragraph text, they receive a short definition (and examples where pertinent) in the support language at the bottom of the screen.

Making Science Accessible Through Language Supports. Recognizing that students' home and English language skills represent critical components of their initial understanding and resources, the "Wolves" module affords students the opportunity to marshal and draw upon all of their linguistic abilities. In making science accessible for ELLs, the design of the "Wolves" module reflects the ideas enunciated earlier that (a) expectations need to take into account the language demands placed on these students, but (b) efforts to lighten the burden of acquiring the new terminology must not negatively impact the process of developing an understanding of the content and vocabulary of science. In support of these commitments, the "Wolves" module incorporates specialized language technology supports to create an accessible and engaging learning opportunity for all students.

Clark, Nelson, Atkinson, Ramirez, and Medina (in press) found that the technology and environment of the "Wolves" module were appealing for students. Most of the study participants stated during interviews that they enjoyed the experience of interacting with the language supports through the computer. During interviews, the students referred to images, interactive tools, language supports, the learning environment, and the content itself as attractive components of the materials. This may be because the "Wolves" project involved con-

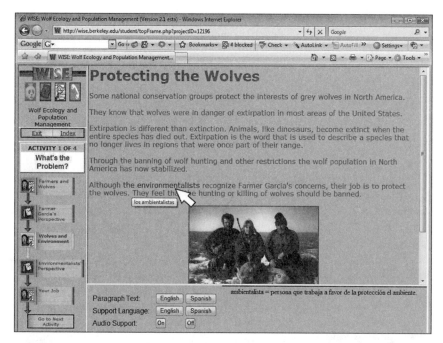

FIGURE 4.3 Screen shot from the TELS "Wolves" module illustrating TODOS language tools implemented in the WISE environment. The navigation bar at the left is used to move between steps and activities. Controls at bottom center allow the student to select languages for main text and supports, and to activate audio support. A pop-up box is shown, which the student can activate to provide a translation of selected text.

ceptually richer content than is often provided to ELL students. This finding supports the importance of providing age-appropriate and conceptually rich content, as opposed to the unfortunate practice of providing content that lowers the conceptual grade level along with the English proficiency grade level (August & Hakuta, 1997; García, 2001; García & Lee, 2008; Thomas & Collier, 1995). Further, ongoing research is investigating how the language supports scaffold students' understanding of the science content.

The inclusion of multilingual, multimodal supports in the "Wolves" module also represents an instantiation of the design principle "Promote autonomous learning." Clark et al. (in press) investigated three potential concerns: (a) Do students actually use the language supports? (b) How do they use the supports? and (c) Do bilingual students engage with the material solely in their native language? To answer these questions, Clark et al. tracked student interactions with the language supports through an integrated logging tool that tracks the time and occurrence of (a) the opening and closing of each page that includes the language supports, (b) all switches made by the student between English and Spanish for either the paragraph or the support language, (c) each word or phrase that the student mouses over to access the audio files and text pop-ups in the support language, and (d) each word or phrase that the student clicks to get extended definitions in the support language.

The findings of Clark et al. (in press) revealed that students purposefully interacted with the language support tools. The increased frequency of usage of the tools as the project progressed suggested that student usage was not driven strictly by curiosity. As well, providing students access to their native language resources did not result in students defaulting solely to their native tongue. Rather, students in all of the studies predominantly made use of the English capabilities, and the Spanish functionality helped the ELL students make sense of the English. Finally, the language supports helped even the English-proficient and English-monolingual students. The data analysis and interviews suggested that English-proficient speakers, including the English-monolingual individuals, may have used the tools to make sense of the content and, in some cases, to learn the pronunciation of English words with which they were not familiar. This finding demonstrates the utility of written and audio language supports for a wide range of students: (a) English language learners, for whom the tools support learning of English as well as science; (b) English-monolingual students, who use the audio tools to help them read the complex English content; and (c) and bilingual students classified as English-proficient, who still derive benefit from switching between languages to make the fullest sense of the text.

Implications and Possibilities for Integrating Language Supports into Online Science Learning Environments. Although the "Wolves" module currently provides supports for only Spanish and English, the technology could easily be expanded to support bilingual students in multiple languages simultaneously in the same classroom. Given the broad native language diversity encountered in many of our schools, this form of online multilingual text and audio scaffolding offers significant advantages for curriculum design. Studies conducted thus far suggest that providing students access to resources in their native language does not result in them defaulting solely to their native tongue. Rather, students in all of the studies made use predominantly of the English capabilities, employing the Spanish functionality to help them make sense of the English. These findings support earlier research suggesting that children can receive considerable instruction in their native language to allow them to catch up in content areas (such as science) without slowing the development of their English language skills (August & Hakuta, 1998; Greene, 1998; Meyer & Fienberg, 1992; Willig, 1985). The dual-language text and audio supports used in the "Wolves" module build on other research suggesting that (a) native-language word or phrase translations provide just-in-time scaffolds (Chun & Plass, 1996; Gettys, Imhof, & Kautz, 2001; Lomicka, 1998), (b) computer-based glossing (providing definitions) scaffolds reading comprehension (Cobb, 1997; Laufer & Hill, 2000; Lomicka, 1998; Roby, 1999), and (c) providing multiple forms of scaffolding allows learners to gather information in the manner most beneficial to them (Martinez-Lage, 1997).

Creating Educative Instructional Supports for Teachers and Students: The CCMS "Light" Action Scenario

Teachers are important mediators of curriculum materials (Gallagher & McLaughlin, 2007). Additional support for teachers working with diverse students may come from the instructional materials themselves. Such materials, which promote teacher learning, have been labeled as *educative* by the CCMS team and provide teachers with tools that enable access to the ideas, reasoning, and attitudes about science that students bring to the classroom. In addition, they help teachers increase their understanding of their professional work. Educative curriculum materials not only support teachers in making connections to students' knowledge and values but also help them understand why these practices are important. Most teachers are able to respond more effectively to students' learning needs when they have such resources available to them (Gallagher, 2007). (For more information about how teachers can be supported to adapt curriculum materials, see Chapter 5.) The CCMS "Light" action scenario illustrates several design features intended to support teachers as they enact curriculum materials that promote integrated understanding of science among wide-ranging learners.

"Seeing the Light: Can I Believe My Eyes?" is included in "Investigating and Questioning Our World Through Science and Technology" (IQWST), a "next-generation" middle school science curriculum that enables a wide range of teachers to effectively instruct middle school students who come to class with varied backgrounds and strengths (IQWST *Teacher's Guide*: Fortus et al., in press; see also Chapters 3 and 8). These new materials, developed by teams of scholars at CCMS partner institutions, include carefully structured sequences of student-centered learning activities and various supports for both teachers and students that promote effective science teaching and learning with highly diverse groups of students. Taking a general approach to addressing diversity, these educative resources help teachers understand students' ideas, suggest effective pedagogical strategies, and explain the intended purpose of specific design features in the curriculum. This helps teachers develop the knowledge and skills required to teach science in a way that enables most students to learn and apply their integrated science understanding.

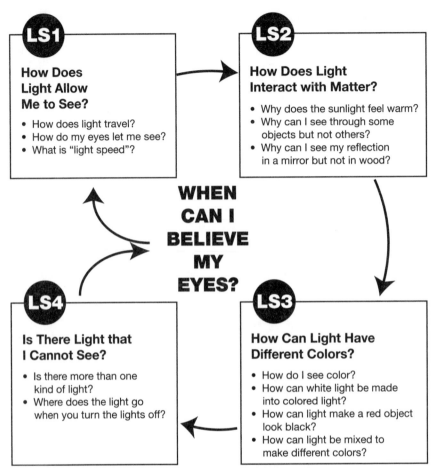

FIGURE 4.4   **Curriculum plan for the CCMS "Light" unit.**
LS = Learning Set. (*Source:* IQWST *Teacher's Guide*.)

Curriculum and Technology Design. IQWST includes four units each year, one each in biology, chemistry, earth science, and physics. The unit selected for this analysis was the sixth-grade physics unit titled "Seeing the Light: Can I Believe My Eyes?" This unit has four sections, as shown in Figure 4.4. The key learning objectives include (a) Light is in constant motion and spreads out as it travels away from a primary or secondary source, (b) Light from a primary or secondary source must enter the eye in order for the source to be seen, and (c) Light interacts with matter by transmission, absorption, or reflection (including scattering).

The following discussion focuses on the design and research related to the second objective. The lesson centers on an anchoring activity intended to provide a common experience for students by demonstrating a color-related physical phenomenon. In the activity, a message or parts of it appear and disappear depending on the color of light used to illuminate the message. Understanding the target science ideas and inquiry processes is instrumental to explaining the anchoring activity (IQWST *Teacher's Guide*).

Students complete several investigations, each time cycling back to the anchoring activity. Each cycle provides them the opportunity delve deeper into the science content and gain a more integrated understanding of (a) how light moves through space, (b) what happens when it meets matter, (c) how our eyes detect light, (d) how colors of light can be perceived to be different from what they really are, and (e) the existence of different types of nonvisible light. During the unit, a model of light and seeing is developed, applied to explain new phenomena, critiqued, modified, and re-applied (IQWST *Teacher's Guide*, p. ii). Students' ideas and reasoning about vision and the behavior of light are explored by the class with guidance from the teacher as the students try to reach consensus about a sound and satisfactory explanation based on the information they have available from their observations and explorations.

***Supporting Instruction and Learning Through the IQWST* Teacher's Guide.** Designers of the "Light" unit created several instructional supports intended to help teachers manage the diversity of student ideas and provide instruction that promotes an integrated understanding of light. Many of these supports are communicated via entries in the *Teacher's Guide*. Four main categories of support include understanding student ideas, pedagogical strategies, managing classroom discourse, and design rationale.

- *Understanding Student Ideas.* The *Teacher's Guide* contains three pretest items to help teachers assess students' entry-level knowledge pertaining to the light concepts presented in the lesson. The *Guide* also includes common student conceptions about ideas related to light and the nature of models. Figure 4.5 illustrates examples of these features. The box on the left contains a pretest assessment item, and the box on the right provides an example of a common misconception that many students hold about light. Designers intend for these supports to alert teachers to potential ideas that may hinder students' integration of relevant science ideas. They also help teachers direct students toward a more normative understanding of scientific models.
- *Pedagogical Strategies.* The *Teacher's Guide* also presents pedagogical strategies to help teachers build on students' ideas and facilitate integrated understanding. As an example, one of the three major goals identified for

Pretest Assessment Item	Common Student Conception Box in *Teacher's Guide*
This girl sees the tree. Draw arrows to show how the light from the sun helps her to see the tree.	**Common Student Conception:** You may have Ss who answer the question above by replying that the light needed to see the tree is coming from the eye rather than to the eye. This is a common response. If they do, ask them to close the flap of the light box back up and look for the tree. Ask them, "If the light is coming from your eye, why can you not see the object when the box is completely closed?" With some help, they should realize that the light must be coming from the outside of the box rather than from their eye.

FIGURE 4.5 Examples of CCMS "Light" unit supports that contribute to teachers' understanding of students' preexisting ideas about light. Awareness of common misconceptions enables teachers to more effectively focus instruction. (Adapted from IQWST *Teacher's Guide*.)

the first set of learning activities in "Seeing the Light" is the development of a basic model of the relationship between light and vision. During initial development of the physical model, students actively engage in expressing their own ideas and comparing them with the ideas of others in the class. The pretest item in Figure 4.5 provides information about the ideas that students bring with them to the instructional setting and provides a basis for subsequent discussions on the topic. Students are guided to think about and annotate the picture with arrows that represent light. In subsequent lessons and learning sets, students apply, revisit, and refine the model, allowing them to increase the model's explanatory power for everyday experiences.

○ *Managing Classroom Discourse.* To support teachers in leading students through the design process for their physical models, the *Teacher's Guide* describes the identifying characteristics of scientific models. This establishes criteria for the teacher to use in evaluating students' models more effectively and leading the whole class toward a "consensus model." The *Teacher's Guide* also communicates strategies for managing classroom discourse as students discuss alternative representations of the light phenomena and work toward consensus.

○ *Design Rationale.* In addition to supporting teachers in anticipating, eliciting, and interpreting the thinking of all of their students, educative curriculum materials promote teacher learning about content and the pedagogical rationale underlying the unit's procedures and activities (Ball & Cohen, 1996; Davis & Krajcik, 2005). In "Seeing the Light," explicit opportunities for teacher learning are identified, such as informing teachers of the pedagogical purposes for particular curriculum features. In one example, the specific reasons for having the students engage in a "synthesizing" discussion as part of the wrap-up activities to a lesson are given. By informing teachers of the original design purposes, teachers are less likely to make modifications that negatively affect the curriculum's instructional goals.

In addition to the *Teacher's Guide*, the IQWST designers created learning resources that provide teachers access to students' ideas. Early in the first lesson, a specialized inquiry tool known as the driving question board (DQB) is introduced. The DQB is a dedicated physical space, such as a colorful bulletin board or whiteboard, where ideas and questions generated by students are displayed after the students' engagement in the unit's anchoring activity. The DQB makes students' alternative conceptions and reasoning skills explicit to the teacher and public to the students. With this knowledge, the teacher can more effectively structure subsequent learning activities. Table 4.3 displays the richness and similarities of student responses on DQBs across three different classrooms in urban, suburban, and rural settings.

The DQB allows teachers to access and track students' ideas throughout the lesson. This enables teachers to build upon students' initial ideas and move toward the learning goals. As the unit progresses, newly produced student products and learning artifacts can be added to the board. Teachers are encouraged to draw attention to the DQB frequently to sustain connections between student understanding and the unit's activities, as well as to make new connections. Ideas and questions posted on the DQB also can be used as prompts for class discussions and debates during the unit.

The Impact of Teacher Supports on Teachers and Students. Including teacher supports in science curriculum materials appears to help teachers address the wide-ranging ideas and experiences students bring to the classroom. Gallagher (2007) found that when teachers attended to students' ideas and reasoning, students typically responded with greater effort, less off-task behavior, and increased enthusiasm for learning. He attributes these changes to teachers' careful attention to students' thinking, which results in students' improved self-perception. This has value for both motivation and learning. In addition, classroom trials of IQWST materials have revealed that teachers increase their confidence and their understanding of the subject matter, students' initial ideas, and strategies for monitoring students' learning trajectories (D. Fortus, personal communication, June 2007).

Although preliminary research findings cannot causally explain how the *Teacher's Guide* and learning activities affect student understanding, some

TABLE 4.3 Questions Generated on Driving Question Boards in Three Enactment Sites Employing the CCMS "Light" Unit*

Learning Set	Classroom 1 (Urban)	Classroom 2 (Suburban)	Classroom 3 (Rural)
1. How Does Light Allow Me to See?	How does light help me see the hidden message in the dark? How far can light travel? How does light affect our eyes? How do our pupils know when to change size when light is seen?	What can cause blindness? Why can't they see? What do our eyes have to do with our seeing? How far does light travel? Does light affect how far you can see? Why do your eyes hurt when the light turns on in a dark room? How does light (brightness) affect your eyes? How fast is light? Why can you still see when the light in the room is off?	How does light let us see? Can my eyes see everything? Will light go on and on or will it only go so far? Can I believe everything that I see? Why are our eyes easy to fool? How can light move so fast? How does light come into our eyes?
2. How Does Light Interact with Matter?	How does light bounce off of an object? How does light interact with organisms? How does light conduct heat? How does light pass through molecules? Is light passed through heat or electricity?	How does light reflect off things? Why does it look really bright when there's snow outside?	How does light do things with matter? Can a chick break out of his egg with a light bulb instead of his mother? How can you see fish in different places in water? Can a light bulb melt the snow?

*Weizman and Fortus (2007a).

88

Sierra's Pretest Reply	Sierra's Posttest Reply
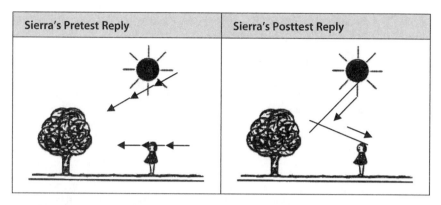	

FIGURE 4.6 A student's response to the assessment item in Figure 4.5 prior to and following instruction.

promising findings about student learning have been reported from classroom trials of the unit. Across urban, rural, and suburban contexts, researchers analyzed over 200 student responses to the three assessment items administered before and after the lesson. Students significantly increased their scores for all three questions (Weizman & Fortus, 2007a). Figure 4.6 shows one student's response to an assessment item. Prior to instruction, this student exemplified a common misconception known as the "bath of light" or "active eye" theory, in which students believe that the light source "lights up objects so they can be seen." Following instruction, the student demonstrated the accepted scientific conception that light from the source strikes the object and is reflected to the viewer's receiving or "passive" eye.

For additional evidence of student learning, researchers interviewed students before and after instruction in Learning Set 1 of the "Light" unit (see Figure 4.4). Table 4.4 provides selected student responses to the interview question "How does light allow the person to see the tree?" These preliminary results show a positive change in students' understanding about the movement of light in relation to seeing. Some common misconceptions had been addressed, and the sixth-grade students in the study appeared to hold a more integrated understanding of light (Weizman & Fortus, 2007a).

Providing teachers with resources that enable them to meaningfully attend to students' ideas gives depth to teacher–student interaction. The teacher supports described for this scenario can equip teachers with knowledge of common misconceptions, assessment tools that elicit students' ideas and reasoning, and learning activities that build from students' existing ideas. These supports help teachers use student work to plan instruction and make instructional decisions, which is essential for moving students toward a powerful and integrated understanding of science.

TABLE 4.4 Selected Students' Interview Responses Before and After Learning Set 1 (CCMS "Light" Unit)*

| Student | Question: "How does light allow the person to see the tree?" | |
	Response Before Instruction	Response After Instruction
SA	Because it's not all dark so the person could see the tree, but in the dark he couldn't because there was no light.	From the light having straight unblocked path into her eyes.... The tree is an object for the sun to light up so she can see it.... The light is going on the tree and into our eyes.
AN	The light shines on the tree so that he could see and there's nothing blocking it from getting to the flag so if he looks at the flag he'll be able to see it.	The light is shining on the tree and then bounces off the tree into your eyes.
HA	If you have light it like shine it all up and you'll be able to see it and won't run into it.	The light can go every direction and spreads out because stuff isn't blocking it. And then the sunlight goes like that and down and makes the reflection and makes your eyes be able to see the tree ... you'll be able to see it because it's lit up.
MG	Light goes to all directions ... it allows people to see so they can look around.	Light goes everywhere ... basically straight ... down to the tree. It heads to the person and he's looking at it.

*Weizman and Fortus (2007b).

SYNTHESIS

Implications for Research and Curriculum Design

The "Asthma," "Wolves," and "Light" action scenarios reveal several design principles and features that can support science educators as they create learning environments to assess and meet the needs of diverse groups of learners. Research described in this chapter highlights active approaches to learning, such as engaging students in complex scientific inquiry. We recommend general and targeted scaffolds that allow diverse groups of learners to situate science as a useful enterprise in their lives and increase their likelihood of constructing an integrated understanding of science. By considering diverse learners, we can uncover design principles that are worthwhile for all students.

Instruction should recognize and incorporate students' prior knowledge, identity, language, and experiences into the design and enactment of curricula. This will position students as co-constructors of classroom culture and learning outcomes. The "Wolves" research presents design features to help educators real-ize this goal. Designers intended for the embedded multilingual, multimodal learning technologies to support students' linguistic practices. They created an environment in which students autonomously monitored their understanding, made decisions about what scaffolds they needed, and ultimately piloted the construction of their science understanding. Throughout the "Wolves" module, linguistic supports were coupled with complex science instruction, allowing edu-cators to maintain high expectations for learning among *all* students.

Another principle that guided the design of the curricula focuses on the inclusion of personally relevant context to (a) engage students in school science topics by providing multiple entry or connection points to science, and (b) help students understand the connections between science and their present and future lives. Research on the "Asthma" module revealed specific design principles related to the selection of context for teaching science content. The designers established criteria for identifying real-world problems that could be transformed into effective community-based science curricula. From the perspective of this research, effective topics should be open-ended, require diverse and intersecting expertise, afford the opportunity for varied scientific inquiry pursuits, and involve community activism. To create the "Asthma" module, the designers relied on a partnership model that integrated multiple perspectives and expertise. Moreover, teachers' and students' ideas and practices influenced the iterative refinements of the curriculum and learning goals. This integration of multiple partners and perspectives increased the potential for multiple connections between school science and students' lives. By offering more points of entry to the world of science, designers are more likely to engage students from a wide range of backgrounds, experiences, and perspectives.

A third design principle underscored in this chapter focuses on embedding assessments to enable teachers to monitor students' developing ideas and reason-ing throughout instruction. This approach encourages teachers to recognize, value, and build upon the diverse repertoire of ideas that students bring to class. The "Light" scenario puts forth specific principles to increase the effective use of such assessments. For example, designed activities that incorporate the assess-ments enable teachers to focus on students' ideas and use those ideas as evidence for instructional planning that benefits *all* learners.

A final design principle highlighted in this chapter focuses on developing cur-riculum materials that are educative for teachers. Teachers need to understand the nuances of the content and the pedagogical choices that designers made to enable integrated understanding of the science content. Explicit instruction through teacher support materials, such as a teacher's guide, provides teachers with back-ground knowledge on the benefits and utility of content and embedded assess-ments in the curriculum. Without such supports, teachers often miss the richness of thought that underlies the overall curriculum plan and the individual activi-ties that comprise it (Ball & Cohen, 1996; Davis & Krajcik, 2005; Chapter 5).

Implications for Policy

We conclude this chapter by suggesting a few strategies and policies for curriculum designers, teacher educators, and students. We advocate policies that encourage school leadership to select coherent curriculum materials that build on students' natural linguistic practices and afford students multiple opportunities to establish science as personally relevant or useful. We additionally endorse policies that provide teachers with tools to manage rich, diverse student ideas in a manner that promotes an integrated understanding of science. In the end, policies related to testing, instruction, and the allocation of resources must work synergistically to enable creation of learning environments that meet the diverse needs of all learners.

Beginning with linguistic policy, we recommend allocation of funds to establish and maintain an infrastructure that supports multilingual education. Policies requiring monolingual instruction only serve to deprive many English language learners of critical resources needed to develop their science (or other complex content) understanding. Schools must offer instruction that builds on students' home language. Such instruction allows students to marshal their linguistic resources as they acquire the complex and highly technical language of science, and it does not impede them in their broader English language learning. In addition, teachers need access to innovations—such as multimodal, multilingual technology and related professional development—that can support these processes.

Our second policy recommendation relates to curriculum selection. As teachers work to help students connect science to their everyday life, they are faced with such an overwhelming number of content standards that in-depth learning is replaced with superficial content coverage. Content standards should not make unreasonable demands on teachers and students, but should guide teachers to select curricula that promote deep connections between students' personal and school science experiences. Policy should also support researchers, teachers, and administrators in identifying critical sequences of content standards that promote an integrated understanding of science among various groups of learners.

We recognize that establishing connections between school science and students' lives can prove difficult, and we advise that school policies support teachers as they develop skills and understanding in this area. To increase the success of such efforts, our third policy recommendation is that policy makers should support science educators as they strive to empower students to use science to make key decisions regarding their health and safety, environmental concerns, and future job responsibilities. Administrative policies should support teachers as they establish professional development and partnerships with fellow teachers, university research groups, and community organizations in pursuit of these goals. In the end, schools must be provided with the necessary resources to create a space where teachers can best serve the needs of their students.

As we design science curricula that serve the needs of diverse students, it is important that assessment practices are aligned with instructional goals in science. Addressing the learning needs of today's diverse population of students requires innovative assessments that capture the various ways students understand and participate in science. As our fourth policy recommendation, we advise policy makers to ensure that evaluative, external assessments such as standardized tests are sensitive to appropriate learning goals and instructional approaches. Furthermore, standardized assessment items should be consistent with classroom assessments that teachers use to monitor and guide instructional planning.

Our fifth and final recommendation proposes increased funding for curriculum designers and researchers in their quest to determine the most effective pedagogical supports for students and teachers. Field testing of curricula should occur in school contexts comprised of students with multilingual abilities and wide-ranging ideas about science topics and their community, and teachers committed to supporting a diverse student body. These studies will not only inform researchers about the effectiveness of learning materials but also can serve as compelling evidence for educators and policy makers when advocating the implementation of innovative curriculum materials in schools across the nation.

Supporting Teachers in
Productive Adaptation

Elizabeth A. Davis and Keisha Varma

TEACHERS ARE CONSTANTLY adapting. Even teachers with access to high-quality, coherent instructional materials adapt those materials for their own classrooms. Maggie, for example, is an elementary teacher in a large, diverse, urban school district. She makes extensive use of the curriculum materials she has, yet based on her knowledge of her students, she continually adapts those materials to improve her effectiveness (Davis, Beyer, Forbes, & Stevens, 2007). The central focus of this chapter is how designers can support this sort of adaptation—changes made before, during, or after classroom enactment to any sort of instructional materials or to one's typical practice.

The Center for Curriculum Materials in Science (CCMS) supports teachers' learning throughout their preservice and inservice careers. At CCMS, educative curriculum materials, technological supports, and teacher education and professional development experiences work in synergy to promote teacher learning, especially with regard to the analysis, critique, adaptation, and enactment of the materials. One of the stated core principles of CCMS, in fact, highlights this emphasis (see http://www.sciencematerialscenter.org/about_core_teacher.htm; see also the Preface, Kali, Koppal, Linn, & Roseman; and Chapter 2, Roseman, Linn, & Koppal).

The Technology Enhanced Learning in Science (TELS) Center supports inservice teachers' use of technology-based curriculum modules. TELS employs a targeted professional development approach, which supports teachers in developing an integrated understanding of science, technology, and student learning via flexible support that is determined by teachers' needs. TELS professional development is supported by technologies to make student learning visible, to support inquiry instruction, and to aid teachers in productive adaptation.

Both centers support teachers' knowledge development by encouraging an integrated understanding of inquiry-based instruction. Together, the centers support teachers across the entire professional continuum (Feiman-Nemser, 2001), from the time they are preservice teachers in schools of education to the time they are experienced teachers ready to try something new. In this chapter we first explore some of the challenges associated with teaching and then focus specifically on the practice of adaptation. Next we present a brief theoretical perspective on teacher learning, followed by a description of some of the ways in which TELS and CCMS support adaptation to enhance teachers' teaching practices and knowledge development. After laying this groundwork, we summarize some of the centers' research on teachers and their adaptation processes. Finally, we discuss policy implications and offer recommendations for further research on adaptation of teaching materials and practices.

CHALLENGES IN TEACHING

Teaching science is a difficult task for a host of reasons—among them content, pedagogical, technological, sociological, and political issues. We cite just a few examples here.

First, what is hard about teaching science as a beginning elementary school teacher? Beginning elementary school teachers require many areas of mastery, yet they generally lack both sufficient coursework and the experience that would contribute to their knowledge base for helping children develop coherent knowledge of science concepts and practices (Davis, Petish, & Smithey, 2006).

Teaching with new materials creates additional challenges. High-stakes testing and curriculum overload require teachers to be acutely concerned about the time cost of incorporating new materials. Innovative, coherent, inquiry-oriented materials require that teachers learn new ideas and incorporate them into their practice. But even when teachers learn relevant new ideas and practices (e.g., about their students' ideas or about inquiry-oriented science teaching), they do not always readily integrate them into their teaching.

Using technology to teach science requires teachers, researchers, and administrators to confront dilemmas related to the technology itself, instruction, and policy. For instance, the technological tools available may be unreliable, outdated, or slow, and access to support may be limited. Teachers may lack strategies for managing students' work on computers. And, administrators may not fully support teachers' use of or access to technology.

A final example concerns teaching science in a way that makes it accessible and meaningful for all students. Teachers need to be prepared for a plethora of differences in their classrooms—differences that manifest themselves in terms of race, ethnicity, class, language, special needs, gender, family structure, and religion, to name just a few. Supporting all of the students in one's classroom in learning science can be a daunting challenge (see Chapter 4, Tate, Clark, Gallagher, & McLaughlin).

ADAPTATION AS A CRUCIAL TEACHER PRACTICE

Looking at how individual teachers use instructional materials in their practice reveals that teachers appropriate tasks (i.e., accept them as-is), adapt tasks, or use the materials as a source of inspiration for developing new tasks (Brown & Edelson, 2003; Remillard, 1999). Each of these, in turn, can promote short- or long-term changes in teachers' practice. We define *adaptation* broadly as the changes a teacher makes before, during, or after classroom enactment to any sort of instructional materials or to his or her typical practice. In conjunction with our discussion of adaptation as a necessary part of working with any curriculum materials, and the importance of high-quality supports for it, we provide a number of examples involving CCMS and TELS materials.

Teachers need to adapt even high-quality instructional materials to better support their own students' learning (Barab & Luehmann, 2003; Baumgartner, 2004; Squire, MaKinster, Barnett, Luehmann, & Barab, 2003). For example, an experienced teacher might adapt a unit to allow students greater opportunity to design their own investigations; a beginning teacher, on the other hand, might adapt the same unit to provide more structure. Another teacher might adapt a unit to incorporate experiences that capitalize on her students' language or cultural backgrounds. Some teachers make productive changes to curriculum materials toward these ends, whereas others—for example, those who do not deeply understand the rationales behind reforms promoted in some materials—may make unproductive changes (Collopy, 2003; Remillard, 1999; Schneider & Krajcik, 2002). Although some science teachers develop their own lessons from scratch, we argue that professional teaching increasingly necessitates the effective use of existing curriculum materials, preferably those developed with an eye toward coherence and innovation.

Taking a broader view of curriculum development—in which teachers play an active role, yet build on resources available to them—is grounded in an assumption that teachers must recognize the strengths and weaknesses of the materials they are using (Ben-Peretz, 1990). Teachers employ their personal resources (such as their knowledge and beliefs) as well as resources within the materials themselves in making changes; their ability to do so is referred to as their pedagogical design capacity (Brown, in press; Brown & Edelson, 2003). When teachers change high-quality, coherent curriculum materials, the changes must be principled—they must maintain the integrity of the original design and must work toward attaining the same goals as were the goals of the original (Ben-Peretz, 1990; Bridgham, 1971; Davis et al., 2006; Pintó, 2005). Sometimes, however, materials are not effective as written (Kesidou & Roseman, 2002), and teachers might need to make more substantial changes.

Even experienced teachers may need significant support in learning to make decisions about using instructional materials effectively, especially when the materials represent an innovative or reform-oriented approach to science teaching that is unfamiliar to the teachers—as is often the case when teachers incorporate inquiry-oriented science and technology into their teaching. Preservice and beginning teachers need these same skills, and should come to recognize that adapting materials to meet their needs is (or can be) in fact a part of the professional role identity of practicing teachers (Schwarz et al., 2008). For all of these teachers, then, it is important for developers of science curriculum materials to provide support for adaptation and for teacher learning.

ADAPTATION, TEACHER LEARNING, AND EFFECTIVE SCIENCE TEACHING

Teacher learning is situated within teachers' own practice (Putnam & Borko, 2000) and is a process of ongoing sense making (Spillane, Reiser, & Reimer, 2002). Teachers are the ones who mediate the influence of any innovation, and using those innovations effectively requires a rich and integrated knowledge base (see, e.g., Remillard, 1999).

The knowledge integration perspective informs TELS and CCMS design of supports for teachers and the centers' descriptions of teachers' learning processes. Knowledge integration (Linn, Eylon, & Davis, 2004; Chapter 2) is a theory of learning consistent with theories of teaching and learning promoted by the learning sciences (Bransford et al., 1999). Although it is often discussed in the context of students, knowledge integration theory can also be used to describe how teachers learn new ideas (Davis, 2004). Teachers have mental representations made up of ideas about the content they teach, about student learning, and about pedagogical practices. Teachers acquire new ideas from a variety of sources (e.g., continuing education courses, classroom experiences, professional development, curriculum materials, student work). When new ideas are encountered, teachers reevaluate and reorganize their knowledge to incorporate the new ideas. As they do this, they link ideas in their repertoires. Knowledge integration theory emphasizes the links between new and existing ideas as evidence of learning. Developing linked and well-organized knowledge positions teachers to use their knowledge flexibly (Ball & Bass, 2000) in their instructional practice—in planning, reflection, and real-time classroom interactions.

SUPPORTING ADAPTATION

CCMS and TELS use three main forms of support in promoting teachers' learning with regard to engaging in productive adaptation. These include technology, curriculum materials, and professional development and teacher education.

Role of Technology in Supporting Adaptation

A cognitive prerequisite for adaptation is that teachers be efficient and effective in their routine practices so that they will be able to perform multiple tasks without exhausting their attentional and cognitive resources. Only then can they advance beyond existing routines to adapt their practices and integrate new pedagogical knowledge (Hammerness, Darling-Hammond, & Bransford, 2005). Technology can streamline some tasks and make others more accessible so that teachers are able to successfully make adaptations. We turn first to ways in which TELS provides such technological support.

TELS and Interactive Assessment. One of the main goals for TELS professional development is to encourage teachers to engage in *interactive assessment*. Interactive assessment begins with developing an understanding of students' repertoires of ideas and proceeds with teachers continually adapting their practices based on students' knowledge.

Interactive assessment is aligned with the tradition of formative assessment and assessment conversations (Duschl & Gitomer, 1997). In most cases, it is a new practice for teachers. Traditionally, science teachers assess student learning via end-of-unit tests or quizzes, as well as summative projects. These practices are informative, but they occur after instruction has ended. Therefore, they do not provide opportunities to address ideas and concepts that students confused, missed, or forgot. If teachers can assess students' knowledge *during* instruction, rather than after instruction has ended, then they can continually adapt their teaching practices to address learning difficulties that students may face or enhance the content to extend students' thinking. This type of interactive assessment can help to ensure that the instruction helps *all* of the students in the classroom be successful learners (Chapter 4). TELS professional development encourages teachers to assess student learning by examining not only the content of students' ideas but also the links they have among their ideas (Chapter 7, DeBoer, Lee, & Husic).

The TELS learning environment includes online tools that teachers can use to assess student learning and provide feedback to students during module enactment. Figure 5.1 shows the "View student work" and "Comment" features of the online assessment tools. This design builds on the idea that teachers can collect information about students' knowledge by initiating assessment conversations as they engage in their normal instruction activities and then use that

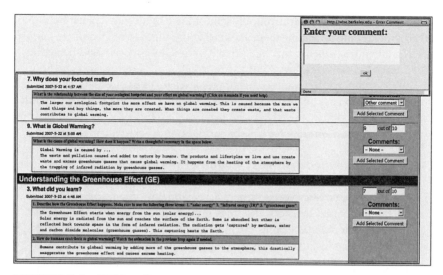

FIGURE 5.1 TELS online management tools to support interactive assessment: "View student work" and "Comment" features.

information to support student learning (Duschl & Gitomer, 1997; Ruiz-Primo & Furtak, 2006).

However, learning to use a new technology to engage in a new assessment practice can be taxing for teachers. Preliminary results from an ongoing longitudinal study of the challenges that teachers face when using TELS modules indicate that, initially, teachers do not attempt to engage in the new assessment practices. Instead, they focus on mastering the logistics of using the module and rely on traditional methods of assessment. Some print out copies of their students' work to grade at the end of the enactment. Others allow students to redo their work to improve their final grade, but do not incorporate additional instruction about the concepts with which students had difficulty. There is no assessment conversation. In these cases, TELS mentors (described in more depth below) reintroduce teachers to the assessment tools and emphasize the value of engaging in interactive assessment practices.

All TELS modules begin by eliciting students' prior knowledge about scientific concepts and phenomena via embedded notes within the module. (For a discussion of the role of eliciting student ideas in promoting integrated understanding, see Chapter 2.) Students' responses to the embedded notes provide a rich measure of their understanding (Linn, Husic, et al., 2006). In the TELS learning environment, teachers have immediate access to students' responses, which gives them the opportunity to adapt their teaching practices in real time to address issues. Teachers can also grade students' work in responding to the embedded notes and use a student feedback tool to electronically send students a message telling them about their progress and informing them about what they need to do in order to perform better. When teachers use this functionality, students are overheard marveling at their teachers' messages; they want to immediately address the issues mentioned. This type of interactive grading encourages teachers to use formative assessment practices and to base adaptations to their teaching practices on students' understanding of the content. (See the design principle "Embed assessment-for-learning within instruction" in Chapter 8, Kali, Fortus, and Ronen-Fuhrmann.)

TELS and Annotated Teachers' Modules. Annotated teachers' modules are TELS curriculum modules with teacher hints embedded at key instruction points. Whereas interactive assessment is used mainly during classroom enactment, the annotated teachers' modules are useful to teachers as they plan to implement a module, as well as during classroom enactments. These modules were created as educative supports (discussed below) to augment and extend TELS targeted support for teachers by promoting an integrated understanding of student learning and their own teaching practices. The annotated modules are especially helpful in helping teachers prepare to use the visualizations embedded in the module activities. Data from teacher interviews, student work, and classroom observations show that visualizations embedded in TELS modules are most effective when a teacher leads a whole-class discussion. The whole-class

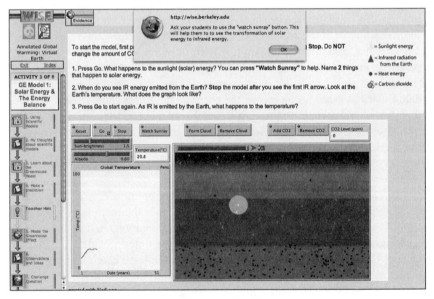

FIGURE 5.2 A visualization-focused teacher hint in the annotated version of the TELS "Global Warming" module.

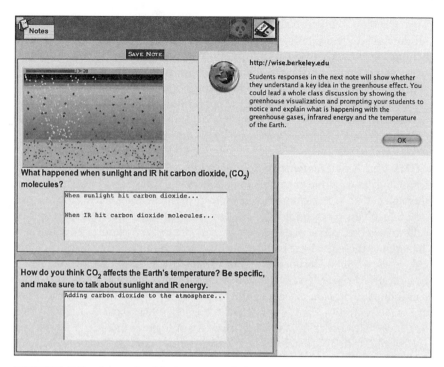

FIGURE 5.3 An embedded note and the associated teacher hint in the annotated version of the TELS "Global Warming" module.

discussion introduces the visualization, shows students how to use it, and probes them about the content that is being taught with it. For example, in the "Global Warming: Virtual Earth" module, students are guided through the process of experimenting with a visualization of the greenhouse effect to learn the roles of different variables (such as solar energy, infrared energy, and greenhouse gases). The annotated module alerts teachers to the complexity of the visualization and suggests that they initially demonstrate how the buttons and slider bars work to control the variables. Figure 5.2 shows a teacher hint for the greenhouse visualization from the "Global Warming" module.

Hints in the annotated module also suggest embedded notes that teachers should evaluate to make sure students are not developing alternative ideas due to faulty experimental design or incorrect data interpretation. Hints also help teachers prepare for issues that are associated with using new instructional approaches, such as online discussions. Figure 5.3 shows an embedded note and the hint that is displayed with it in the annotated module.

During classroom enactment, teachers can have the annotated module open and available to them as their students are working in the curriculum module.

This provides access to real-time classroom support. The annotated teachers' modules also include information about the curriculum designers' rationale behind specific activities. This information helps teachers make informed decisions about adapting their teaching to support the learning goals that are addressed in the design of the module. This is especially important if teachers are considering making changes to the curriculum module.

We turn next to a discussion of the role of technology in supporting teachers in CCMS curricula, which has some parallels to the annotated modules from TELS.

CCMS and New Elementary School Science Teachers. One way in which technology plays a role in supporting teachers in CCMS curriculum materials is through CASES (Curriculum Access System for Elementary Science, http://cases .soe.umich.edu), a technology-mediated learning environment aimed specifically at new (i.e., preservice and early career) elementary school science teachers. To support these teachers as they learn to teach inquiry-oriented science more effectively, CASES incorporates inquiry-oriented unit plans that are intended to be educative for teachers, as well as a personal online journal, an online teacher community discussion space, and other resources for science teaching. Unit plans are made educative for teachers (Ball & Cohen, 1996; Davis & Krajcik, 2005; Schneider & Krajcik, 2002) through a variety of features intended to work synergistically, such as science content background, information about students' likely alternative ideas, and multiple representations of inquiry. Some features are aimed directly at supporting teachers in making productive adaptations of the CASES lesson plans.

CASES is grounded in three main design principles for supporting teachers' learning. Here, we discuss these design principles in light of how they support adaptation. The first design principle, called "Guidance on demand" (Bell & Davis, 2000), states that new teachers should be allowed the opportunity to request contextualized guidance when they need it. This can take the form of hints similar to the teacher hints in the TELS annotated teachers' modules described above. Educative hints in CASES provide teachers with ideas, for example, about *how* to enact instructional recommendations. The hints also give the rationales behind particular instructional decisions within a specific lesson (see Figure 5.4). Understanding the reasoning behind particular instructional recommendations helps teachers make productive changes—especially new teachers. Reflection prompts—another form of guidance on demand—can provide sentence starters asking teachers to consider students' ideas that might emerge in a lesson or changes teachers might make to a particular lesson. Teachers, like other learners (Davis, 2003), often have trouble reflecting productively (Davis, 2006a; Hatton & Smith, 1995) and thus need support.

The second design principle, called "Images of inquiry," states that new teachers need multiple representations of inquiry-oriented science teaching to develop

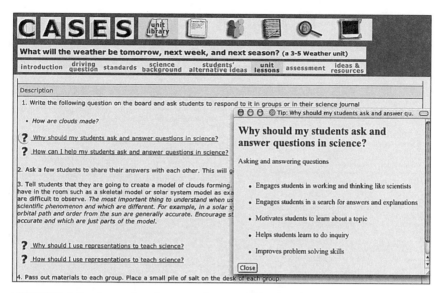

FIGURE 5.4 A teacher hint in CCMS CASES, a technology-mediated learning environment designed especially for new teachers.

an understanding of how inquiry plays out in the classroom. It is important in any learning environment to provide learners with multiple representations of what the learner is intended to understand (Kozma, Russell, Jones, Marx, & Davis, 1996; Spiro, Feltovich, Jackson, & Coulson, 1991). Because a main goal of CASES is for teachers to develop an improved understanding of inquiry-oriented science teaching, multiple images of inquiry are provided, in narrative, graphical, and tabular form (Davis, Smithey, & Petish, 2004). Figure 5.5 shows examples of each. The tabular and narrative images are focused in part on supporting teachers' adaptation. Narrative images of inquiry describe changes one or more teachers have made to a particular CASES lesson, given the teachers' goals (Dietz & Davis, in press; Smithey & Davis, 2004). Tabular images of inquiry, on the other hand, provide generic guidance to support teachers in making lessons more or less student directed—in other words, in moving along the inquiry continuum (NRC, 2000a). Such guidance can serve as a general support to help teachers help all of their students learn (Chapter 4).

The third design principle, called "Social supports," states that new teachers need opportunities to share ideas and see role models that can inform their practice. Teacher communities provide opportunities for the development of expertise (Grossman, Wineburg, & Woolworth, 2001) and identity (Overbaugh, 2002). CASES incorporates a commercial threaded asynchronous discussion program; the online discussion can be focused on adaptation. In addition, CASES

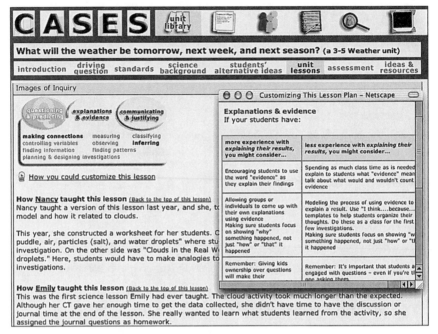

FIGURE 5.5   Images of inquiry in the CCMS CASES environment: Graphical, narrative, and tabular representations focusing, in part, on supporting teachers' adaptation of curriculum materials.

provides role models through the use of the narrative images of inquiry mentioned above. For example, one set of narratives explores how a teacher, Maggie, thinks about adapting her curriculum materials in light of her diverse students' ideas and backgrounds.

CCMS and Urban Middle School Teachers.   Knowledge Networks on the Web (KNOW, http://know.umich.edu; Fishman, 2003; Fogleman, Fishman, & Krajcik, 2006) is an online professional development environment aimed at an audience of experienced middle school teachers. KNOW was developed as an extension of the inquiry-oriented middle school science curriculum materials from the Center for Learning Technologies in Urban Schools (LeTUS) (in particular for print-based educative curriculum materials developed with the Detroit Public Schools; Singer et al., 2000) and later of materials from the "Investigating and Questioning Our World Through Science and Technology" (IQWST) curriculum associated with CCMS (Krajcik & Reiser, 2006; Krajcik et al., 2008; Chapter 3, Krajcik, Slotta, McNeill, & Reiser). In addition to providing access to electronic versions of the print materials, KNOW provides two types of video: "Images of practice" videos that provide windows into classrooms, and "How to" videos that give step-by-step visual instruction on how to use scientific apparatuses or software. KNOW also provides a broad range of student work samples and teacher tips, as well as a discussion environment linked to each unit. Such support can help teachers make productive use of adaptations to the lessons.

Shared Design Principle. A design principle that summarizes the shared perspective of TELS and CCMS on the role of technology in supporting teacher learning with regard to adaptation can be stated as follows:

> *Teachers can be supported through technology to make productive adaptations to curriculum and instruction based on their students' ideas. This support can be provided during planning and enactment as well as post-enactment, and can cover a continuum from fairly generic to quite specific supports. This technological support is important because teachers need to engage in productive adaptation through interactive planning, instruction, and assessment. If teachers are not supported in making productive adaptations to curriculum and instruction via technology, teachers may not be able to engage in interactive assessment and instruction with students. Additionally, print educative curriculum materials can quickly become unwieldy due to their length.*

In sum, technology can play an important role in supporting teachers in engaging in productive adaptation of materials. We argue, however, that technology is unlikely to be effective on its own. Instead, we argue for roles for curriculum materials and professional development, as well. We turn next to the role of curriculum materials—not surprisingly a major focus of CCMS, the Center for Curriculum Materials in Science.

Role of Educative Curriculum Materials

As noted earlier, educative curriculum materials (i.e., curriculum materials intended to promote teacher learning as well as student learning) can provide support for teachers, either independently or in conjunction with other forums for teacher learning such as face-to-face professional development. Researchers and curriculum developers hypothesize that educative curriculum materials can promote teachers' identity development, as well as their learning (Ball & Cohen, 1996; Davis & Krajcik, 2005).

Design Heuristics. Work from the CASES project, the hi-c³e group (i.e., the Center for Highly Interactive Classrooms, Curricula, and Computing in Education), and other CCMS projects was synthesized by Davis and Krajcik (2005) to produce a set of design heuristics for educative curriculum materials. These heuristics focus on supporting teacher learning in subject matter knowledge and pedagogical content knowledge for science topics and for scientific inquiry. Although Davis and Krajcik are careful to note that the design heuristics should not be considered to be design principles, because too little empirical research exists on educative curriculum materials, the authors put them forward as recommendations for guiding the design of such materials. When materials are designed with educative features in place, then empirical research can be conducted to test the efficacy of the heuristics. Each design heuristic is written to recommend the inclusion in educative curriculum materials of three crucial elements: (a) baseline instructional guidance, (b) rationales, and (c) implementation and adaptation guidance.

Davis and Krajcik (2005) build on Ball and Cohen's (1996) discussion of using curriculum materials to support the development of pedagogical content knowledge and recommend providing *baseline instructional guidance* for teachers. For example, Design Heuristic 1, which is focused on engaging students in scientific phenomena, suggests that educative curriculum materials should "warn of potential pitfalls with specific physical experiences" (Davis & Krajcik, 2005), such as experiments or demonstrations.

For the goal of adaptation of curriculum materials, other forms of support are at least as important. Researchers emphasize the importance of using curriculum materials as a way of providing *rationales* behind instructional decisions (Ball & Cohen, 1996; Davis & Krajcik, 2005), and Remillard (2000) talks about using curriculum materials to "speak to" teachers rather than "speaking through" them (p. 347). For example, Design Heuristic 7, which is focused on the scientific practice of explanation, states in part that "The supports should include rationales for why engaging students in explanation is important in scientific inquiry and why these particular approaches for doing so are scientifically and pedagogically appropriate" (Davis & Krajcik, 2005; see Chapter 3 for further exploration of engaging students in scientific explanation). Because teachers often engage students in science experiences without making sense of the science, helping teachers understand why curriculum materials recommend this inquiry practice is especially important. More generally, if teachers understand the rationale behind a particular instructional recommendation, then they may be more likely to enact the curriculum materials in keeping with the developers' intent. Davis and Krajcik argue that such rationales may also support the development of more generative and integrated knowledge among teachers; rationales may, for example, provide support for the development of more principled knowledge that can be applied in units other than the one in which the rationale is incorporated. As an example of materials designed in this way, the teacher materials for the "Investigations in Environmental Science" high school environmental science curriculum developed by the GEODE (Geographic Data in Education) Initiative (Edelson, 2005) emphasize design rationales. All of the activities are labeled by the role that they play in the learning-for-use learning cycle (Edelson, 2001) that was used to design the materials. The goal is for teachers to understand the implications of modifying or deleting a particular activity.

In addition to implementation guidance and rationales behind instructional decisions, educative curriculum materials can also provide direct *implementation and adaptation guidance* (Davis & Krajcik, 2005). For example, Design Heuristic 5, which is focused on collecting and analyzing data, suggests in part that educative curriculum materials should "help [teachers] adapt and use these approaches across multiple topic areas even when the data being collected seem fairly different" (p. 11). For example, as described earlier, the CCMS CASES curriculum materials incorporate tabular images of inquiry that suggest adaptations to move toward more or less student-directed inquiry—an important support for beginning teachers who may feel uneasy about highly student-directed inquiry, or for any teacher who is new to inquiry-oriented science teaching. This guidance may serve as curricular resources that can contribute, along with teachers' personal resources, to the teachers' pedagogical design capacity (Brown, in press).

Shared Design Principle. A design principle guiding the work of CCMS and TELS around educative curriculum materials can be stated as follows:

> *Curriculum materials can and should be designed to promote teacher learning in addition to student learning. Incorporating baseline instructional guidance, implementation and adaptation guidance, and rationales for instructional recommendations into curriculum materials can promote informed decision making and can promote knowledge integration and generative learning among teachers. If curriculum materials are not used as a vehicle to support teacher learning, educators dismiss an opportunity to promote change to teachers' knowledge and practice situated in their daily classroom work.*

In sum, educative curriculum materials can support teachers in learning with regard to adaptation and in making productive adaptations to materials. Curriculum materials on their own, however, are less likely to successfully promote teacher change. Additional supports are crucial, as we argue next.

Role of Professional Development and Teacher Education

Effective teachers constantly make adaptations to curriculum materials, but some teachers do not view adaptation as a legitimate or high-priority part of their job (Bullough, 1992; Eisenhart, Cuthbert, Shrum, & Harding, 1988). Additional sustained efforts may be necessary to complement the approaches discussed above.

TELS Targeted Professional Development. A professional development approach called *targeted professional development* has been developed by TELS to support teachers as they learn to incorporate technology innovations into their classes, engage in inquiry instruction, and cultivate best practices. The key idea is that teachers must be empowered to design their own professional development. They are encouraged to try a 5-day module, reflect on the value of the experience, and determine the support they need to effectively execute modules with their students. Targeted professional development is a variant of the mentored professional development approach that has been used successfully in other research (Slotta, 2004; Spitulnik & Linn, 2006). The mentored approach is well suited for teachers using technology in support of inquiry instruction in science classrooms. The mentor–teacher relationship is based on a model of cognitive apprenticeship (Brown, Collins, & Duguid, 1989), where the mentor introduces new ideas and models new strategies that are most effective when using TELS modules. This approach entails *planning* enactment of a module, *enacting* the module, *reflecting* on instruction, and *adapting* the module and/or instruction prior to subsequent enactments (Slotta, 2004; Spitulnik & Linn, 2006; Varma, 2006).

The mentor–teacher relationship is important across all phases of the TELS professional development program. Participating teachers receive support during the planning, enactment, and reflection phases of their module implementation. Additionally, TELS professional development support is flexible enough to support teachers to adapt their classroom practices or the actual TELS module based on their enactment experiences and their reflections on student learning. These phases form iterative cycles that allow teachers to refine their practice, and allow mentors to refine the support they provide based on what is learned during each phase.

Using technology in the classroom requires hours of *planning* (Hew & Brush, 2007). TELS supports teachers to engage in the planning process across multiple activities. Teachers familiarize themselves with the tools in an initial meeting. Then, during and following the classroom enactment, teachers are encouraged to reflect on students' work within the TELS module to plan future instruction and enactments. As teachers plan, a mentor from their school's technology support staff or from TELS helps them to assess their technology resources.

Most of the TELS professional development program takes place in teachers' classrooms, because teacher knowledge develops in classroom and school contexts (Putnam & Borko, 2000). Targeted support during the *enactment* phase ensures that teachers can successfully implement the module. Teachers report that this type of personal mentoring is one of the most valuable aspects of professional development support (Peers, Diezmann, & Watters, 2003). Classroom mentoring addresses the potential gap between the curriculum designers' intentions and actual classroom practices (Ball & Cohen, 1996) without discounting the fact that teachers need to make curricula their own. After the first day, the teacher and mentor decide on the extent and form of additional classroom support. Engaging in immediate practice with the research mentor in the classroom demystifies inquiry-based science and instills confidence. The role of the mentor can vary from providing technology support to modeling effective teaching practices to facilitating instruction with the teacher (Cobb, Confrey, diSessa, Lehrer, & Schauble, 2003).

The *reflection* phase helps teachers modify their teaching practices according to their students' needs. During and following a module enactment, the mentor and teacher may have informal discussions about student learning, the progression of instruction, and how to adapt practice in the future. Mentors usually use embedded student work to begin such discussions, thus promoting the practices teachers should engage in on their own. Mentors encourage teachers to continually examine student work and provide feedback to them to increase the impact of the inquiry learning experience. Professional development materials have a tendency to present innovations from a best-practices approach. Although this is a valuable perspective, it may set up unrealistic goals for teachers (Bielaczyc, 2006). Participating in these cycles of targeted professional development supports teachers in a trajectory of phases in their individual development.

CCMS Teacher Education and Professional Development. Preservice and practicing teachers both need to be able to recognize key features of curriculum materials, such as their coherence, and develop skill in adaptation. In general, however, preservice and practicing teachers face different challenges and thus have different needs. Work within CCMS extends across the professional continuum of teaching (Feiman-Nemser, 2001) in an attempt to meet that range of needs as related to curriculum materials.

Preservice elementary science methods courses at both Michigan State University (Schwarz et al., 2008) and the University of Michigan (Davis, 2006b; Forbes & Davis, in press-a) focus on helping preservice elementary teachers learn to effectively select, critique, adapt, and use existing curriculum materials for science—a set of related knowledge and skills. A parallel effort for preservice secondary science teachers resulted in modules that are intended for widespread use among teacher educators (Fortus & Kanter, 2005; see http://ed-web2.educ .msu.edu/CCMS/Webpages/SecTEMod.htm). A common theme across all these efforts is a focus on the use of criteria through which curriculum materials can be analyzed—either the curriculum materials analysis criteria of AAAS Project 2061 (Kesidou & Roseman, 2002), modified versions of these criteria, or criteria developed by the preservice teachers themselves. It is crucial for beginning teachers to develop knowledge and skills around this principled analysis; although preservice teachers may have a tendency to simply like or dislike curriculum materials, engaging in principled analysis allows them to put a finer focus on their likes and dislikes, to identify strengths and weaknesses with justification, and to adapt the materials in a thoughtful manner.

For inservice teachers, however, general professional development tends not to be successful due to both lack of interest among teachers and the difficulty of applying general principles to specific contexts (Wilson & Berne, 1999). Thus, within CCMS, professional development for inservice teachers is largely practice-based and curriculum-driven, and it emphasizes using innovative, coherent, inquiry-oriented curriculum materials developed by CCMS partners. For example, sustained and long-term professional development opportunities within CCMS may engage teachers in examining learning activities, considering how and how well they target the intended learning goals and support teaching and learning those goals. Professional development opportunities also include analyzing student work and videotapes of classroom teaching to gauge the effectiveness of the materials, and considering what modifications could address difficulties identified in the data. CCMS researchers have also worked with district leaders to understand the process of building district capacity to provide professional development that supports teachers using reform-rich curriculum materials, in the hope of developing facilitator materials for district-based workshop leaders (Fogleman et al., 2006). Others at CCMS emphasize scaffolded planning and reflection in curriculum-driven, practice-based professional development (Kanter & Schreck, 2006; Mawyer, Johnson, & Edelson, 2008).

Shared Design Principle. A design principle that summarizes the perspectives of TELS and CCMS emphasizes the need for practice-based, materials-centered experiences as follows:

> *Teacher education and professional development can be designed to support teachers in planning with, critiquing, adapting, and using instructional materials, throughout cycles involving planning, enacting, and reflecting. A generalized, one-size-fits-all approach is not likely to be successful. Instead, teacher education and professional development should engage teachers in thinking about, enacting, and adapting the actual materials they will use or are using with their students. This is important because instruction is not generic, and teachers need help in learning to identify ways in which instructional recommendations can be adapted to work effectively in their classrooms. If such an approach is not taken, teachers may not engage in productive adaptation of materials.*

In sum, research and development at both centers explores how to support teachers in adapting and using instructional materials. The opportunities share a focus on the centrality of instructional materials in shaping teachers' learning, and more generally share an emphasis on situating teachers' learning in their practice.

RESEARCH ON SUPPORTING
PRODUCTIVE ADAPTATION

We have described multiple approaches for supporting teachers in productive adaptation, including the use of technology, curriculum materials, teacher education, and professional development. At both TELS and CCMS, research is ongoing to explore how their approaches support teachers' productive adaptation. We summarize findings from some of this research next, beginning with an overview of the main strands of each center's work. We include teacher cases to illustrate and clarify selected findings from each center; as with all small-scale, in-depth research on teachers, these cases cannot be taken as typical of all teachers but can be used to characterize issues that some teachers face.

Research on Supporting Teachers' Adaptation at TELS

Two studies at TELS investigate teachers' adaptation. One looks at changes in the targeted professional development support required to help teachers adapt their teaching practices to successfully enact TELS modules. Another study examines how teachers adapt their assessment practices as they enact TELS modules (Varma, 2006). Targeted support allows teachers to choose the number of days they would like a mentor to help them in their classroom. They can elect to receive no support (0 days), minimal support (1–2 days), typical support (3–4 days), or extensive support (5–7 days). The *level* of support that teachers require decreases as teachers' experience using TELS modules increases. During initial enactments, most teachers require the typical level of support. A mentor comes to the classroom for 3 or 4 days and helps register students in the TELS learning environment, models classroom management and teaching strategies, and helps identify and resolve technology issues. Teachers who experience more technology issues require more extensive support. Also, teachers who participate in research on student learning using TELS modules require extensive support. During subsequent enactments, fewer teachers require extensive support, and most are able to be successful with only minimal support.

The *type* of support teachers request also changes over time. During the first year of the TELS professional development program, most teachers request support for technology issues. Interviews following the second year of the program show that many teachers request support to better use the student assessment tools in the TELS materials. They also seek assistance in creating rubrics to focus more on changes in students' understanding. Initial findings indicate that after teachers develop a level of expertise with technology-enhanced instruction, they begin to focus on how the instruction impacts student learning. Once teachers become more comfortable with TELS modules, they may begin to make adaptations to their assessment practices. This is the focus of the second study on supporting teachers' adaptations.

TELS examines teacher learning by focusing on changes in teachers' assessment practices and transformations in their ideas about assessment. Professional development support and the teacher tools in the TELS learning environment help teachers to elicit students' ideas, reflect on them, and adapt instruction. Initial findings show that after enacting their first module, teachers typically have isolated ideas about assessment and student learning. For example, a high school physics teacher said, "The kids that got it all done, I gave them most all the credit, simply because they actually did it." Similarly, a high school biology teacher, also reflecting on the first enactment of a TELS module, said, "I found myself grading for completion." During subsequent enactments, teachers' assessment practices change, and they show evidence of a more integrated understanding of assessment and their teaching practices. For example, after her second enactment, a middle school life science teacher said, "I graded the project three times. I went through to see where they were really missing the boat. And that's when I realized they're really missing the idea of what a cancer medicine should do, so that's when I intervened with the whole class." Another middle school life science teacher said, "I graded as we went along so I could anticipate problems and clarify things because it was good for me to know what they were putting in there and guide them and give them a chance to go back and fix their answers." These responses and others show that teachers are making links between their teaching practices, the science content, and student learning.

In summary, teachers initially enact TELS modules with the pedagogical strategies that are most familiar to them. When they are using technology-enhanced curriculum modules, they spend a lot of time addressing technology, classroom management, and logistical issues (e.g., registering students, reserving time with computers, determining Internet access, etc.; see Varma, 2006). Ongoing research shows how teachers adapt their practice across multiple enactments and documents the type of professional development support that best supports adaptations to their practice and to the curriculum materials.

Additional work associated with TELS also extends the professional development approach itself. For example, the MODELS (Mentored and Online Development of Educational Leaders for Science) project provides professional development support via summer workshops and extensive classroom mentoring. The support is designed to help teachers make adaptations to technology-enhanced modules before they use them in their classrooms. Findings from this project show that teachers' adaptations improve over time and that higher quality adaptations are related to increased student learning (Spitulnik & Linn, 2006).

The cases of two TELS teachers, Jane and Rhoda, illustrate how targeted professional development helps teachers to successfully enact new modules and how they adapt their practice across multiple module enactments. Both teachers

requested and received extensive support during their first TELS module enactment. During their second enactments, both teachers developed a more integrated understanding of the curriculum modules, their teaching practices, and
their students' learning. Their learning is evident in data collected from classroom observations and ideas expressed in individual interviews.

Jane requested various types of professional development support during the
planning phase of her first module enactment. Initially, Jane had multiple individual meetings with a TELS professional development mentor to explore the
module she planned to teach and to check the technology that would be used during the enactment. She also asked to visit the classroom of an expert TELS teacher
who was implementing the module so that she could see how a TELS classroom
actually worked.

During her first enactment, Jane requested and received extensive classroom
support from a TELS mentor. Although she was able to integrate the module into
her regular curriculum schedule, she did not make links between the content of
the module and her regular curriculum content. She modified her teaching practices somewhat by letting the students be more independent as they used the
module. Overall, however, she let the mentor take the lead instructional role. This
is common during initial enactments. Initially, Jane did not readily initiate whole-
class discussions to address students' difficulties.

During brief reflection meetings, the mentor discussed what was happening in
the enactment, showed Jane how to use the online assessment tools to access student work and use it to plan future instruction. However, Jane's primary focus was
on classroom management challenges and technology issues. Rather than making
major adaptations to her teaching practice, she continued to do what she was most
comfortable with. Classroom observations showed that she engaged in inquiry
instruction with her students during their typical instruction, but not during the
TELS module instruction. Jane did grade her students' work in the TELS module
using the online tools, but only at the end of the module to give them a final grade.
TELS research shows that teachers are usually overwhelmed with technology
issues during initial classroom enactments and are unable to make major adaptations to specific instructional practices (Varma et al., in press).

Jane chose to implement a second module during the same school year. The
changes during the second enactment were striking. She requested no support
prior to the enactment and only required minimal support during the initial
registration portion of the module implementation. During the reflection meetings, she asked questions about better integrating the module content into her
curriculum. During the enactment, she used some of the strategies that were
modeled by the mentor, such as asking more probing questions as she worked
with individual groups during instruction, and initiating more whole-class discussions. During these whole-class and individual discussions, she made links
between the TELS module and the classroom curriculum. She encouraged

students to think about the content in the module during their typical classroom activities such as the "daily warm-up," when students provide written responses to questions on the board and then discuss their responses. She also changed some of her traditional practices to include the new module content and new teaching strategies.

During the second enactment, Jane looked at students' work periodically and addressed issues that she observed primarily via one-on-one discussions. She primarily encouraged students to make progress in the project and to use good writing strategies in their note taking. Her main plan was still to be able to assign students a final grade at the end of their participation. She did note that during her grading she found that many students did not understand some of the ideas addressed in the module and decided to ask students to write about the ideas during the daily warm-up to give them another opportunity to reflect on them.

This case reveals that, at the outset of her participation, Jane viewed TELS professional development as a means to get technology support for using the new modules. However, as she enacted a second module, she became more interested in enhancing her teaching practices and requested support to do so. Subsequently, she was able to incorporate more of the teaching practices necessary for successful implementation and increased student learning during her second module enactment (Varma, 2006).

A second case illustrates how Rhoda, a teacher new to TELS and new to teaching, adapted her practices to better incorporate the content in the module and to promote inquiry thinking in her students. Before enacting her first module, Rhoda attended a summer workshop designed to introduce teachers to the learning environment, the modules, and the assessment tools. As she prepared for her classroom enactment, Rhoda exchanged e-mail with a TELS mentor about scheduling the computer lab and some of the activities in the curriculum module. She scheduled her enactment at the same time as another teacher in her school so that she could watch an experienced teacher enacting a TELS module. Rhoda used traditional teaching strategies in her classroom as she implemented the module. Her main goal seemed to be to complete the module activities, and she did not link the activities to her regular curriculum. She interacted with individual students only in response to their questions or to make sure that they were staying on task and making progress. She did not ask probing questions or initiate whole-class discussions.

During her second enactment, Rhoda did not receive any classroom support. Observations and a reflection interview revealed that Rhoda had adapted her practice in multiple ways. She incorporated the content from the module into her regular curriculum and instruction by adding her own hands-on activities to extend students' understanding. As students worked, Rhoda still interacted with individuals to make sure they were on task, but she also asked some probing questions and made links between the module activities and the regular curriculum. She did not initiate whole-class discussions except to remind students to monitor their behavior and their progress. She did, however, begin to use the online assessment tools to grade students' work as they participated in the project. She sent comments to them to guide their thinking and designed extension activities based on ideas the students showed difficulty in understanding.

These teachers received different types of support based on their individual needs. They were both able to increasingly adapt their practice in productive ways as they became more familiar with TELS curriculum modules and using technology in their classrooms. During their second enactments, both teachers engaged in more scientific inquiry instruction.

These cases are part of ongoing longitudinal work. Future research at TELS will examine the nature of the targeted support that teachers request and receive after they have reached a level of comfort that allows them to make initial adaptations to their practice. Additionally, targeted support will be offered to specifically increase teachers' knowledge about inquiry instruction, assessment, and student learning. Research will document links between the professional development support, teachers' adaptations to their practice, and their knowledge development.

Research on Teachers' Adaptation at CCMS

Groups within CCMS have explored teachers' adaptation of curriculum materials in multiple ways. As noted earlier, supporting preservice teachers in critiquing and adapting existing curriculum materials has been a prominent focus for CCMS, especially partner institutions the University of Michigan (in Davis's CASES group) and Michigan State University (in Schwarz and Smith's Elementary Teachers and Curriculum Materials [ETCM] group and Fortus's secondary science methods work). For example, the CASES group has explored how preservice elementary teachers engage in a series of activities incorporated into an elementary science methods course, with the critique and adaptation of curriculum materials as one primary focus. Preservice elementary teachers were found to hold a sophisticated set of criteria for critiquing instructional materials. For example, they paid attention to scientific inquiry and instructional goals (Davis, 2006b; see also Forbes & Davis, in press-a). Even with explicit support, however, the preservice teachers did not engage in substantive critique about how scientific content is represented (Davis, 2006b). Thus, the findings indicate that preservice teachers can critique and adapt curriculum materials adequately when provided with appropriate supports. They do not, however, reach the level that science educators would hope for among expert teachers, a finding also supported by Schwarz's research (Schwarz et al., 2008).

Another strand of work at CCMS explores teachers' curricular role identity, or how teachers relate curriculum materials to their professional role as teachers. Curricular role identity development for preservice elementary teachers is tied in part to their practicum experiences. Many preservice teachers rarely interact, or observe cooperating teachers interacting, with curriculum materials and do not perceive curriculum materials (or their adaptation) as a fundamental part of classroom-based practice. Thus, it is important to make this teaching practice visible to preservice teachers (Forbes & Davis, in press-b). Related findings from ETCM indicate that preservice teachers may perceive that they are navigating multiple communities of practice (i.e., their science methods courses, field placements, and college science courses) that hold different and conflicting values and norms about the use of curriculum materials and that may in fact conflict with the preservice teachers' own perspectives (Schwarz et al., 2008).

Preservice teachers engaging in curriculum analysis and adaptation sometimes find the process—which uncovers inadequacies in published curriculum materials—to be destabilizing. They are troubled by the notion that they may not be able to rely on curriculum materials as-is (Schwarz et al., 2008). Given the challenges faced by beginning elementary teachers of science, this feeling of destabilization must contribute to their lack of confidence.

Findings from the CASES longitudinal work following elementary teachers from their preservice years into their first several years of teaching, however, show the importance of developing knowledge and capabilities related to adaptation. The beginning teachers do engage in extensive adaptation of curriculum materials (Forbes & Davis, 2007). They draw from a variety of resources in crafting an approach, but experience a tension between an investigation orientation and a text orientation. Some teachers worry that using text will "give away the inquiry," whereas others use trade books and textbooks as ways of supporting children's inquiry learning in science.

The CASES longitudinal study also indicates that having and using a stable set of curriculum materials over an extended period may help to promote teachers' development of pedagogical content knowledge and pedagogical design capacity (Forbes & Davis, 2007). Beginning teachers whose curriculum materials change each year seem less able to draw productively on additional resources to make constructive changes to their curriculum.

Finally, the CASES longitudinal study indicates that the beginning teachers critique and adapt the instructional representations embedded in the curriculum materials along a set of dimensions including accessibility, content, and management (Stevens & Davis, 2007). As with teachers' critique of curriculum materials in general, the teachers' critiques of instructional representations within the materials are mediated by their classroom experiences and their subject matter knowledge. Once in the classroom, teachers seem better positioned to think about instructional representations than they were as preservice teachers (cf. Davis, 2006b).

Two teachers from Davis's longitudinal study provide examples on which to reflect. Catie took an elementary science methods course from Davis that represented the first instance of a focus on critique and adaptation in the course (Davis, 2006b). Maggie had taken the course a few years earlier, when it did not have an emphasis on curriculum materials but did emphasize inquiry-oriented science teaching. These teachers are similar to elementary teachers across the United States in that they are White females from middle- or upper-middle-class families (National Center for Education Statistics, 2003). Highlights from these two cases illustrate a few key points about how teachers may engage in adapting curriculum materials.

In enacting the CASES educative materials with a focus on scientific explanation, Catie—at that time, a third-year second-grade teacher—developed a more sophisticated understanding of scientific explanation than she originally had (Beyer & Davis, in press). The curriculum materials for the CASES unit on plants (organized around the driving question "Where did the trees in our playground come from?") include numerous supports for engaging students in the construction of scientific explanation, with a particular emphasis on using evidence to support claims. These supports take the form of guidance on demand, images of inquiry, and the supports built into the student materials emphasizing the relationship between claims and evidence. Catie adopted learning goals for some lessons that emphasized this inquiry practice, and developed instructional practices to foster students' construction of explanations. However, Catie emphasized learning factual content above generating explanations in her learning goals and instructional and assessment practices. She did not see using evidence in the construction of scientific explanations as an instructional strategy for facilitating students' understanding of the science content, nor did she see it as an educational goal in its own right. Catie enacted the CASES curriculum materials largely as they were written, showing an effect of the curriculum materials, but CASES researchers hypothesize that in part Catie's adherence was because of the researchers' presence in her classroom. Because she did not value scientific explanation as a learning goal, she acknowledged that if left to her own devices, she would have focused student assessments only on content (Beyer & Davis, in press). Later data collection involving Catie's use of the same unit the next year revealed very little indication of a focus on evidence-based explanation. Instead, Catie emphasized engaging her young students in making careful observations. Catie's changes to the CASES curriculum materials were reasonable, and consistent with her learning goals for her students—yet because of a mismatch between Catie's learning goals and those espoused by the CASES curriculum materials, her adaptations were not consistent with the intentions of the curriculum developers (Davis et al., 2007).

Maggie was a somewhat more experienced teacher. In discussions during the summer after her sixth year of teaching, Maggie revealed that the previous year was the first time she had recognized what she called the art of modifying curriculum materials to map onto her students' needs. Maggie taught in an urban, culturally and linguistically diverse school, and she emphasized the importance of adapting her instruction based on her students' specific prior knowledge and experience. In fact, Maggie drew extensively on her personal resources (including her knowledge of her students and their family and school contexts, as well as her own previous teaching experiences) and curricular resources within and outside of CASES to make productive changes to the CASES curriculum materials. For example, Maggie adopted an instructional strategy described in the narrative images of inquiry associated with the unit she was teaching, and she also used or modified ideas from the main unit calendar as she identified additional lessons to enact with her students. Maggie would be characterized as a teacher having high pedagogical design capacity (Brown, in press; Davis et al., 2007). Features of her current and prior school contexts seemed to influence her development as a teacher capable of making productive adaptations to curriculum materials.

Catie and Maggie were similar in some ways. Each had taken an elementary science methods course at the same university with the same instructor. Each also used CASES educative curriculum materials and the CASES learning environment in her planning, and thus was supported through curriculum materials and technology. These experiences produced somewhat different end results, however. Maggie came to appreciate the importance of adaptation of curriculum materials, and performed effective adaptations in keeping with designer intent. Catie made important changes to her practice in one enactment of the curriculum, but these changes were not applied to a later enactment, which was performed in a manner more consistent with her own learning goals. Each teacher is effective in her own way, yet each reflects the notion of adaptation differently.

Lessons Learned

What does this series of studies from TELS and CCMS—as reflected by these case accounts, as well as other center research—mean for our understanding of teachers' adaptation of curriculum materials and their own practices? We focus on beginning teachers and teachers who are using new technologies, although the work in both centers extends beyond these two groups.

First, teachers may need ongoing support to engage in productive adaptation. Beginning teachers have resources on which they can build when it comes to critiquing and adapting existing curriculum materials, including their own understanding of inquiry-oriented science teaching. However, adapting along some dimensions is more challenging for teachers, even when they are provided with support. Similarly, teachers using new technologies in their instruction must address logistical challenges and make small adaptations that are closely aligned with their current teaching practices during initial enactments. Initial support must focus on increasing their comfort with using technology. Ongoing support may be necessary to help teachers like these develop a better understanding of best practices for engaging in inquiry instruction. Such support could be built into educative curriculum materials, technological tools, teacher education, and professional development programs intended to promote teacher learning.

Second, teachers change as they embark on new kinds of work. Beginning teachers experience shifts in their identities with regard to their use of curriculum materials. Although preservice teachers see the value of using curriculum materials, they may not see their cooperating teachers engaging in substantive critique and adaptation of those materials, and thus they tend not to see this task as an authentic task of teaching. On the other hand, once teachers reach their own classrooms, they can, like Maggie, come to see the centrality of adapting existing materials to meet the needs of their students. Similarly, experienced teachers using a new technology innovation understand the positive impact that it could have on their students' learning. However, initially they may view it as an "extracurricular" activity rather than an integrated part of their regular curriculum. Although they seek support to help them adapt their teaching practices, they devote so much of their cognitive resources to monitoring the success of the technology that they do not focus much attention on truly adapting their practices. During reflective interviews, for example, Jane and Rhoda both expressed the desire to focus more of their attention on their teaching practices, including assessment, during subsequent enactments.

Third, teachers do engage in the adaptation of instructional materials, and the materials they have available to them influence how they engage in that adaptation. A caveat is in order, though: Productive adaptations are those that are founded on a careful analysis of the materials at hand and that work toward coherent support of a diverse body of students in developing an integrated understanding of science content and practices. Imagine one teacher who receives from her district a set of existing curriculum materials. Often, these materials are poor (Kesidou & Roseman, 2002). They may not support students in developing robust and integrated understanding of science concepts, they may be more activity-oriented than inquiry-oriented, or they may not reflect a coherent instructional sequence. The teacher who receives these materials may want to make wholesale changes to the materials, to better meet her learning goals and to better align with her orientation toward teaching. In fact, science educators hope to support teachers in making significant changes to such materials and in becoming leaders in their schools to work toward adoption of more coherent materials. Now imagine another teacher who, in contrast, receives a thoughtfully developed set of materials. For example, this teacher may participate in a field test of the IQWST materials, which are driven by articulated learning goals (Krajcik et al., 2008; Chapter 3). This teacher, then, should be supported in making productive changes to the given materials to better match his students' needs—yet one hopes that these changes would be in keeping with the intent of the curriculum developers. This teacher, too, needs support in developing the knowledge and capabilities associated with productive adaptation. Supports such as the annotated teacher modules of TELS or the educative curriculum materials of CCMS may help in either case.

Teachers naturally adapt their practices as they incorporate new materials into their science classrooms. Ideally, the changes that they make improve their content knowledge and inquiry instruction strategies and promote an integrated understanding of science teaching—and thereby help to increase student learning. Research at TELS and CCMS indicates that teachers can do so effectively, with support, and points to specific areas that may be particularly challenging.

SYNTHESIS: IMPLICATIONS FOR RESEARCH AND POLICY

In this chapter we have discussed the roles that technology, educative curriculum materials, teacher education, and professional development can play in supporting teachers in engaging in productive adaptation. Chapter 6 (Bowyer, Gerard, & Marx) describes the additional crucial support role played by principals and other school administrators.

We have also provided a summary of some of the relevant research being conducted by TELS and CCMS. This work has implications for policies at the school, district, state, and possibly federal levels. For example, school or district policies that require time to be dedicated to situated, practice-based, materials-centered professional development would help to ensure teachers' opportunities to learn to engage in reform-oriented instructional practices and, more specifically, to engage in productive adaptation of materials and of their own practice. More generally, school policies should support teachers in engaging in innovative science teaching practices in the first place, because school context clearly matters in how and to what extent teachers adopt and adapt inquiry-oriented practices. Furthermore, teachers need access to technology and the support to use it in their science classrooms.

State or federal policies have the potential to influence the adoption of curriculum materials and textbooks that are intentionally designed to be educative for teachers. Such commercial materials do exist (Beyer, Delgado, Davis, & Krajcik, 2006), but they tend to be less widely adopted than are more traditional textbooks. Placing educative curriculum materials on state adoption lists could play an important role in promoting teacher learning on a wide scale.

The work reported in this chapter has policy implications across the professional continuum (Feiman-Nemser, 2001). For example, state policy could influence teacher education at public universities through mandates to increase emphasis on preservice teachers' learning to use resources available to them and to engage in reform-oriented practices, shifting emphasis away from the primarily content-focused expectations currently in place. The findings reported here indicate that schools of education have an important role in teacher preparation. Strong subject matter knowledge alone is not sufficient for effective science teaching. Preservice teachers need to be—and can be—supported in learning to engage in productive adaptation. Although this chapter has not focused on the preparation of teachers to use technology for science instruction, certainly this is another important role for schools of education, and one that goes beyond the preparation teachers would receive through their content-specific studies. Finally, cooperating teachers who mentor preservice teachers need support in providing high-quality mentoring for student teachers.

This work also has policy implications relating to induction or early-career teachers. A major concern is the high level of attrition among beginning teachers (Ingersoll, 2001; Smith & Ingersoll, 2004). How can this attrition be reduced? Supporting induction teachers would likely improve the situation, because low morale and decisions to leave the teaching field are often linked to low levels of support (Smith & Ingersoll, 2004). Thus, districts and other education personnel need to provide increased and high-quality support for induction teachers, and reward excellence and innovation among them.

Finally, the work reported here has implications for policies related to experienced teachers. Policy makers often wonder how teachers can be supported such that they will remain in the profession of teaching and remain effective. First, of course, policies should require districts to provide high-quality professional development oriented toward adaptation for all teachers, in addition to requiring teachers to maintain a certain level of commitment to engaging in professional development each year. Furthermore, districts must invest in high-quality professional development up front, under the assumption that the support will be able to fade over time. Finally, as with induction teachers, districts should reward excellence and innovation in experienced teachers. Innovative teachers are willing to try new curriculum materials and learn about new teaching strategies in their classrooms, but they need support to invest the time and effort required to adapt their curricula and teaching practices to best meet their students' needs. Districts must provide incentives and rewards for these teachers.

Additional research on teachers' adaptation of instructional materials is needed to further explore the roles of teachers' knowledge, beliefs, orientations, identities, and school contexts as they engage in this practice. Related research should focus on adaptations teachers make to address the diversity of their students' backgrounds, primary language, and prior scientific knowledge. In this era of accountability, investigation of the relationship between the quality of teachers' adaptations and how they impact student learning will be important, as will study of how long-lasting the adaptations are. Finally, to better understand teacher development, research could explore teachers' personal and career trajectories as they learn to engage in productive adaptation.

Although TELS and CCMS differ in the specifics of the supports provided for teachers and in the research being conducted, the centers share a focus on meeting teachers' needs through situating their learning in their own practice, using technology, curriculum materials, professional development, and teacher education as venues to do so. Only through such situated learning opportunities, we argue, will teachers develop the knowledge, beliefs, abilities, and orientations to make productive adaptations and, more generally, to move toward instructional practices aligned with current reforms in science education.

6

Building Leadership for Scaling Science Curriculum Reform

Jane Bowyer, Libby Gerard, and Ronald W. Marx

THIS CHAPTER examines the role of leadership and its impact on scaling science curriculum reform. Over the past decade substantial efforts have been made to improve the quality of science instruction in public schools in the United States. Prioritization and support from the National Science Foundation have resulted in a rich collection of science curricula and technology-enhanced science curricula that have extensive research documenting positive effects on student learning. Yet few students have access to these curricula (Blumenfeld, Fishman, Krajcik, Marx, & Soloway, 2000; Elmore, 1996; Fishman et al., 2004). There are several reasons for this. In the case of science curricula that have technology components, the major scaling barrier relates to lack of access to adequate technology (Becker & Riel, 2000). A fundamental problem common to all efforts to scale science curriculum reform relates to district and school leaders' prioritization and active support for teachers' implementation of reform curricula. The good news is that research is beginning to suggest that the early and continuing involvement of administrator, principal, and teacher leaders in reform is directly linked to the successful integration of reform curricula into the school system (Anderson & Dexter, 2005; Borko, Wolf, Simone, & Uchiyama, 2003; Coburn, 2003; Gerard, Bowyer, & Linn, 2008a). This makes scaling exemplary science curricula so that all students have access a realistic possibility.

Unfortunately, the area of science and technology instruction receives very weak support from district and school leaders in terms of leadership for curricular reform (Blumenfeld et al., 2000; Zhao, Pugh, Sheldon, & Byers, 2002). This stems in part from leadership's unfamiliarity and inexperience in the areas of science and instructional technologies (Fishman & Gomez, 2000; Gerard, Bowyer, & Linn, 2008b; Prestine & Nelson, 2005). It is also explained by the nature of administrators' and teachers' daily work demands (Elmore, 2000; Fink & Resnick, 2001; Little, 1999). Certainly, increasing accountability pressures in mathematics and language arts have diverted school leaders' attention from science education in particular (Burch & Spillane, 2003).

This chapter examines the successes and challenges of several professional development programs for administrators, principals, and teacher leaders that are designed to foster the leadership capacity necessary to scale and sustain research-based science curriculum innovations. The programs described here were developed by two of the National Science Foundation's Centers for Learning and Teaching: the Center for Curriculum Materials in Science (CCMS) and the Technology Enhanced Learning in Science (TELS) Center. Prior research and project development work from these two groups that was foundational to the focus of this chapter is also included where appropriate.

SCIENCE AND TECHNOLOGY CURRICULUM LEADERSHIP

Much has been written about the difficulties in creating a fit between curricular innovation and the school system, particularly inquiry-oriented, computer-based science instruction (Blumenfeld et al., 2000; Elmore, 1996; Fishman et al., 2004; Marx & Harris, 2006). In this chapter we will use a conceptual model designed to evaluate the usability of innovations to examine the CCMS and TELS leadership approaches for scaling science curricula. The model, developed by CCMS researchers (Blumenfeld et al., 2000; Fishman et al., 2004), focuses on key school organizational structures: culture, capability, and policy/management. The framework looks at the relationship between these three school variables and the value the curriculum innovation places on them. The more convergence there is between the school and the values of the curriculum on each of the three variables (culture, capability, and policy/management), the greater the possibility for successfully scaling the curriculum.

In the framework, *culture* refers to the existing norms, beliefs, and values of the districts and schools; *capability* refers to the conceptual and practical knowledge about the curriculum possessed by district administrators, principals, teacher leaders, and teachers; and *policy/management* refers to the internal district and school policies that govern allocation of resources. A good fit or close alignment between the goals and requirements of the curriculum, and the culture, capability, and policy/management of districts and schools creates a stable system that can incorporate and sustain complex curricular innovation. For example, in terms of the capability variable, a principal might place a high priority on supporting teachers' development of strategies that foster students' critical thinking. If a potential curriculum also has the development of students' capacity for thinking critically as a major goal, that convergence of values increases the likelihood that the curriculum will be adopted and scaled.

The culture variable is often difficult to match in terms of the district/school structures and the values of the technology-enhanced science curriculum. Research suggests that instructional programs that are inconsistent with local norms, routines, and practices are often rejected or, more often, transformed to fit traditional routines (Cuban, 2001; Elmore, 1996). Inquiry, technology, and science fundamentally challenge traditional school values and norms. For example, studies of inquiry-oriented science indicate that the "test prep" culture prevalent in most schools creates a hostile environment for implementation of inquiry-oriented science curriculum (Diamond & Spillane, 2004). High-stakes testing in mathematics and language arts has led many administrators to focus attention only on math and language arts, and in turn has reduced the attention given to science (Marx & Harris, 2006). In addition to testing pressures, the student-centered nature of inquiry-oriented instruction challenges common teacher-directed approaches to science instruction, as Davis and Varma described in Chapter 5 of this volume (Songer, Lee, & Kam, 2002). Zhao et al. (2002), for instance, found that when teachers with more traditional pedagogical beliefs attempted to integrate technology designed to facilitate student inquiry, the teachers often modified the lessons to fit their traditional teacher-directed approach, or canceled the lessons altogether. Effective district and school leaders are able to create a close fit between the curriculum reform culture and the school culture. One way that strong leaders can support teachers to broaden their pedagogical beliefs is by articulating a clear vision for technology-enhanced instruction that explicitly links the new computer-based lessons with school-wide values and norms (Gerard, Bowyer, & Linn, 2008b). And one way effective leaders are able to balance the emphasis on mathematics and language arts with a focus on science is by linking outcomes of inquiry learning in science to the goals for students' critical thinking in mathematics and language arts (Marx & Harris, 2006).

The capability variable presents significant challenges in terms of aligning the district and school capability with the demands of the science curriculum innovation. Technology-enhanced science curricula, as described in Chapter 5, require teachers to have knowledge of the science concepts, understanding of how those concepts manifest in computer-based scientific visualizations (e.g., dynamic models, graphs), and familiarity with computer operations. Currently few teacher and administrator preparation programs provide opportunities to experience technology tools for scaffolding student inquiry. Nor are teachers or administrators prepared for the classroom management and resource challenges presented by computer-based instruction (Becker & Riel, 2000; Fishman, Gomez, & Soloway, 2002). Despite administrators' and teachers' overall lack of experience with instructional computer technology, there remains remarkably little high-quality professional development to help them become proficient (CEO Forum on Education and Technology, 2000; Holland & Moore-Steward, 2000). In addition to learning the role of technology in the classroom, science teachers need adequate pedagogical knowledge in relation to science reform curricula. Administrators require understanding of the curricular reform goals, strategies, and materials. Yet the ongoing professional support needed for administrators and teacher leaders to successfully implement, sustain, and scale reform is rare. For example, activity-based instruction programs developed by scientists and well financed by the government in the late 1960s had demonstrable positive effects on student learning (Shymansky, Kyle, & Alport, 1983). Yet this approach failed to gain widespread adoption. Lack of ongoing attention to the principals' and teachers' understanding of the reform curriculum goals, methods, and materials is cited as the primary reason for the limited success of the activity-based approaches (Elmore, 1996). Successful leaders can maximize curriculum and school convergence along the capability variable. One way that leaders address this issue is by providing and participating in regular formal and informal opportunities to discuss curricula, and teaching in relation to goals for student understanding (Fullan & Stiegelbauer, 1991; Hallinger, 2003).

A third challenge to scaling curriculum innovation is creating convergence between the school system's policy and management structures and the requirements of the technology-enhanced science curriculum. Innovations typically call for new policies that require changes in responsibility among different levels of the system, computer scheduling, and resource distribution (Fishman et al., 2004; Spillane, Diamond, Walker, Halverson, & Loyisa, 2001). For example, gridlock among district, school, and classroom often occurs with regard to student use of computers. In most schools, the teaching of technology-based curricula is the responsibility of principals and teachers, although control of the computer network typically resides with district administrators (Fishman et al., 2004). To further complicate matters, in most schools computers reside in a computer lab room dedicated to teaching computer skills. As a result, the computers are rarely available to the science teacher for use during regular class time (Coffland & Strickland, 2004). Technology personnel to support these computers are available in only a small minority of public schools (Davidson, 2003). One way that effective leaders can increase convergence of the technology-enhanced science curriculum and policy/management is by reallocating resources to ensure that the science teacher has adequate access to computers during classroom instruction time and an appropriate level of on-site technology support (Spillane et al., 2001).

PROFESSIONAL DEVELOPMENT
AND LEADERSHIP

A potential explanation for the failure of research-based curriculum innovations to take root in school systems is the lack of high-quality leadership development opportunities provided for district administrators, school principals, and teachers (Borko et al., 2003; McLaughlin & Mitra, 2001; Stein, Hubbard, & Mehan, 2004). Sarason's study (1971, 1996) on new math reform in the 1950s and 1960s concluded that a central reason for the failed adoption of new math instruction was the lack of sustained professional support for administrators and teachers. A similar argument was made about the lack of ongoing professional learning opportunities provided for school and district leaders in the large-scale National Science Foundation curriculum reform projects of the 1950s and 1960s (Elmore, 1996).

The professional learning community offers a promising leadership development approach in the context of reform. The reform literature repeatedly cites teacher professional community as the key factor in successfully scaled and sustained instructional reform (Franke, Carpenter, Levi, & Fennema, 2001; Little, 1999; Wood, 2007). This chapter draws on the foundational research-based definition of a professional learning community articulated by Louis and Kruse (1995). Characteristics of a professional learning community include (a) shared norms and values with regard to participants' goals for the instructional innovation; (b) discussion and analysis of specific practice-based problems that deprivatize practice; (c) reflective dialogue in which participants hold practice, pedagogy, and student learning under scrutiny in order to reevaluate participants' roles in supporting innovation; and (d) collaboration focused on a mutual aid to get work done efficiently. Researchers continue to examine teacher professional communities through this lens, and their work highlights the opportunities and challenges inherent in these characteristics for supporting ongoing professional learning (see Atchinstein, 2002; Borko et al., 2003; Grossman et al., 2001; Little, 2003; Wood, 2007).

Although there are few examples of learning communities designed to support administrators' professional development, research on administrators' learning supports this professional development approach. Two central mechanisms in teacher professional communities—analysis of practice-based problems and reflective dialogue—are found in the literature to be instrumental in scaffolding administrators' understanding of instructional reform. For example, Leithwood and colleagues (Leithwood & Montgomery, 1982; Leithwood & Stager, 1989; Leithwood & Steinbach, 1992) found that expert principals rely more on relevant practical evidence than do typical principals, when responding to hypothetical school leadership problem scenarios. Similarly, researchers report that expert principals respond to school leadership dilemmas by connecting district or school-based student data to educational policies (Goldring, Spillane, Barnes, & Supovitz, 2006). In professional development for leaders involved in curriculum implementation, the principals develop a more complete understanding of innovation when engaged with data from multiple levels within a school setting (Fink & Resnick, 2001). For example in the area of mathematics, principals' direct interactions with mathematics curriculum standards, teacher pedagogical practices, and students' mathematical reasoning gave them an advantage in supporting mathematics curriculum reform (Stein & Nelson, 2003). In the area of science and technology, principals' analysis of student data helped them link the curriculum innovation to schoolwide teaching and learning goals across subject areas (Gerard, Bowyer, & Linn, 2008b).

The other central mechanism, reflective dialogue, promotes leadership development by supporting administrators and teacher leaders in examining issues from multiple perspectives. When principals are involved in professional development, discussion with other principals helps them to reflect on their own progress from the lens of an outside observer (Smylie, Bennet, Konkol, & Fendt, 2002). A key component for discussing practice in these groups is trust. To gain new insights, leaders must feel safe in order to reveal their limitations in understanding and to experiment with new ideas (Fullan & Stiegelbauer, 1991; Prawat & Peterson, 1999). Collegial interactions with members of the school community such as teachers, students, and other administrators enables principals to develop more powerful solutions to problems and integrate curriculum scaling data with school values (Murphy, 2002).

A key function of reflective dialogue in a professional learning community is to support administrators, principals, and teachers in reevaluating and reconceptualizing their work (Grossman et al., 2001; Wood, 2007). Most administrators and teachers play a limited role, if any at all, in scaling and sustaining instructional reform. This is due in part to the fact that there is typically little reward and often considerable risk for administrators and teachers that associate themselves with reform (Wood, 2007). Further, professional isolation and a workday consumed by solving immediate problems prevents administrators, principals, and teachers from reflecting on ways to fundamentally improve curricula and instruction (Elmore, 2000; Fink & Resnick, 2001). The professional community provides a venue for widening administrators' and teachers' professional responsibility and honing their professional judgment (Murphy, 2002; Wood, 2007). The community situates expertise and responsibility within its domain, and in doing so encourages participants to reflect on their role in shaping and supporting instructional innovation and to hold one another accountable for continued improvement (Grossman et al., 2001).

Potential benefits of the professional learning community are significant, especially for developing leadership for scaling reform. Key outcomes identified by Louis and Kruse (1995) are a greater sense of efficacy, increased motivation to improve teaching and learning, and increased collective responsibility for leading innovation or change. Grossman et al. (2001) highlights the key role of the professional community in broadening teachers' knowledge of subject matter and in developing teachers' leadership capacity. Little (2003) explicates the benefits of the professional community in breaking down insularity among educators and broadening participants' understanding of teaching methods, curricula, and student knowledge. Lewis, Perry, and Hurd (2004) note that improved lesson plans and increased commitment to reform can result from teachers and administrators jointly participating in a professional learning community.

Unfortunately, the most common forms of professional development for administrators and teacher leaders are the district inservice day and the summer institute (Peterson, 2000). The district inservice training focuses almost exclusively on managerial techniques or pedagogical strategies for immediate implementation; the summer institute, on the other hand, typically attempts to refresh educational leaders through short workshops focused on big ideas (Grossman et al., 2001; Peterson, 2000). Grossman et al. (2001) argue that the professional learning community bridges these two approaches. It provides a venue for administrators and teachers to create an intellectual community that sustains focus on integrating curriculum and pedagogical innovation within the intricate details of the school system. The TELS and CCMS leadership development projects discussed in this chapter provide instances of professional learning communities for district and school leaders for the purpose of scaling technology and science curriculum reform. These leadership development projects relate to curriculum coherence and eventually to promoting students' integrated understanding.

CCMS AND TELS LEADERSHIP DEVELOPMENT PROJECTS

TELS and CCMS have iteratively designed and tested different forms of leadership professional development with three different populations: district administrators, principals, and teachers. The structure and content of the CCMS and TELS leadership development projects are informed by educational research on practitioner learning and professional development. In all cases, the researchers were active participants in the leadership development meetings and served as the leadership development organizer or facilitator. An *organizer* is defined as one who invites people to the professional development meetings and arranges the location and food. A *facilitator* is defined as one who guides the leadership development discussions by encouraging participants to find their own solutions to tasks or problems. Researchers collected and analyzed data from each leadership project to better understand administrators' and teacher leaders' developing capacity in relation to scaling science curriculum reform. The primary data sources for this chapter are documents about leadership development projects conducted by TELS and CCMS and two other affiliated research projects, MODELS (Mentored Online Development of Educational Leaders for Science) and ARC (Administrator Reform Community). Documents include published articles, doctoral dissertations, conference presentations, and grant proposals. The data for these documents consist of transcripts of interviews with participating leaders, transcripts of leadership development meetings, artifacts from leadership development meetings, postmeeting reflections, observational field notes, and in some cases scaling outcome data. The analysis for this chapter involved identifying and describing key aspects of each CCMS and TELS leadership development project in terms of the (a) the leadership development project goal and central challenge, (b) leadership development model, and (c) scaling outcomes according to the dimensions involved in the Blumenfeld et al. (2000) curriculum innovation framework—culture, capability, and policy.

CCMS Administrator Reform Community

Challenge and Goal. In 1994 CCMS began working with four large urban school districts to implement technology-enhanced science reform curricula aligned with national and district science curriculum standards. Senior administrators in each of the districts were interested in the success of CCMS reform because it was a part of their districts' larger systemic reform initiative to integrate standards-based, technology-mediated instruction. Administrators wanted to develop deeper understanding of instructional technology and how to address complex issues related to integration of instructional technology districtwide. In, 1998, the ARC was formed. The goal of ARC was to bring together senior-level district administrators to share resources, administrative practices, and insights for leading systemic standards-aligned, technology-enhanced curriculum reform (Gomez & Fishman, 2001).

Leadership Development Model. Distinguishing features of the ARC model include activities relevant to administrators' day-to-day work and discussion among leaders focused on administrative reform issues. Participants in ARC included the superintendent, assistant superintendent, chief information officer, and other senior district leaders involved with curriculum and technology from each of the four school districts. School administrators and classroom teachers were also included to maintain close contact with local enactment of the reform. On average, a mix of 12 leaders participated in each ARC meeting.

ARC met face-to-face quarterly. The first meeting was held in a district nationally recognized for its successful implementation of technology-mediated curriculum reform. After this initial meeting, ARC participants gathered at each of the partner district sites, rotating among the four locations. The goal for each meeting was to increase administrators' exposure to technology-mediated curricula and share ideas about how to leverage resources, develop infrastructure, and design instructional programs that meet the goals of the curriculum standards while integrating new technologies. This contributed to the CCMS goal of developing district capacity for scaling technology-enhanced science curricula (Murray, Fishman, Gomez, Williams, & Marx, 2001).

The CCMS researchers organized the date, food, and transportation for the ARC meetings; the administrators who hosted the meeting shaped the agenda and led the activities. Meetings began with an open discussion or "plenary session" focused on goals and issues in scaling technology-mediated curricula. This was followed by small-group walk-throughs of the host district to see technology reform in action. Then, the host district responded to specific questions from other ARC leaders about their technology programs and organizational supports. Finally, participants reflected on their own respective technology practices in light of the observed work. A critical element of this approach was that the discussion focused on the work of the administrators, not the teachers or students. For example, participants discussed teachers' enactment of technology curriculum reform in the classroom, but focused on how administrators in the district and schools worked to acquire resources and to provide teacher professional development to enable teachers' successful enactment of instructional reform (Gomez & Fishman, 2001).

Leadership Development Model in Action. The Union City, New Jersey, school district was considered by ARC leaders to be a model of systemic technology-mediated instruction aligned with curriculum standards. District leaders wanted to see firsthand what this actually looked like in classrooms and district offices. ARC leaders chose Union City because it was both innovative and successful, as measured by teacher acceptance of reform, districtwide implementation of reform practices, and improvements in student learning as measured by state assessments. ARC leaders worked in collaboration with Union City administrators to craft a 2-day agenda for an observational visit (Murray et al., 2001).

The Union City visit began over breakfast with informal talk of the challenges that ARC administrators faced in implementing technology reform. One administrator commented, "breakfast gave me the chance to really talk about my district's technology plans and goals with people who I want to talk to—other supervisors, principals, technology facilitators, superintendents." Researchers passed out digital and disposable cameras and encouraged ARC administrators to capture as much of the observational visit as they could on film (Murray et al., 2001). After breakfast, the group divided into smaller groups to walk through different schools and district offices that Union City administrators believed demonstrated how technology facilitated teaching and learning.

Administrators took numerous photos during their Union City visit that illustrated the reform practices they wanted to implement in their respective school districts. One administrator who wanted to encourage a more facilitative pedagogical approach among the teachers in her schools (as opposed to overreliance on teacher-directed pedagogy) took several pictures of a teacher scaffolding a student's interaction with a computer-based model. Other district administrators and school principals took photographs of hand-held technologies students used in conjunction with the computers, such as scientific probes. Others documented the different physical layouts of computers in classrooms that allowed students to move easily back and forth between teachers, peers, computer, and textbook. Administrators from two districts were so impressed that they scheduled a follow-up visit to Union City so they could bring their colleagues (Murray et al., 2001).

After ARC leaders explored Union City classrooms, they convened to discuss what they had observed and reflected on the implications for their own districts and schools. Participants commented on the importance of configuring classrooms so that students can work in pairs on computers and transition fluidly among different collaborative work groups. Strong leadership was considered by ARC participants to be the most important criterion for the successes they had witnessed in Union City. They observed that distributed leadership among administrators, principals, and teachers led to coherent technology-mediated instruction across sites. One administrator noted, "the Union City leadership made sure that everyone is on the same page ... from students, to teachers, to principals, to administrators, they all knew what their objectives were and how they fit with the reform agenda ..." (Murray et al., 2001).

Scaling Outcomes. ARC enabled participants to reflect on practices in their own districts, and identify gaps between their vision for technology-enhanced instruction and their actual district culture, capability, and policies.

Culture. ARC participants examined together their goals and values for districtwide technology reform and their current district values and norms. There was widespread agreement that technology should be used as a tool to enable student learning. One ARC member remarked, "The word technology is thrown out there a lot. Technology doesn't mean much to me though unless I see students using technology and generating questions." Like this administrator, other leaders in ARC focused on the use of technology to promote critical thinking. Some identified gaps between this goal and their teachers' values. "If you came to my schools, you would see that there are still teachers here for the wrong reasons.... I want people to be here because they want to break new ground in using technology to teach and not because the school is walking distance to their house!" one administrator remarked. Other administrators noted gaps between their vision for technology and their principals' curricular technology goals: "After our last meeting I surveyed my principals about technology and they said they want to use technology as a remedial tool—that totally misses the point." By highlighting these gaps between the reform vision and the reform enactors' views, ARC motivated senior administrators to generate professional development plans for teachers and principals that would shift district culture in greater alignment with their vision for technology reform (Murray et al., 2001).

Capability. ARC increased administrators' capabilities by broadening their knowledge of technology-based reform and the districtwide support systems that it requires. Conversations with leaders from other urban districts and observations of students in diverse settings working intently with technology-mediated curricula "opened [administrators'] eyes about the instructional uses of computers" (Murray et al., 2001). Leaders reported observations of classroom configurations that allow students to move fluidly between computer and textbook, pedagogical strategies that scaffold students' interaction with computer-based science simulations, and a range of hand-held technology devices that support scientific inquiry. The observations led many ARC members to reframe their systemic technology reform vision and, with the help of ARC peers, more effectively communicate their revised goals and rationale to their constituent groups. Shifts in districtwide capability hinged to a large degree, therefore, on the leaders' ability to articulate what technology practices they observed in ARC visits and how these practices would benefit their respective districts. Some administrators used their photographs of students engaged with computer-mediated curricula as evidence to counteract teacher and principal resistance to technology reform, a major issue faced by senior administrators in all four districts. Other administrators invited teachers and principals from the ARC partner districts to share their experiences using particular curriculum technology programs with stake holders in their respective districts. The increased awareness of technology-mediated curricula across the participating districts strengthened the districts' capability for systemic technology reform.

Policy. District and school leaders who participated in ARC developed new ideas about organizational policies that support integration of technology-mediated instruction aligned with state curriculum standards. For instance, several senior-level administrators acknowledged that initially they "thought that the reform effort would mean students need access to the computer lab," but after seeing other districts they realized that "computers need to be right there in the classroom and not scheduled in a lab" (Murray et al., 2001). The revised thinking of senior administrators had significant implications for districtwide distribution of resources and configuration of school space; one ARC district alone had over 600 schools. In addition, ARC helped administrators identify ways to balance state policies requiring high-stakes assessment of curriculum standards with the ARC participants' goals of using technology for scaffolding students' critical thinking.

TELS Community of Principals

Challenge and Goal. For two decades university curriculum researchers and developers have designed and iteratively refined the TELS curricula. Enthusiastic teachers have provided trial sites for this development work. Often these teachers have continued to teach with the TELS units after the developers completed their work. Unfortunately, other teachers in school science departments have not adopted and integrated the curriculum despite national assessment data demonstrating its effectiveness, particularly in helping students understand science concepts (Linn, Lee, et al., 2006). The goal of the Community of Principals leadership development model is to actively involve and support the principal as the key leverage point for scaling and sustaining TELS curriculum reform.

Leadership Development Model. The primary feature of this model is the development of a learning community of principals sustained over time for the purpose of creating a space away from the daily demands of principals' work to consider issues of curriculum reform and scaling. Direct interaction with data, face-to-face collegial discussion, and a facilitator with expert knowledge regarding the TELS curriculum materials distinguish this approach. A subset of seven California principals participated from the population of 22 schools across the country where TELS research development efforts are under way. These seven schools are located within a 5-mile radius.

The Community of Principals began meeting in 2005 and continued to meet every 6 weeks. At the time of writing this chapter the Community had met for 2 consecutive years and was continuing to meet every 6 weeks. Principals' "need to know" questions determine the agenda for each meeting (Table 6.1 provides some examples). The TELS research facilitator arranges an off-campus meeting site and works with principals to identify and organize relevant data to address principals' questions. In addition, the facilitator generates three open-ended questions prior to each Community of Principals meeting to focus principals' reflection and discussion.

Leadership Development Model in Action. The Community evolved in such a way that principals developed a trust that allowed them to listen to each other respectfully, admit their own vulnerabilities, and learn from others. The following example demonstrates the nuances of these interactions and the culture of inquiry that developed over time.

Principals wanted to know, "How can I support my teachers to use TELS?" Two middle school TELS science teachers, at the suggestion of the principals, were invited to come to one of the Community of Principals meetings. Before the teachers arrived, the principals talked among themselves. One high school principal noted:

TABLE 6.1 Representative Principals' Questions and Resulting Professional Development Agendas for the TELS Community of Principals

Date	Principals' Question	Meeting Agenda
August	What is TELS?	Interact with TELS computer curricular visualizations and student work
October	What are the challenges in supporting TELS?	Principals share strategies for providing computer resources and addressing teacher resistance
November	How can I support my teachers to use TELS?	Interview two TELS teachers
December	How does TELS influence my students' thinking?	Talk with three high school students who use TELS
January	How can state policy support my use of TELS?	Presentation/discussion by former State Superintendent
February	What classroom set-up maximizes learning in TELS?	Observe "TELS-in-Action" in a middle school classroom
March	What leadership practices best support my teachers?	Read and discuss a research article on leadership for reform
May	What are our long-term goals for TELS reform?	Discuss TELS reform with a science education researcher

We have very little staff development funds, and so we are using some of our GATE money for … teacher training in advanced placement courses … and helping faculty to work on developing learning communities and departmental assessments … none of this focuses on teaching technology-science curriculum.

About 30 minutes later the two TELS middle school teachers arrived. The principals began asking them about their experience implementing the TELS units. "How long does it take for new teachers to go through the whole TELS project before feeling comfortable? How does the computer model change your interaction with your students?" The teachers helped the principals understand the realities and obstacles teachers face in relation to integrating computer-based, inquiry teaching methods in their science classrooms. The principals learned that the pedagogical and subject matter knowledge required was greater than what most of their teachers currently possessed.

After the teachers left the meeting, the principals stayed to discuss what they had heard. The high school principal who initially had no budget plans for supporting his TELS teachers revised his thinking:

> *Often times we give teachers new curriculum and we say, "Go ahead, why don't you do this?" But, we don't really give the teachers any time to look at the curriculum, to learn what this new approach is all about. Then the teachers don't do a good job, they get frustrated, and they say "Oh well, this didn't work. I'm going to stick with my book." I think that if we gave teachers some time and training with TELS, they would be enthusiastic about the curriculum.*

The other principals suggested strategies that they use to support their teachers when adopting new curricula, particularly in the area of language arts and mathematics. The high school principal listened, and after a few moments he responded:

> *We have five or six teachers signed up to run a TELS project and they have not had any training at all. I really need to work with our [one] teacher who has used TELS before … and find out what the teachers are going to need to be successful. Even if I can get the teachers to stay after school for an hour to walk through a project together before using it in the classroom, that would help.*

In this specific example the principal reconceptualized his approach to building TELS professional capability in his teachers (Gerard, Bowyer, & Marx, 2008).

Scaling Outcomes. The Community of Principals provided space, time, and audience for principals to think coherently about technology-enhanced science curriculum reform. Principals increased the convergence between TELS curricula and their individual school culture, school capability, and school policy (Gerard, Bowyer, & Marx, 2008).

Culture. The principals examined the values embedded in the TELS curricula to explore how they aligned with their own school culture. Although all of the values of the curriculum actually matched quite well with most principals' expectations for their teachers and students, values such as "Students experiment with scientific models," "Students ask questions and explain answers," and "Teachers facilitate, not lecture" presented particular challenges. The degree to which principals were able to enact these values correlated highly with their schools' performance on the No Child Left Behind (NCLB) high-stakes examinations. Most of the principals in schools with consistently high performance across subject areas on the NCLB examinations had the freedom to use TELS as a catalyst for focusing on technology integration, student experimentation, formative assessments, and inquiry-driven teaching. Others in the Community of Principals understandably could not make science or inquiry a top school priority. Their schools were in the midst of a state mandate to raise test scores in mathematics and language arts or face closure. These principals, still eager to support the values embedded in the TELS curriculum materials, checked in regularly with their TELS science teachers regarding individual successes and challenges. They informally observed their science teachers enact TELS curriculum modules. So, although the school principals could not prioritize the implementation of TELS because of outside pressures, informally they communicated the shared values of the TELS curricula and their school goals for teaching in science.

Capability. An outcome of participation in the Community of Principals was that principals developed an awareness of the gap between the complex knowledge, particularly around technology, needed to enact TELS curriculum units and their current teachers' capabilities. The varying levels of teacher quality in the principals' schools determined to a large extent their ability to scale the reform. Principals whose science departments included many highly qualified teachers collaborated with other principals in the Community of Principals to design opportunities that supported their novice TELS teachers. Principals engaged more experienced TELS teachers within and across schools for collaborative teacher professional development.

Other principals in the Community of Principals, however, faced major science teacher capability issues, such as frequent teacher turnover and lack of adequate subject matter preparation. One principal, for example, did not have a fully staffed science department. Substitute teachers were filling in as he searched desperately to identify qualified teachers. Obviously, for this principal, the gap in his teachers' capabilities and what was required for successful implementation of TELS was far too wide to begin any scaling effort. During the professional development meetings the principal talked with his colleagues about this challenge. In the second year of the Community of Principals meetings, this discouraged individual reflected to his colleagues, "I know I said before that my teachers can't do TELS, but, I know that as the principal I am the one that has to make it happen." Another principal in the Community who shared a similar challenge began brainstorming ideas with him, and collaboratively they began advocating to their school site councils for increased technology resources and incentives to recruit highly qualified science teachers.

It should be noted that this 3-year study involved collection of data on the number of teachers using TELS in all 22 of the TELS curriculum research and development schools from Years 1, 2, and 3. Community of Principals meetings

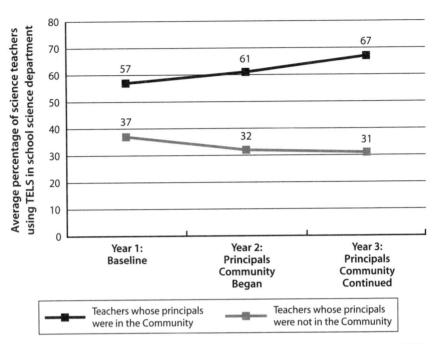

FIGURE 6.1 Change in the percentage of science teachers using TELS curriculum materials (over 3 years) in relation to their principals' participation in the Community of Principals.

were conducted in Years 2 and 3 with seven of these principals. The Community was continuing to meet at the time this chapter was written. All schools received technology and teacher support from an adjacent university. The percentage of teachers using TELS modules in schools where principals participated in the Community of Principals increased gradually, as shown in Figure 6.1. In schools where principals did not participate in the Community of Principals for various reasons, the number of teachers using TELS gradually decreased. Data from the first half of Year 4 appear to continue this trend (Gerard, Bowyer, & Linn, 2008a).

Policy. The participants in the Community of Principals understood that they have responsibility for implementing district and state policies, but they also knew that they were responsible for creating internal school policies with regard to specific curriculum reform (Shen, Gerard, & Bowyer, 2008). For example, some principals in the Community created a policy mandating all science teachers to enact one TELS curriculum unit each year. Others established scheduling policies to increase science teachers' access to the schools' technology resources during regular classroom instruction time. Others implemented teacher hiring policies that prioritized the hiring of TELS-qualified and interested teachers Although scaling an exemplary curriculum like TELS—which satisfies school-wide, district, and state policies regarding student science learning—is advantageous to all stake holders, federal and state policy issues can gridlock the scaling process. The power of principals engaged in a Community of Principals appears to provide one mechanism for counteracting this problem.

CCMS Lead Teacher Development

Challenge and Goal. CCMS researchers have worked with Detroit Public Schools since 1994 to reform districtwide middle school science instruction. For the first eight of these years, CCMS researchers facilitated extensive professional development for teachers. After this initial effort, CCMS researchers worked with Detroit Public Schools to move primary responsibility for all professional development focused on science curriculum reform to the Detroit school district. Like most urban school districts, Detroit experiences high teacher turnover, necessitating continual staff development. After 3 years of exclusive district-led teacher professional development, CCMS researchers became reinvolved. The challenge was to establish district leadership that could conduct professional development that preserved the essential character of the curriculum reform without day-to-day involvement of the CCMS researchers (Fogleman et al., 2006). The CCMS Lead Teacher Project was created to support the development of lead teachers who would assume full responsibility for planning and conducting CCMS professional development workshops (Fogleman et al., 2006).

Leadership Development Model. Two distinguishing features of the lead teacher model were the lead teacher selection process and the leadership development delivery system. The Detroit Public Schools CCMS coordinator (who is also a district science curriculum specialist) had the major responsibility for selecting the lead teachers. Lead teachers were selected on the basis of their abilities as a "capable enactor" and the respect they had garnered from their peers and CCMS researchers (Fogleman et al., 2006). A capable enactor is one whose students' academic performance gives evidence that the teachers have sufficient content knowledge, pedagogical knowledge, and pedagogical content knowledge to implement CCMS curricula (Shulman, 1986). In addition to having sophisticated knowledge of the reform, each lead teacher was formerly a participant in CCMS-led professional development workshops, where the teacher had demonstrated his or her ability to communicate and to collaborate with colleagues (Fogleman et al., 2006).

The "work circle" is the organizational structure that supported the personal and professional development of lead teachers. A work circle is defined as a group that includes people with different expertise meeting regularly to address problems related to implementation and scaling of reform. The work circle for the Lead Teacher development program included the Detroit Public Schools science curriculum specialist, lead teachers from each middle school grade level, and several CCMS researchers. The work circle met for 2 hours after school, 1 or 2 weeks before lead teachers conducted the Saturday CCMS teacher workshop. In addition to conducting Saturday workshops, lead teachers also facilitated more extensive CCMS summer workshops. At the work circle meetings, teachers discussed ways in which they have enacted CCMS curricula in their classrooms, focusing on challenges they used to engage students and develop their understanding. These discussions often got very detailed, as the lead teachers worked to consider how teachers who are learning to use the materials might be more successful. They also discussed ways of securing resources for teachers, as well as adaptations to the curriculum materials and implementation in the service of the school district's goals for student learning (Fogleman et al., 2006).

Leadership Development Model in Action. Several CCMS curriculum reform units require students to learn how to explain scientific phenomena, and students are required to write their explanations. In this work circle example, the district curriculum specialist recognized that writing scientific explanations is a task with which students districtwide struggle on the high-stakes science examination. The goal of the work circle was to plan professional development that helps new teachers understand the models and strategies presented in the CCMS curriculum materials for supporting students' construction of scientific explanations (Fogleman et al., 2006).

Two of the lead teachers began the discussion by sharing teaching and assessment strategies they had created to support students' writing of scientific explanations. One lead teacher, for example, presented a graphical organizer that she observed her students use to construct better sentences for each component of their explanation. But, the lead teacher pointed out, she was having difficulty fading this scaffold and transitioning her students to writing their scientific explanations in paragraphs. CCMS researchers presented posttest results that confirmed the lead teacher's observation, as well as research-based information regarding pedagogical approaches to successful professional development. Other lead teachers presented concrete examples of student work and classroom assessments to illuminate their students' difficulties in generating written scientific explanations (Fogleman et al., 2006).

The work circle discussions progressed as the lead teachers from different grade levels looked for ways to align strategies that supported students' explanations across grades. The team made revisions in the curriculum units so that the explanations students were asked to construct increased in complexity from Grades 6 to 8. The lead teachers noted the importance of providing opportunities for students to practice writing explanations and the importance of teachers providing formative feedback. Lead teachers discussed strategies for modeling this process to novice teachers in the upcoming CCMS professional development workshop. The CCMS researchers, district curriculum specialist, and lead teachers collaboratively developed pedagogical strategies for implementing the CCMS reform. Ultimately, the lead teacher work circle discussion resulted in powerful professional development activities that scaffolded students' abilities to write scientific explanations (Fogleman et al., 2006).

Scaling Outcomes. The Lead Teacher Project increased alignment between the district's culture, capability, and policy, and the goals and requirements of CCMS reform. Through their interactions, deliberately selected lead teachers increased their own capabilities, which advanced the reform effort.

Culture. The lead teacher professional development work circle promoted a culture of learning among lead teachers, researchers, and district personnel that reflected many of the values embedded in the CCMS curriculum reform materials. The CCMS units are designed according to principles described in the Preface (Kali, Koppal, Linn, & Roseman), Chapter 1 (Roseman, Linn, & Koppal), and Chapter 3 (Krajcik, Slotta, McNeill, & Reiser). The work circle used guiding principles such as "Engage in the process of scientific inquiry" and "Collaborate and engage in discourse" as members discussed the curriculum and planned professional development activities. For instance, lead teachers gathered and discussed research-based information, concrete examples of student work, and classroom assessments to formulate strategies for helping teachers scaffold students' scientific explanations. Work circle participants regularly engaged in discourse regarding their goals for teacher and student learning, pedagogical and curricular scaffolding, and their professional development plans. A shared understanding of reform priorities, norms, and practices evolved in the work circle, and a norm for collaboration and inquiry among district administrators and teachers was established.

Capability. The lead teacher professional development work circle dramatically increased the district's capability for scaling CCMS reform. It increased lead teachers' understanding of CCMS curriculum content, pedagogy, and professional development. Work circle participants learned to synthesize theory and research with knowledge of pedagogical strategies and structures. This new level of integrated understanding enabled lead teachers to plan professional development activities that would engage novice CCMS teachers with innovative instructional strategies to support students' reasoning in difficult science topic areas.

One of the noteworthy features of the work circle activities described in this example is that the process demonstrated how it is possible to close the capability gap two ways. One way is to increase the capability of the lead teachers to help novice teachers enact reform curriculum. This is the classic way in which reform is scaled. The other way is to adjust the curriculum so that it is more usable in the district. In this example, CCMS researchers revised the curriculum materials based on lead teachers' suggestions so that the various curriculum units across the grade levels would treat the teaching of explanations in an appropriate manner as students learned through the middle school years.

Policy. The CCMS lead teachers designed professional development that not only met the district's reform goals but also addressed mandated statewide policies and national standards. This was evidenced particularly in terms of the national science standards and the Michigan high-stakes science examination. Aligning professional development with state and district policy increased opportunities to institutionalize the reform as a part of the district's organizational fabric. For example, the curriculum materials developed through CCMS research were adopted by the district, making them officially acceptable as a means by which schools can enact a science curriculum to meet district science goals, state standards, and assessment requirements. Further, the lead teacher development program provided evidence that a districtwide policy granting central responsibility for professional development to carefully selected lead teachers is a powerful mechanism for scaling and sustaining instructional change. The status of lead teachers was ultimately made an official district position, and lead teachers continue to lead CCMS professional development today.

TELS/MODELS Mentor Teacher Development

Challenge and Goal. University-led professional development programs are difficult to sustain when grant funding ends. For example, often in science reform, new curricula are introduced to teachers in university-led summer workshops or weekend seminars. When teachers return to their classrooms and try to integrate the new curriculum materials with the realities of everyday teaching, they often encounter multiple obstacles and discard the new approach if they do not have ongoing support. The goal of the TELS/MODELS Mentor Teacher Project is to foster professional development of school-based mentors who can support novice teachers in enacting TELS curriculum materials and reform practices after university support ends.

Leadership Development Model. A distinguishing feature of the MODELS mentor teacher approach is the long-term support given to the developing mentors and their respective school science departments for the purpose of cultivating a teacher community focused on inquiry-oriented, technology-enhanced instruction. Although the program is structured so that the mentor teacher scaffolds the novice teachers, both mentor and novice benefit from the extra set of eyes and ears focused intently on curriculum and teaching. The selection process for mentor teachers varies depending on individual school dynamics. In some schools, the mentor teacher is selected by an administrator based on the teacher's experience with technology; in other schools, the mentor position rotates annually among teachers in the science department. In one school, a mentor volunteers from each grade level. Although the selection processes vary, all selected mentors are eager to integrate new technology-enhanced curriculum materials into their classrooms and collaborate with peers. University researchers provide the mentor teachers with "buy-out" time for one period each day so that the mentor has adequate time to support teachers learning to teach with technology for the first time (Spitulnik, Corliss, & Kirkpatrick, 2008).

University researchers with expert knowledge of the TELS curriculum materials facilitate leadership development opportunities for selected mentor teachers. For a period of 2 years, the MODELS mentor program facilitators communicated weekly with the mentor teachers via phone, e-mail, and face-to-face meetings, and conducted an annual 2-day summer workshop. Weekly communication with mentors included discussion of emerging questions and issues related to the mentors' plans and activities to support novice teachers at their respective schools. The summer workshop focused on curriculum content, pedagogical strategies, and student assessment. Mentors learned the curriculum standards targeted by each TELS module and the inquiry theme or driving question that guides each project. They worked with student assessment data to identify topics and activities that are difficult for students, discuss possible pedagogical strategies for addressing these challenges, and identify methods to track students' ideas, such as pre- and posttests (Spitulnik et al., 2008).

After participating in mentor teacher professional development activities, the mentors provided customized professional support for the teachers in their respective science departments. For instance, the mentor might suggest strategies to scaffold students' interaction with the computer simulations, think with teachers about questions they might ask, or consider ways to incorporate hands-on laboratory activities. Because teachers are often rushed to provide feedback to students while they engage in a project, mentors and teachers might discuss common assessment findings and prepare comments in advance that the teachers can quickly give students as they work (Spitulnik et al., 2008).

Finally, mentor teachers served as liaisons between the teachers enacting TELS reforms and the curriculum developers. The mentors relayed their teachers' concerns regarding the curriculum content, format, and requisite technology tools to the developers. The curriculum developers then used this information to adapt the TELS modules so that they more smoothly integrated with classroom practices. The curriculum developers relayed their instructional goals and research findings for TELS modules. Mentors used this information to support teachers in reflecting on teaching strategies and better supporting students' sense making (Spitulnik et al., 2008).

Leadership Development Model in Action. School-based mentors wore multiple hats. To illustrate, we will describe the case of Patricia, a school-based mentor who juggled leadership development activities, supported teachers in using projects, and managed technology and computer maintenance for the issues that typically arise when adopting a technology-based reform. Patricia had 12 years of teaching experience and 3 years of experience integrating TELS projects into her classroom. She taught 7th-grade life science in a California middle school and, at the time we discuss, had completed her second year as a school-based mentor (Spitulnik et al., 2008).

Patricia was actively involved with the university-based research team, including the mentor program facilitators and the curriculum developers. She regularly attended weekly 2-hour research meetings at the university, and provided feedback regarding the difficulty of the scientific concepts presented in the TELS modules and the relevance of the guiding inquiry questions. She communicated ideas for possible revisions to the TELS modules based on her observations of teachers enacting them and on teachers' feedback. After each of the weekly meetings, Patricia met with the mentor program facilitators to discuss her own questions and problems with regard to her role as a school-based mentor. For instance, during one conversation Patricia related that one of the teachers did not feel comfortable having her observe his teaching. The facilitators suggested alternative ways for Patricia to scaffold this teacher's understanding of the TELS curriculum materials, such as meeting with him immediately after he enacts a project (Spitulnik et al., 2008).

After participating in university-led professional development activities, Patricia provided support for TELS at her school site. During her first year as a school-based mentor, Patricia dealt primarily with issues of school technology resources. She convinced her school administration to upgrade the school's computer lab, and she invested hours in building and maintaining a computer calendar for the science department that ensured each science teacher had adequate and equitable computer access. After taking care of the necessary technology issues, Patricia focused on providing pedagogy support for teachers. During her second year as a mentor, Patricia supported teachers in reviewing a TELS project before using it in their classroom. Teachers frequently had many questions, such as "How do I monitor student progress? How do I assess students?" Patricia not only served as extra eyes and ears in the classroom while the teacher enacted the TELS module, but she also modeled particular teaching strategies for teaching with technology, and documented scientific concepts or curriculum activities that challenged students. Patricia led strategic curriculum planning meetings. Her leadership was instrumental in aligning the school's TELS-enhanced science program with the California state science standards (Spitulnik et al., 2008).

Patricia's balancing act between her role as a mentor and a colleague raised some new challenges. She strived to make mentoring a collaborative experience rather than an authoritative one. Some teachers were more open to discussing their practice than others. Although she had a good relationship with teachers in her science department, Patricia needed to be sensitive to how individual teachers wanted to receive feedback concerning their instruction. Patricia's role as a mentor teacher changed over 2 years. In the first year, much of her energy was spent maintaining and scheduling the computer lab, and working to keep some of the teachers simply using the TELS materials. In the second year, Patricia was able to focus on student work within the TELS projects in her discussions with fellow teachers. She also helped teachers improve the feedback they give to the students as they engaged with the scientific visualizations and graphs (Spitulnik et al., 2008).

Scaling Outcomes. The Mentor Teacher Project increased the capability of the mentors, which in turn improved the knowledge and skills of their respective science departments. The shift in capability led to changes in the teaching culture of the science departments and in internal departmental policies governing computer usage.

Culture. The culture established between the mentor teachers and their peers determined the degree to which the mentors increased their colleagues' knowledge and skills for enacting TELS modules. When the mentor created a collaborative relationship with the other teachers, the mentoring relationship was mutually beneficial. The positive exchange of ideas cultivated a learning culture characterized by a collective commitment to improving science instruction. The mentor supported teachers in their departments by regularly discussing classroom strategies, planning lessons, and sharing instructional assessments. Mentor program facilitators provided ongoing support to help mentors reflect on how to customize their support for colleagues to fit individual needs and personalities.

Capability. The Mentor Teacher Project provided recurring opportunities for the mentor to engage with TELS curriculum content, pedagogy, assessment, and educational research. These activities aimed to strengthen the mentors' conceptual knowledge of TELS instructional approaches and their practical skills for promoting students' scientific reasoning in a computer-based environment. The mentors then worked collaboratively with teachers before they used a TELS module to help them become more familiar with the science content, identify challenging concepts, and anticipate students' ideas. Evidence for teachers' increased capability is the growing number of teachers that use TELS materials in each mentor's school, including those who work with students outside of the science department, such as special education and English language learner specialists (Spitulnik et al., 2008). Just as the mentor teacher caused shifts in the capability of their respective science departments for scaling TELS reform, the mentor also improved the capability of the TELS curricula. By communicating teachers' ideas about particular TELS technology requirements, curriculum content, and inquiry structures, the mentor teacher helped curriculum developers revise the modules to more tightly integrate with classroom instruction and routines. Critical curriculum changes include increased scaffolding for students and embedded pedagogical suggestions for teachers. Thus, the capability gap was reduced both by increasing the skill and knowledge of the teachers and by modifying the curriculum materials so that they were more usable.

Policy. The Mentor Teacher Project for leadership development resulted in internal policy changes that affect the sustainability and scalability of the TELS curricula. The most frequent policy change was related to computer scheduling in the schools. The mentor teacher, as illustrated in the case of Patricia, created a schedule for the computer lab that allowed TELS science teachers to use the computers for an extended period during regular class hours. Additionally, mentor teachers convinced administration to acquire new computers specifically for TELS activities. These are essential policy changes, because over the past two decades of curriculum development research, teachers have frequently reported that they do not complete TELS projects due to limited computer access (Varma, Husic, & Linn, in press). Beyond its ability to resolve a mechanical issue such as computer scheduling, the mentor teacher program provides evidence regarding a much more significant issue: Enactment of a district policy granting teacher leaders (such as mentors) release time to support novice teachers in their department is a promising approach for scaling complex curriculum reform.

DISCUSSION

The research reported in this chapter suggests that leadership development projects can substantially affect the capacity of districts and schools for scaling and sustaining science technology innovation. Table 6.2 summarizes the findings reported.

As noted in Table 6.2, administrators and teacher leaders in these projects developed convergence between innovative curricula and school-system environments. In these projects, leaders interrupted their frenetic administrative pace to provide time for extended inquiry, reflection, and collaboration around science and technology curriculum reform. They crafted practical visions for a student-centered learning culture based on what they learned about the curricula and their knowledge of their own school's priorities and challenges. They increased their school system's capability for innovation by designing leadership development for teachers focused on curricular integration, and by actively participating in leadership development themselves. In the case of the ongoing Community of Principals, a dramatic increase in the number of teachers implementing the science curriculum innovations resulted (see Figure 6.1). Leaders

TABLE 6.2 TELS and CCMS Leadership Development Projects: Scaling Outcomes in Terms of Culture, Capability, and Policy*

Project	Culture	Capability	Policy
CCMS Administrator Reform Community	Administrators and teacher leaders identified gaps between district vision and schools' technology implementation.	Administrators more effectively communicated their technology vision with constituents. They generated professional development plans to shift their districtwide cultures to align with new district visions for technology reform.	Administrators redistributed resources and reconfigured school space to support new uses of technology. They balanced state assessment policies with district curricular technology goals for critical thinking.
TELS Community of Principals	Principals identified congruence between the technology science curriculum and their schools' values. They struggled with conflict between the values congruent with science curriculum innovation and No Child Left Behind pressures.	Principals' participation in professional development resulted in more teachers using the TELS curriculum in their schools. Principals organized professional learning opportunities for novice TELS teachers.	Principals created school policies customized to their schools' needs to support curricular scaling. Principals reported reform innovation updates to their school leadership teams, making themselves accountable for ongoing reform progress.
CCMS Lead Teacher Project	Lead teachers and district administrators created a shared understanding of reform priorities and values. They established a district norm for collaboration and inquiry.	Lead teachers contributed to curriculum improvements and developed knowledge and skills to conduct districtwide professional development for science curriculum innovation.	Curriculum materials were adopted as the official district curriculum. The district created lead teacher positions to drive the reform.
TELS/MODELS Mentor Teacher Project	Collaborative relationships between mentor and novice teachers promoted a focus on inquiry and technology.	Mentors contributed to curriculum improvements. Their participation led to increased teachers' use of the curriculum materials (including special education and English language learner teachers) in the mentors' schools.	Mentors influenced school policies, which resulted in increased computer hardware and increased computer access for science teachers.

*Blumenfeld et al. (2000).

created school and district policies that mandated the use of the science curriculum reforms, recruited technologically skilled science teachers, created districtwide professional development opportunities focused on science reform, and increased computer resources for science departments. Face-to-face interactions between the leaders proved critical in bringing about change.

Findings from the four leadership development projects discussed in this chapter suggest that a change in culture, capability, or policy can in fact catalyze reform in one or more of the other dimensions. In other words, the three dimensions are interconnected, and one dimension often functions as the leading edge for change. For example, in the TELS Community of Principals, culture functioned as the leading edge. The principals' initial focus on generating a collective vision for technology-enhanced science spurred principals to invest in teacher professional development for technology-enhanced science (capability), and to acquire and/or redistribute technology resources specifically for the science department's use (policy/management). Likewise, in the CCMS Administrator Reform Community, a newly developed vision among administrators (culture) catalyzed them to implement changes in their districts' teacher professional development for technology (capability) and reconfigure school space to support new uses of technology (policy).

Whereas culture operated as the leading edge for scaling reform in the administrator and principal communities, significant shifts along the capability dimension functioned as the leading edge in the two teacher leadership development projects. For example, in the CCMS Lead Teacher Project, lead teachers collectively cultivated new understandings of science reform and conducted professional development workshops to share this new knowledge with their teacher colleagues (capability). Their facilitation of professional development led to a districtwide shift to prioritize inquiry and collaborative learning (culture), as well as the creation of a new district-appointed job title for science reform "lead teachers" (policy). The variability in schools and districts in terms of the challenges for scaling suggests that no one school or district will follow the same sequence of change in scaling technology-enhanced science. By starting with change in the dimension that is most compelling to the administrators or teacher leaders, momentum to catalyze change along the other dimensions of the school system builds.

Shifts in the systemwide capacity for scaling science technology also depended on the skills of school and district leaders in communicating with their constituent groups. Both TELS and CCMS administrator leadership development projects promoted development of communication strategies in the structure and content of their leadership meetings. The Administrator Reform Community, for example, gave administrators cameras to photograph their observations of technology use in colleagues' districts and schools; they were then able to use these photographs to visually communicate their new vision for district technology use to stake holders. In the TELS/MODELS Mentor Teacher Project, mentors focused on customizing their feedback regarding novice teachers' use of technology-enhanced science to support the individual challenges and personalities of the novice teachers. In sum, to leverage the vision of leadership and expertise in technology-enhanced innovation in science instruction, knowledge must be coupled with effective communication.

Design Principles: Leadership Development for Scaling Science Innovation

Design principles that emerge from the CCMS and TELS leadership development efforts described in this chapter offer robust mechanisms for building professional leadership communities to support widespread use of exemplary science curricula. The three design principles described below are part of a more general design principle—"Promote productive interactions" (Chapters 3 and 5; Chapter 8, Kali, Fortus, & Ronen-Fuhrmann). This broader design principle advocates creating opportunities for learners at various levels (students, teachers, principals) to interact with each other in ways that promote their learning. The specific design principles described below provide guidelines for promoting the types of interactions that are specifically valuable for leadership development.

Make Visible Leadership Work for Scaling Curricular Innovation. CCMS and TELS curriculum research and development projects provide unique examples of what can occur as the result of an investment in leadership development. The four leadership development projects discussed in this chapter transformed complex school systems into places where technology-enhanced science curriculum innovation flourished. Making this leadership work visible to funding agencies, policy makers, and constituent groups within the school community is key. It provides specific evidence to inform decision makers.

In addition, making leaders' work visible to their colleagues contributes significantly to administrators' and teacher leaders' own professional learning and development (Louis & Kruse, 1995). By observing collectively in classrooms, leaders in the four TELS and CCMS leadership development projects were able to see the implementation of technology-enhanced curricula, experience the teaching challenges associated with using computer visualizations, and become informed about the complex infrastructure necessary to scale curricular innovation. By sharing detailed stories of the successes and challenges of technology-enhanced innovation in science instruction, the district and school leaders could see the key school-system variables involved in the curriculum reform and appreciate the complex matrix of actors and settings. The challenges of merging leaders' visions for science curriculum reform with the realities of their classroom/school/district systems were made visible. Further, by making leadership goals and work explicit and visible, administrators and teacher leaders made themselves accountable to each other for ongoing improvement in technology and science instruction.

Sustain Leadership Focus on Innovation. Successfully scaling reform is a dynamic and continual process that requires a sustained focus on innovation. Reform teeters between scale on one end and resistance to change on the other; the direction of its tilt in either direction hinges on the vision and commitment of the school and district leadership. Issues related to principal/teacher capability, school/district values, and technology resources emerge and dissipate at different points in the reform process. In most cases, this continual disequilibrium discourages reform. As obstacles are encountered, the new curriculum is put aside in favor of the traditional and reliable, and in most cases *less* effective, instructional approaches. In the CCMS and TELS leadership development projects discussed in this chapter, a community of leaders meeting at regular intervals over several years for the purpose of scaling innovation buffered innovation from this nonlinear, dynamic process. In this scaffolded setting, leaders continually evaluated the fit between the innovation and the school or district, shared strategies, and generated new expectations for both technology innovation and instruction systemwide.

A community of leaders, as evidenced by each of the projects in this chapter, depends on the organizational support and curricular expertise of a facilitator. A mutual interest in reform from several school/district leaders located geographically close to one another is another characteristic of a successful leadership community. Finally, partnership with a university curriculum research development team is optimal. A built-in obstacle to long-term sustainability of a leadership community, however, occurs when the research team's funding is terminated. The CCMS Lead Teacher Project faced this challenge, and successfully established an official district position for lead teachers. This example provides a promising model for leadership sustainability.

Prioritize Leadership Collaboration and Learning Across Schools and Districts. The four leadership development projects discussed in this chapter, with extensive support from the National Science Foundation, created venues for learning what happens when time is set aside for district and school leaders to actively engage in critical inquiry with their colleagues. Administrators, principals, and teachers committed to developing a new vision for science education. They proposed and organized professional learning experiences that included observing innovative uses of technology at each other's sites and inviting teachers to share their experiences and challenges with innovative technology-enhanced science curricula. Additionally, the leaders developed a community of support and collegiality that created the conditions that would allow them to borrow strategies from each other or run low-cost scaling simulations of risky innovations (Ven de Ven, Polley, Garud, & Venkataraman, 1999). Over time, the recurring meetings and professional dialogue led not only to changes in school-system structure to support scale but also, and perhaps more importantly, to changes in administrators' and teacher leaders' conceptions of teaching and learning in science. As one TELS principal remarked, "I was shocked to learn that these students actually think of themselves as scientists".

Too often, as one principal in our study noted, "our staff development consists of going to these talking head meetings where they just give you all these binders and you walk out of there more overwhelmed than when you came in.... There is no time to actually reflect and really talk about curriculum and teaching." The professional leadership communities described in this chapter provide a promising alternative.

Obstacles to Developing Leadership for Scaling Science Innovation

The successes of the TELS and CCMS leadership development projects described in this chapter underscore the promise of what can be accomplished with enlightened leadership and dedicated support. However, it is important to be prepared for obstacles. First, the culture of leadership in schools traditionally places high value on running a tight ship where things get done quickly and efficiently (Peterson, 2000; Wood, 2007). Participating in long-term leadership development and learning from colleagues could seem to run counter to this speed and efficiency ideal. Second, high teacher and administrative turnover creates discontinuity in school and district leadership and can fragment a developing leadership community. Finally, the traditional school system's lack of prioritization of time and resources for leadership development poses a significant challenge. Principals and teachers are overloaded with day-to-day responsibilities, and few schools have funds to hire external facilitators to organize leadership development meetings.

CONCLUSIONS: POLICY IMPLICATIONS

An important role of educational research is to bridge fundamental knowledge of learning and development with applied knowledge of learning in schools. We agree with Burkhart and Schoenfeld (2003) that "traditions of educational research are themselves not strongly aligned with effective models linking research and practice" (p. 3). Put bluntly, educational research has little impact on the practical rough and tumble of education. Yet educational research journals contain many examples of empirically validated programs that, if scaled to broader settings, could greatly improve the quality of education in America.

CCMS and TELS are two examples of well-funded, long-term partnership efforts that are attempting to systematically address this issue by focusing on leadership as a lever for systemwide change. This work has important implications for education policy. CCMS and TELS attend to the multiple ingredients for reform—curriculum design, professional development of teachers, usability of technology, and the needs and capacities of diverse learners. Multiple institutions with scholars from diverse fields including computer science, psychology, literacy, teacher education, science education, and science disciplines conduct research and development for reform in each of these areas. Funding organizations such as the National Science Foundation, the U.S. Department of Education, and private foundations have invested several million dollars per year for over two decades in this reform-oriented, collaborative research. As a result of this work, both centers have developed exemplary curricula that can improve students' understanding of science and cultivate a passion for science inquiry. Now, the focus is scale. The variables are in place to enable the broader impact that Burkhart and Schoenfeld (2003) describe as the highest level of research and development—systemic change. The leadership development projects described in this chapter bring district and school leaders together with researchers to synergize components for reform with conditions in the school system. This nonlinear and dynamic process is ongoing, and it hinges on the sustained focus of the leadership. Without strong leadership, it is unlikely that innovations can go to scale and that once at scale can be sustained.

7

Assessing Integrated Understanding of Science

George E. DeBoer, Hee-Sun Lee, and Freda Husic

QUALITY ASSESSMENT is an essential part of quality instruction. Assessment can be used to monitor student progress toward stated learning goals and to measure the effectiveness of instruction. In an era of public accountability, assessment instruments have enormous potential to pull curricula and instructional practices toward what is included in those assessments. When the goal is for students to develop an integrated understanding of science, assessment can support this goal through careful structuring of the kinds of assessment tasks students perform and through provision of feedback on how well students are moving toward accomplishing the goal. In this chapter, we focus on (a) ways of designing test items to measure a variety of learning outcomes, including development of particular knowledge and skills, mental models of science processes, and hypothesized mental constructs related to an integrated understanding of science; (b) the use of qualitative and psychometric analyses to obtain information on the quality of assessment instruments; and (c) the use of assessment results to revise the curriculum materials being developed. We use examples from the Center for Curriculum Materials in Science (CCMS) and the Technology Enhanced Learning in Science (TELS) Center to illustrate how assessment can lead to the development of integrated understanding in science.

DECIDING WHAT TO ASSESS: DEFINING THE CONSTRUCT

The first step in developing assessment items and instruments is to clearly define what is to be measured. This might be knowledge of a particular scientific fact, principle, or interconnected set of ideas; the ability to use scientific knowledge to make predictions and explanations of real-world phenomena; or the ability to engage in scientific practices such as designing experiments. At both CCMS and TELS, the primary focus is on measuring students' ability to use knowledge to solve problems and explain scientific phenomena, and on identifying gaps in knowledge that limit students' understanding of events in the natural world.

In the section that follows, we provide three examples of constructs used to guide the item-development process. In the first example, we describe a 2-year item-development cycle being used by researchers at Project 2061 of the American Association for the Advancement of Science (AAAS) to design test items aligned with ideas in the national content standards, specifically ideas in *Benchmarks for Science Literacy* (AAAS, 1993) and the *National Science Education Standards* (NRC, 1996). In the second example, we illustrate how CCMS researchers have adapted the Project 2061 approach in their development of assessment items that measure students' use of science practices linked to science content, specifically students' ability to generate scientific explanations of phenomena related to the properties of substances. In the third example, we describe how TELS researchers design assessments to measure students' ability to connect multiple science ideas to solve problems in the real world, a major component of the TELS knowledge integration construct.

Aligning Assessment Items with Science Ideas in the National Content Standards

Recognizing the importance of high-quality assessment items that are aligned with the science ideas in state and national content standards and the poor quality of many of the items currently being used (American Federation of Teachers, 2006), Project 2061 has been engaged in a multi-year project to develop assessment items precisely aligned with middle school content standards in science (DeBoer, 2005).

Project 2061 has developed a five-stage process for creation of assessments: (a) clarifying each content standard targeted for assessment; (b) applying a set of alignment criteria in devising assessment items that are aligned with the specific ideas in the content standards; (c) obtaining feedback on the items from students during interviews and pilot testing, and revising the items based on that feedback; (d) having the items formally reviewed by science specialists and experts in science education, and making revisions based on those reviews; and (e) field testing the items on a national sample of students.

Clarify the Content Standards. Both *Benchmarks for Science Literacy* (AAAS, 1989) and the *National Science Education Standards* (NRC, 1996) are organized around ideas and skills that all students should learn by the end of certain grade bands in order to effectively engage in a world in which science and technology play such an important role. In addition to identifying what should be learned, these standards documents also organize the knowledge and skills into coherent and well-integrated accounts of events and processes in the physical and biological world. These standards provide guidance for developing curriculum, instruction, and assessment at CCMS.

Although the standards provide considerably more detail than a topic list does, they are also acknowledged to be just the first step in defining what students should know. The accounts of natural processes in the standards documents are not intended to be complete, and by themselves the statements do not provide enough information to assessment developers about exactly what students can or should be held accountable for. Therefore, to increase precision of content alignment and precision in diagnosing gaps in students' knowledge that may interfere with their understanding of natural phenomena, Project 2061 researchers subdivide the content standards into finer grained statements of knowledge, or *key ideas*. The key ideas are then clarified and elaborated to specify what the boundaries of that knowledge are for purposes of assessment. Consider the following key idea for a benchmark from the topic of plate tectonics:

> *The outer layer of the Earth—including both the continents and the ocean basins—consists of separate plates.*

Clearly there are concepts in this statement about earth's plates that need to be described beyond the simple statement that the outer layer of the earth is made of plates. Exactly what knowledge should students have of what a plate is? Researchers used three questions to guide clarification of the key idea:

1. Is this description of plates what is needed for students at this age to form a mental image of the Earth's plates that will allow them to predict and explain phenomena involving plates?
2. Is this description of plates what is needed for students to understand later ideas and the accompanying phenomena they will encounter?
3. Will the specified terminology contribute enough to students' ability to communicate about the targeted ideas to make that terminology worth learning?

The *clarification statement* answers these questions to provide a more detailed description of what students are expected to know:

> *Students are expected to know that the solid outer layer of the Earth is made of separate sections called plates that fit closely together along the entire surface where they are in contact, such that each plate touches all the*

plates next to it. They should know that any place where two plates meet is called a plate boundary. They should know that plates are continuous solid rock, miles thick, which are either visible or covered by water, soil, or sediment such as sand. They should know that the exposed solid rock of mountains is an example of plate material that is visible. Students are not expected to know the term bedrock. Students should know that there are about 12–15 very large plates, each of which encompasses large areas of the Earth's outer layer (e.g., an entire continent plus adjoining ocean floor or a large part of an entire ocean basin), which together are large enough to make up almost the entire outer layer of the earth. They should also know that there are additional smaller plates that make up the rest of the outer layer, but they are not expected to know the size of the smaller plates or how many there are. Students are expected to know that the boundaries of continents and oceans are not the same as the boundaries of plates. They should know that some boundaries between plates are found in continents, some in the ocean floors, and some in places where oceans and continents meet. Students are not expected to know the names of specific plates or the exact surface areas of plates. Students are not expected to know the terms lithosphere, crust, or mantle; the difference between lithosphere and crust; or that a plate includes the crust and the upper portion of the mantle.

In addition to providing detailed guidance for assessment, these elaborations of the term *plate* can also be used to guide instruction that will lead to a mental model of a plate that students will use when learning subsequent ideas about plate motion and the consequences of plate motion, which come later in the instructional sequence. In particular, this mental model will help students understand such things as mountain building and where earthquakes and volcanoes form when the students are introduced to those ideas. With respect to terminology, it was decided for assessment purposes not to expect students to know certain technical terms such as lithosphere, because these terms were not likely to contribute significantly to explaining phenomena related to plate motion. Although individual teachers may choose to show students the relationship between lithosphere, upper mantle, and plates during instruction, the assessment items do not include the term.

Expectations for students are also based on what research on student learning tells us regarding the age-appropriateness of the ideas being targeted and the level of complexity of the mental models that students can be expected to develop. Research on student learning also describes many of the misconceptions that students may have, which are then included as distracters in the items so that these nonnormative ideas can be tested alongside the targeted ideas.

After the ideas that are to be assessed have been identified and clarified, the next step is to determine how these ideas relate to other ideas within a topic and across grade levels. The objective here is to be as clear as possible about the boundaries around the ideas that are being explicitly tested and the prior knowledge students can be assumed to have. For example, if students are being tested on their understanding of digestion at the molecular level, in which molecules from food are broken down to simpler molecules that have a different number and arrangement of atoms, can it be assumed that students already know that molecules are made of atoms? If not, are questions on chemical digestion, written in terms of atoms of molecules, to some extent also testing whether students know the relationship between atoms and molecules?

In making judgments about which ideas precede a targeted idea, Project 2061 researchers make use of the conceptual strand maps published in the *Atlas of Science Literacy* (AAAS, 2001, 2007). The strand maps were developed to visually represent the interconnections among ideas in *Benchmarks for Science Literacy* and the *National Science Education Standards*. The map for the topic of "Diversity of Life" in Figure 7.1, for example, has three strands: classification, similarities and differences, and diversity and survival. The interconnections among the ideas in these strands are visually represented—or mapped—to show the progression of ideas within each conceptual strand through four grade bands and the links between ideas across strands. In the *diversity and survival* strand, a benchmark at the 6–8 grade level says, "In any particular environment, the growth and survival of organisms depend on the physical conditions" (AAAS, 2007, p. 31). This is preceded on the map by a benchmark at the 3–5 grade level that says, "For any particular environment, some kinds of plants and animals thrive, some do not live as well, and some cannot survive at all" (AAAS, 2007, p. 31). In testing whether students know that organisms in ecosystems depend on the physical conditions, it is assumed that they already know that not all organisms are as successful as others in a given ecosystem. As a rule, unless there are good reasons to believe otherwise, it is assumed that students already know the ideas listed at an earlier grade band, and the ideas and language from those earlier ideas are used freely in item development for the grade band that follows. But it is also recognized that these earlier ideas are a good place to look when students do not know a targeted idea. Not knowing an earlier idea, such as the idea that not all organisms are as successful as others in an ecosystem (or the idea that molecules are made of atoms), is often the reason why students have difficulty with the idea being tested. The relationships identified in the *Atlas* maps (see Figure 7.1) can help developers focus on ideas that may be needed for understanding the targeted ideas and encourage them to think about whether or not it is reasonable to assume that students already know that earlier idea.

Design Assessment Items Aligned with Content Standards. Test items should always be written in such a way that teachers and researchers can draw

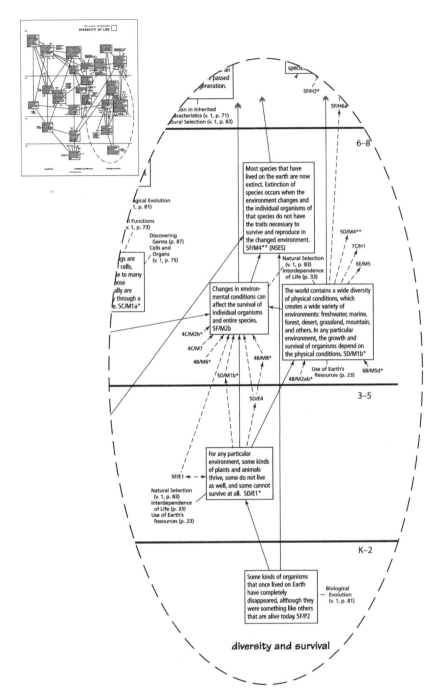

species...

5F/H3*

5F/H6a

6-8

...on in Inherited
...aracteristics (v. 1, p. 71)
...tural Selection (v. 1, p. 83)

...gical Evolution
1, p. 81)

...l Functions
v. 1, p. 73)

Discovering
Germs (p. 87)

Cells and
Organs
(v. 1, p. 75)

...gs are
...cells,
...e to many
...hose
...ally are
...through a
...e. 5C/M1a*

Most species that have
lived on the earth are now
extinct. Extinction of
species occurs when the
environment changes and
the individual organisms of
that species do not have
the traits necessary to
survive and reproduce in
the changed environment.
5F/M4** (NSES)

5D/M4**

7C/H1

Natural Selection
(v. 1, p. 83)
Interdependence
of Life (p. 33)

6E/M5

Changes in environ-
mental conditions can
affect the survival of
individual organisms
and entire species.
5F/M2b

The world contains a wide diversity
of physical conditions, which
creates a wide variety of
environments: freshwater, marine,
forest, desert, grassland, mountain,
and others. In any particular
environment, the growth and
survival of organisms depend on
the physical conditions. 5D/M1b*

4C/M2b*

4C/M7

4B/M6*

4B/M8*

5D/M1b*

Use of Earth's
Resources (p. 23)

4B/M2ab*

6B/M5d*

5D/E4

3-5

For any particular
environment, some kinds
of plants and animals
thrive, some do not live
as well, and some cannot
survive at all. 5D/E1*

5F/E1

Natural Selection
(v. 1, p. 83)
Interdependence
of Life (p. 33)
Use of Earth's
Resources (p. 23)

K-2

Some kinds of organisms
that once lived on Earth
have completely
disappeared, although they
were something like others
that are alive today. 5F/P2

Biological
Evolution
(v. 1, p. 81)

diversity and survival

FIGURE 7.1 *Atlas of Science Literacy* strand map for the topic
"Diversity of Life" (AAAS, 2007, Map 5A).

valid conclusions from them about what students do and do not know about the ideas being tested. Unfortunately, many test items have features that make it difficult to determine whether a student's answer choice reflects what that student knows about an idea. When an item is well designed, students should choose the correct answer only when they know an idea, and they should choose an incorrect answer only when they do not know the idea.

The first thing to consider when designing test items is the alignment of the item with the targeted idea. Project 2061 researchers use two criteria to determine whether the content that is being targeted by an assessment item is aligned with the content specified in a particular key idea. The *necessity* criterion addresses whether the knowledge in the learning goal is *needed* to successfully complete the task, and the *sufficiency* criterion addresses whether the knowledge in the learning goal is *enough by itself* to successfully complete the task. If the targeted knowledge is not needed to answer the question, then the item is obviously not a good indicator of whether students know the targeted idea. And, if *additional* knowledge is needed to answer correctly, it is difficult to know if an incorrect response is due to not knowing the targeted idea or not knowing the additional idea. The criteria of necessity and sufficiency are used both in the initial design of the items and in subsequent analyses and revisions of the items. (See DeBoer [2005] for a further discussion of the application of the necessity and sufficiency criteria in item development.)

Despite its critical importance in item development, content alignment alone is not enough to determine whether or not an item should be used. There are many other factors related to construct validity that can also affect the usefulness of an assessment item in providing accurate insights into student understanding of the targeted content. For example, students should not be able to answer correctly by using test-taking strategies that do not depend on knowing the idea (a false positive response) or be so confused by what is being asked that they choose an incorrect answer even when they know the idea being tested (a false negative response). To improve the validity of conclusions that can be drawn from assessment results, it is important to identify and eliminate as many problems with comprehensibility and test-wiseness as possible. (The criteria for judging alignment and threats to validity are detailed in Project 2061's Assessment Analysis Procedure, available on the Project 2061 Web site at http://www.project2061 .org/assessment/analysis.)

Obtain Feedback from Students. Rigorously applying a set of criteria to determine the alignment of test items with learning goals and to identify features that obscure what students really know are both important steps in the item development process. However, findings from research indicate that this analytical approach works much more effectively when used in combination with one-on-one interviews with students or pilot tests of items in which students are asked to explain why they chose the answer that they did (DeBoer & Ache, 2005). By comparing the answer choices that students select with their oral or written explanations, it is possible to determine if an assessment item is measuring what it is supposed to measure or if students are giving false negative or false positive responses to the item. In the Project 2061 item development work, students are asked the questions shown in Figure 7.2 to get feedback on problems they may have in interpreting the items and to find out what ideas they have about the content being assessed, especially the misconceptions they have. Pilot tests are carried out in urban, suburban, and rural middle schools serving a wide range of students (DeBoer, Herrmann Abell, & Gogos, 2007).

The following examples illustrate the kinds of information that can be obtained from these pilot tests. The examples also show how this information can be used to improve the items' alignment with the key ideas and improve their validity as measures of student learning.

Example A: Atoms, Molecules, and States of Matter. The item shown in Figure 7.3 tests whether students know that molecules get farther apart when they are heated and whether they know that this molecular behavior explains why most substances expand when heated. The item includes answer choices that test

1. Is there anything about this test question that was confusing? Explain.			
2. Circle any words on the test question you don't understand or aren't familiar with.			
[3 to 6. Students are asked to explain why an answer choice is correct or not correct or why they are "not sure."]			
3. Is answer choice A correct?	Yes	No	Not sure
4. Is answer choice B correct?	Yes	No	Not sure
5. Is answer choice C correct?	Yes	No	Not sure
6. Is answer choice D correct?	Yes	No	Not sure
7. Did you guess when you answered the test question?	Yes	No	
8. Please suggest additional answer choices that could be used.			
9. Was the picture or graph helpful? If there was no picture or graph, would you like to see one?	Yes	No	
10. Have you studied this topic in school?	Yes	No	Not sure
11. Have you learned about it somewhere else? Where? (TV, museum visit, etc.?)	Yes	No	Not sure

FIGURE 7.2 Project 2061 questionnaire for student interview on an assessment item.

Key Idea: *For any single state of matter, increasing the temperature typically increases the distance between atoms and molecules. Therefore, most substances expand when heated.*

The level of colored alcohol in a thermometer rises when the thermometer is placed in hot water. Why does the level of alcohol rise?

A. The heat molecules push the alcohol molecules upward.

B. The alcohol molecules break down into atoms which take up more space.

C. The alcohol molecules get farther apart so the alcohol takes up more space.

D. The water molecules are pushed into the thermometer and are added to the alcohol molecules.

Students who chose each answer:

	A	B	C	D	Not Sure/ Blank	Total
#	48	7	28	5	20	108
%	44.4	6.5	25.9	4.6	18.5	100

FIGURE 7.3 Project 2061 assessment item development questionnaire for students: Atoms, molecules, and states of matter (Coffey, Douglas, & Stearns, 2008).

common misconceptions related to thermal expansion and the behavior of molecules, especially the idea that there are "heat molecules."

Pilot testing showed that 25.9% of the students answered this question correctly. The most common response (44.4%) was that "heat molecules" push the alcohol molecules upward. Pilot testing also revealed that a number of the students were not familiar with the terms "alcohol" or "colored alcohol," at least not in the context of a thermometer. Based on the results of pilot testing, the following revisions were made: First, because answer choice A is the only one that has the word "heat" in it and students may choose that answer choice because they connect the liquid rising in the thermometer with heat rising, the word "heat" was added to other answer choices. Also, the word "alcohol" was changed to "liquid" to remove a word that some students find confusing in the context of thermometers.

When students were interviewed about this item, a number of them had difficulty reconciling what they expected to be a very small expansion of the liquid in the bulb of the thermometer into what appears to be a very large expansion of the liquid in the narrow tube of the thermometer. One student who knew that substances expand when heated did not believe the liquid could expand that much and chose answer choice A ("heat molecules"). Even though her commitment to "heat molecules" did not appear to be strong during the interview, it seemed to her that something besides thermal expansion had to explain such a large increase. Because of developmental issues regarding children's ability to easily engage in proportional reasoning in middle school, the thermometer context may be a difficult context for general testing of middle school students' understanding of thermal expansion. But it is also possible that focused instruction might help students see that a small change in the volume of a liquid is amplified in a narrow tube. The thermometer could then be used as an example of how measuring devices in general are often designed to amplify the effect being measured. Often a close examination of student reasons for selecting answer choices during assessment leads to insights that can be applied to instruction as well as to assessment.

Example B: Control of Variables. The item shown in Figure 7.4 was developed to determine whether students understand that the way to determine if one variable is related to another is to hold all other relevant variables constant. The item also tests a number of common misconceptions that students often have regarding the control of variables, including the idea that all of the variables should be allowed to vary in a controlled experiment.

The results of pilot testing showed that 53.9% of the students answered correctly and that 26.3% chose answer choice A, which targets the misconception that both variables should vary at the same time. Answer choices B and C were less popular distracters. Answer choice B was chosen by only one student. Of the six students who chose C, three said they rejected answer choices A and B because there were no weights in one of the carts for those answer choices. Also, three students thought the word "trials" in the stem referred to the answer choices and circled three answer choices as correct. Six students (including some of those who chose the correct answer) thought that the word "blocks" in the stem referred to the parts of the ramp rather than the weights in the cart. Based on the results of pilot testing, the blocks in the carts were replaced by metal balls and the number of balls in each cart was increased so that there were no empty carts. The stem was changed to read, "Which set of tests should he compare?"

External Review. Following pilot testing, the items are reviewed by panels of experts in science and science education to ensure content accuracy, alignment with the targeted content standards, and construct validity. The reviewers are

> **Key Idea:** *If more than one variable changes at the same time in an experiment, the outcome of the experiment may not be clearly attributable to any one of the variables.*

A student wants to test this idea: The heavier a cart is, the greater its speed at the bottom of a ramp. He can use carts with different numbers of blocks and ramps with different heights. Which three trials should he compare?

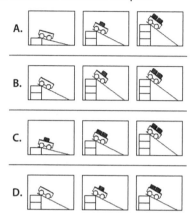

Students who chose each answer:

	A	B	C	D	Not Sure/ Blank	Total
#	20	1	6	41	8	76
%	26.3	1.3	7.9	53.9	10.5	100

FIGURE 7.4　Project 2061 assessment item development questionnaire for students: Control of variables (Coffey et al., 2008).

trained in the use of Project 2061's Assessment Analysis Procedure (see http://www.project2061.org/assessment/analysis), which uses the criteria of necessity and sufficiency for content alignment, and focuses reviewers' attention on issues of test-wiseness, comprehensibility, accessibility, and appropriateness of task context. The reviewers also make use of the results of pilot testing, including students' written comments, to help them in the analysis of the items. The reviewer ratings and comments, combined with the pilot test data, are then examined by Project 2061 staff, and the items are then revised and prepared for field testing.

Field Testing.　Each test item is field tested in topic clusters of 12–25 items per cluster with a national sample of approximately 1,000 students from a wide range of urban, suburban, and rural schools across the country. The results are analyzed using item response theory (IRT) and classic test item analysis procedures to determine relative difficulty of the items, the factor structure of the cluster of items, the contribution that each item makes to assessing student understanding of the topic, and whether or not the items function similarly for the various subgroups tested. Data are analyzed by gender, race and ethnicity, and whether English is the students' primary language.

For example, on a set of 14 items designed to measure middle school students' understanding of control of variables, it was found that boys and girls performed equivalently on the set of items as a whole. However, although they performed equivalently on most of the individual items, some of the individual items functioned differently for boys and girls. These differences demonstrate how important it is to be aware of item context when writing test questions. Test writers may use their best judgment in predicting how boys and girls (or members of different ethnic groups) will respond to the scenarios they create, but an analysis of actual test results is needed to see if those predictions are accurate. Providing test items that are accessible to a wide range of students and on which subgroups of students will perform similarly is an issue of equity and one of the goals of this assessment work. Equity is also a core principle of CCMS and TELS. (See Chapter 4, Tate, Clark, Gallagher, and McLaughlin, for further discussion of how equity issues are addressed at the two centers.)

Connecting Science Content to Science Practices

In the second example, we illustrate how CCMS researchers have designed assessment items to measure student ability to engage in scientific practices involving real-world phenomena related to a targeted science idea (Harris et al., 2006; McNeill & Krajcik, 2008a). The stated goal is for students to be able to use their knowledge of science content as they engage in a particular science practice. The example is taken from the "Investigating and Questioning Our World Through Science and Technology" (IQWST) middle school curriculum unit focusing on properties of substances and chemical reactions (McNeill et al., 2004). The particular science practice that is targeted is the ability to provide a scientific explanation for a claim the student makes based on data provided.

The assessment task shown in Figure 7.5 requires students to apply two science ideas. First, they must know that different substances have different characteristic properties. Second, they must know that a property such as density, color, or melting point is a characteristic property of a substance that does not change when the amount of the substance changes. The students are judged on the basis of their ability to (a) make accurate claims from the data using their knowledge of properties of substances, (b) justify their claims about these substances using the available evidence, and (c) provide a reason why the evidence

	Density	Color	Mass	Melting Point
Liquid 1	0.93 g/cm^3	No color	38 g	–98 °C
Liquid 2	0.79 g/cm^3	No color	38 g	26 °C
Liquid 3	13.6 g/cm^3	Silver	21 g	–39 °C
Liquid 4	0.93 g/cm^3	No color	16 g	–98 °C

Write a scientific explanation that states whether any of the liquids are the same substance.

FIGURE 7.5   IQWST assessment item: Scientific explanation for properties of substances.

justifies the claim (i.e., link their claim and evidence to the general rule or scientific principle that is being targeted). This claim-evidence-reasoning format is taught explicitly in the IQWST curriculum (see Chapter 3, Krajcik, Slotta, McNeill, & Reiser) and is tested using items such as the one in Figure 7.5.

Identify and Unpack the Content Standard. The first step in writing an IQWST assessment task is to identify the content standard to be assessed. The content standard is then unpacked to identify exactly which science ideas are to be tested, those statements are elaborated, and boundaries are set around the expectations for students. What comes earlier and later in the learning trajectory is also noted so that specific expectations for the age range can be determined. Item developers also consider which nonnormative ideas or misconceptions students may have about the content, and these misconceptions are then used in the design of the assessment task either as distracters in multiple-choice questions or as part of a scoring rubric for open-ended questions.

Unpack the Scientific Inquiry Practice. The next step that IQWST developers take is to consider which scientific inquiry practices (e.g., modeling, designing an investigation, or providing a scientific explanation) they want to measure. In the chemistry example in Figure 7.5, the science practice that was chosen was scientific explanation. This science practice was unpacked into three separate components: claim, evidence, and reasoning. Unpacking the scientific practice specifies what it is that students will be expected to do with their understanding of the science content. Each constructed response assessment task requires a separate scoring rubric for each content area and each scientific inquiry practice, although a base rubric can be developed for a particular science practice and applied to different contents (McNeill et al., 2006).

Create Learning Performances. Learning performances are then developed to make explicit what students should be able to do with the targeted content knowledge (Krajcik et al., 2008). A learning performance combines both a content standard and a science practice. In the case of the chemistry example (Figure 7.5), the learning performance clarifies how science principles related to properties of substances are to be used in reasoning about scientific phenomena involving substances and their properties.

Write the Assessment Task. The next step is to design assessment tasks that ask students to apply both their content knowledge and their ability to engage in scientific explanation.

Review and Revise the Assessment Task. After creating the assessment task, three questions adapted from Project 2061's assessment framework (DeBoer, 2005; Stern & Ahlgren, 2002) are used to review the assessment tasks.

1. Is the knowledge *needed* to correctly respond to the task?
2. Is the knowledge *enough by itself* to correctly respond to the task, or is additional knowledge needed?
3. Are the assessment task and context likely to be *comprehensible* to students?

These questions help to determine whether the assessment task aligns with the desired learning goal and whether or not it will be accessible to the students.

Develop Specific Rubrics. The next step is to create a rubric for each assessment task by determining what counts as appropriate application of the science practice in the context of the question being asked. In this case, the scoring rubric is used to evaluate the appropriate use of scientific explanation (claim, evidence, and reasoning) for a question involving the properties of substances.

The approach described here can be applied to many other combinations of science content and science practice. (See McNeill and Krajcik [2008a] for an example of scientific explanations dealing with predators and prey.) In addition to providing scientific explanations of phenomena, students can also be tested on their ability to use science ideas to predict what will happen given a set of conditions, generate physical models of abstract science ideas, or use their knowledge of science ideas to design investigations.

Measuring Students' Ability to Link Ideas Together

In the third example, we describe how the TELS knowledge integration construct is used to guide item development and scoring processes. TELS researchers have developed assessment items that act as prompts for students to connect multiple science ideas together to explain scientific phenomena they encounter in the real world, which is a central component of the knowledge integration construct. By examining the scientific relevance of students' ideas and the connections they make between those ideas, different levels of integrated understanding can be identified. (See Chapter 2, Roseman, Linn, and Koppal, for a detailed discussion of the knowledge integration construct and of the notion of integrated understanding.) Student explanations are coded for the following levels of knowledge integration:

- *Level 0: No Information.* If students do not provide an answer to an item, their understanding is scored at the "no information" level.
- *Level 1: Irrelevant.* If students answer an item incorrectly, perhaps because they do not have the knowledge relevant to the item or the motivation to take the item seriously, and if they show no evidence of understanding, their level of understanding is "irrelevant." These students may provide nonsense explanations that have nothing to do with the science context being described, descriptions that reveal their lack of motivation such as "I do not like science," or confessional statements such as "I do not know."
- *Level 2: No Link.* If students appear to have made an attempt to answer an item with scientifically invalid reasons based on nonnormative ideas or links, their understanding is scored at the "no link" level.
- *Level 3: Partial Link.* If students respond to an item with at least some relevant and correct ideas but do not meaningfully connect the ideas to the task, their understanding is scored at the "partial link" level. To illustrate, consider the Spoon Item, which asks students to explain why a metal spoon just taken from a cup of hot water feels hotter than a wooden or plastic spoon. Students might say "metal is a heat conductor." Although the statement is correct, without explicitly comparing the heat conductivity of metal with that of plastic or wood, the statement does not explain why the metal spoon feels hotter than the other materials.
- *Level 4: Full Link.* If students explicitly link a set of correct and relevant ideas to the item, their understanding is scored at the "full link" level. In the case of the heat conductivity of the spoons, they would indicate first that heat conductivity is a relevant concept to consider and second that metal has the highest conductivity of the three materials.
- *Level 5: Complex Link.* If students can meaningfully link three or more normative and relevant ideas together in answering an item, their understanding is scored at the "complex link" level. For instance, on the Spoon Item a student might indicate that heat conductivity is a relevant concept, that metal is a much better heat conductor than wood or plastic, and that better heat conductors both absorb and release heat faster when they come in contact with other objects, such as a hand.

○ *Level 6: Systemic Link.* If students can systematically apply a particular science concept to multiple contexts by recognizing common features relating to the particular science concept, their understanding is scored at the "systemic link" level. For example, students at this level can consistently explain the heat conductivity concept in contexts using a variety of combinations of materials including gases, liquids, and solids. This level of knowledge integration is determined by examining student responses to a number of items that address the same science concept across different contexts.

Figure 7.6 summarizes the relationship between hypothesized levels of the knowledge integration construct and scoring of the items on the knowledge integration scale. The placements of "incorrect" and "correct" responses to multiple-choice items on the scale in Figure 7.6 are estimations. Because there are only two (dichotomous) scoring levels for multiple-choice items, we assume that students with relevant ideas would provide a correct answer to a multiple-choice item, whereas students lacking relevant knowledge (irrelevant) or understanding (no link) would provide incorrect answers. We will discuss whether the TELS assessment data support this assumption in the next section.

To obtain information about knowledge integration levels, TELS researchers use concrete contexts in which key scientific ideas are elicited to solve real-world problems or explain phenomena (Lee & Songer, 2003). Items based on abstract contexts, esoteric terminology, or simple computations are typically not used because they are less effective in eliciting what students know or providing them with opportunities to link ideas together. The TELS items also make use of tables, graphs, pictures, and models because these devices help students visualize the situation presented in the item. These strategies are expected to make items more accessible to students and to provide more complete information about their knowledge and its connection to the problem being presented.

TELS researchers use an argumentation structure to frame many of their items by asking students to choose an answer to a question and then provide a written explanation to justify their choice. To illustrate, consider the item shown in Figure 7.7A. The Spoon Item consists of a multiple-choice question and a follow-up question that asks students to explain their answer to the multiple-choice question. The stem reads, "A metal spoon, a wooden spoon, and a plastic spoon are placed in hot water. After 15 seconds which spoon will feel hottest?" The four options provided are "the metal spoon," "the plastic spoon," "the wooden spoon," and "the three spoons will feel the same." This multiple-choice question is an item released by the Trends in International Mathematics and Science Study (TIMSS, 1995) for public use. To this multiple-choice question, TELS researchers added the follow-up portion: "Explain your choice." Providing students with choices such as "metal," "wooden," and "plastic" spoons and "the three spoons will feel the same" facilitates their search for their knowledge relevant to the item.

Direction of Increasing Knowledge Integration Levels ↑

Student Characteristics	Responses to Open-Ended Items	Responses to Multiple-Choice Items
Systemic Link Students have a systemic understanding of science concepts across science contexts.	Make multiple scientifically valid links among relevant and normative ideas across different but related contexts.	
Complex Link Students have an understanding of how three or more normative and relevant ideas interact in a given science context.	Elicit three or more normative and relevant ideas and elaborate two or more scientifically valid links among the ideas.	
Full Link Students have an understanding of how two normative and relevant ideas interact in a given science context.	Elicit two normative and relevant ideas and elaborate one scientifically valid link between the two ideas.	
		Choose a correct choice.
Partial Link Students have normative and relevant ideas in a given science context.	Elicit normative and relevant ideas but cannot fully elaborate the links among them.	
		Choose an incorrect choice.
No Link Students have inadequate ideas and links in a given science context.	Elicit relevant ideas that are not nonnormative but make nonnormative links among them.	
Irrelevant Students do not access knowledge and experience relevant to a given science context.	Elicit ideas that are relevant to the science context but are non-normative. Elicit ideas that are irrelevant to the science context.	
		Do not answer the item.
No Information Students do not have any ideas on a given science context.	Do not answer the item.	

Direction of Decreasing Knowledge Integration Levels ↓

FIGURE 7.6 TELS knowledge integration construct map.

A | A metal spoon, a wooden spoon, and a plastic spoon are placed in hot water. After 15 seconds which spoon will feel hottest? — **Item Stem**

(a) The metal spoon
(b) The wooden spoon
(c) The plastic spoon
(d) The three spoons will feel the same

— **Claim: Multiple-Choice**

Explain your choice.

Metal is a much better conductor than wood or plastic so it would both gather heat quicker and exert that heat faster on to you when you touch it.

— **Explanation: Open-Ended**

B

Score	Level	Description	Examples
0	No answer	• No information is gathered about the student	• Blank
1	Irrelevant	• Mentions experience, opinion, or interest considered not relevant to the science context	• I don't know • I do not like science
2	No link	• Refers to nonscientific personal experience, opinion, or interpretation • Includes only non-normative ideas • Includes only non-normative links	• Because when a metal spoon gets hot it stays hot for a little while • The metal spoon traps heat the best and will stay hot longer • Because the metal attracts the heat • The metal has atoms that transfer heat and wood and plastic don't have many heat transfers
3	Partial link	• Mentions heat absorption ability of one material **AND** • Does not compare with the other materials • Does not consider heat absorption over time (heat transfer rate)	• Because metal absorbs heat more than wood or plastic • The metal spoon because metal heats up very much in a small amount of time
4	Full link	• Compares heat transfer rates (e.g., conductor, heat absorption rate, heat absorption over time) among three materials	• The metal gets hot the fastest • Metal transfers heat faster than plastic or wood
5	Complex link	• Compares heat transfer rates in absorbing heat from the hot water to the spoon and transferring heat from the spoon to the hand	• Metal is a much better conductor than wood or plastic so it would both gather heat quicker and exert that heat faster on to you when you touch it

FIGURE 7.7 Spoon Item: (A) Multiple-choice question (TIMSS, 1995) and follow-up explanation question; (B) Knowledge integration scoring rubric.

This strategy enhances the "outcome space" (Wilson, 2005, p. 63) of written explanations and reduces the likelihood of responses that are completely unrelated to the scenario described in the item stem. From the explanation portion of the item, it is then possible to determine how many relevant ideas students reveal and how well they connect those ideas.

ANALYZING DATA TO OBTAIN PSYCHOMETRIC PROPERTIES OF TEST ITEMS

Our discussion up to this point has focused on the development and use of individual test items to reveal what students do and do not know about particular science ideas and their ability to apply that knowledge in the solution of real-world problems. We now continue the discussion by describing how psychometric analysis can be used in item and instrument development. Although similar analyses are made in both the TELS and Project 2061 item development work, the examples discussed here are from the TELS work. The examples are used to demonstrate how some items are more useful than others in estimating students' knowledge integration abilities.

To compare how each item in a test contributes to the measurement of knowledge integration, TELS researchers conducted IRT analyses based on the Rasch partial credit model (Liu et al., 2008). IRT analyses produce various statistical outputs that allow assessment developers to inspect how each item functions compared with the other items in a test, as well as how the test functions as a whole to measure the underlying construct. This section illustrates analysis of a middle school physical science test that included 2 short-answer items, 12 multiple-choice items, and 7 explanation items. Seven of the 12 multiple-choice items were linked to the 7 explanation items. An example of an item with linked multiple-choice and explanation questions is the Spoon Item shown in Figure 7.7A. The full list of items can be found at the TELS Web site (http://www.tels center.org). Half of the test addressed heat and temperature concepts, and the other half addressed kinematics concepts such as distance, velocity, motion, and force. Three multiple-choice items and two short-answer items were selected from released standardized tests such as TIMSS and the National Assessment of Educational Progress (NAEP). The rest of the questions were designed by TELS researchers. The set of these 21 items had a Cronbach's alpha reliability coefficient of .84.

The discussion that follows focuses on the information provided in the Wright map shown in Figure 7.8. The numbers on the left side of the Wright map represent the knowledge integration scale. The higher the number, the higher the knowledge integration level. For example, students at the −1.0 level have a lower estimated knowledge integration ability than those at the 1.0 level. The left side of the Wright map also shows the knowledge integration ability distribution of all students who took the test ($N = 1,129$). Each "x" on the map

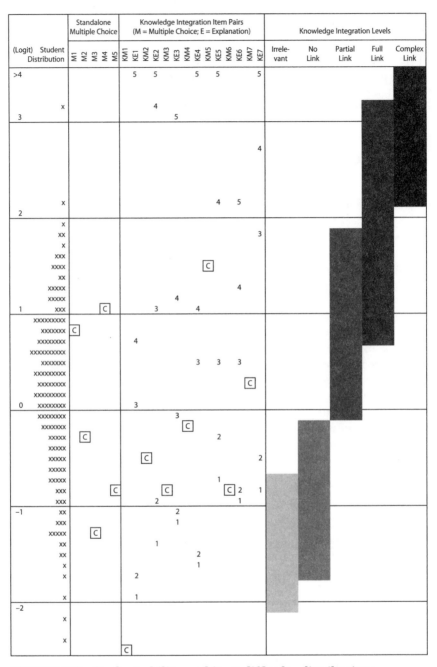

FIGURE 7.8 Student ability and item difficulty distributions on Wright map. Each "x" represents about seven students. "C" in the multiple-choice item columns refers to the correct choice. Numbers in the explanation item columns indicate "1" irrelevant, "2" no link, "3" partial link, "4" full link, and "5" complex link. N = 1,129.

represents about seven students, and their position on the scale is determined by their performance on the set of 21 questions. Most of the students fall between −1.0 and 1.0.

The distribution of students on the knowledge integration scale also can be used to show the relative difficulty of the items. Because the multiple-choice items are scored as either correct or incorrect, there is just a single difficulty location marked with a "C" for each item. The first multiple-choice item (M1) has a location "C" at 0.82, which means that students with a knowledge integration ability estimate of 0.82 will have a 50% chance of getting the M1 item correct. From its position at 0.82, we can see that the item is somewhat more difficult than some of the other items, because students with an ability estimate of 0.82, which is considerably above the average, have only a 50% chance of getting the item correct. Students with a knowledge integration ability estimate higher than 0.82 will have a greater than 50% chance of getting the M1 item correct, and those with a knowledge integration ability estimate lower than 0.82 will have a less than 50% chance of getting this item correct. In contrast to the multiple-choice items, the explanation items have five score locations on the map because they were scored on a scale of 0 to 5. A location of "1" represents the transition from getting a score of 0 to a score of 1 or higher on the knowledge integration scale; "2" represents the transition from getting a score of 1 to a score of 2 or higher; and so forth.

Figure 7.8 shows the item difficulties of the 19 items used in the TELS physical science test, plus the 2 short-answer items that were used for comparison between multiple-choice and explanation item formats. From their positions on the distribution, we can determine whether the student responses collected from the test match the conceptualization of the knowledge integration construct shown in Figure 7.6. Results show that although the locations "1" and "2" are very close to each other for most explanation items and could probably be represented as a single level, the locations for all of the items on the map match the order of increasing levels of knowledge integration ability.

To further illustrate the knowledge integration spectrum, the bars on the right side of the Wright map diagram represent the range of ability estimates for the entire set of 21 items. See, for example, that the range of ability estimates for students who were scored at level "3" is from −0.03 (KE3) to 1.84 (KE7), and that this is represented as the "partial link" bar in the right column. The diagram also shows that there is a distinct ordering of the levels, which matches the initial conceptualization of the knowledge integration construct shown in Figure 7.6.

From the Wright map analysis, it is also possible to obtain information about how each item contributes to the measure of the knowledge integration construct. First, it can be seen that for the most part, the multiple-choice items do not effectively estimate high levels of knowledge integration at the full and complex link levels. (Note the positions of the "C"s for each multiple-choice item on the Wright map.) For multiple-choice items to be located at the higher levels on the map, they would have to require students to draw upon a set of ideas in the solution of a problem (or, at least, scores on those items would have to be correlated with the ability to make such connections). Nor do the multiple-choice items match well where students fall on the knowledge integration scale as measured by the corresponding explanation items. For example, although 92.5% of the students answered the multiple-choice Spoon Item *correctly*, suggesting that they understood the science content, when their written explanations for the Spoon Item were analyzed using the scoring rubric shown in Figure 7.7B, 39.9% of those students could not adequately explain their multiple-choice answer and were placed in the no link level or below on the knowledge integration scale (see Figure 7.9A).

Of the 85 students who answered *incorrectly* on the multiple-choice question, the match between student answers on the multiple-choice and explanation questions is much better. Here, 82 of the 85 students (96.5%) who answered the multiple-choice question incorrectly are also placed in the lowest levels of the knowledge integration scale based on their answer to the explanation question (see Figure 7.9A). These students chose the incorrect answer (or left it blank) on the multiple-choice question and also showed a lack of knowledge in their written explanations. This demonstrates that this item is more useful as an indicator of what students do not know than of what they do know.

Although the Spoon Item context is often used in research on heat conductivity (Clough & Driver, 1985; Erickson, 1979; Harrison, Grayson, & Treagust, 1999), the multiple-choice portion of this item did not prove to be useful for differentiating better from worse understanding of heat conductivity. As shown on the Wright map (item KM1, Figure 7.8) and in Figure 7.9B, even students whose ability estimate is at the extreme low end of the knowledge integration scale (as determined by the full set of questions) still have a better than 50% chance of getting this multiple-choice question correct. Although some of the students who answered correctly may have an understanding of the targeted idea, many do not. This suggests that this particular item has limited usefulness on an instrument that measures knowledge integration. The reason so many students got this item correct without understanding the science concept involved is probably because many students know from experience that when a metal spoon is used to stir a liquid it feels hotter to the touch than a spoon made of plastic or wood, without knowing why that is true. When there is a mismatch between the multiple-choice portion of an item and the explanation portion of an item, the item can be examined to find out why the mismatch occurred. As was discussed in the first part of this chapter, there are a variety of reasons why multiple-choice items may yield false negative or false positive responses, but there are also ways to correct many of those problems.

Other multiple-choice items in the TELS instrument produced results that more closely matched what was learned from the explanation items. The multiple-

A What knowledge integration levels are represented in correct and incorrect responses to the multiple-choice question?

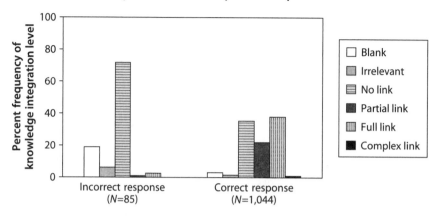

B Does high knowledge integration lead to a correct response to the multiple-choice question?

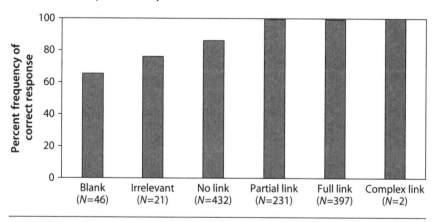

FIGURE 7.9 Spoon Item: Effectiveness of the multiple-choice question as an indicator of knowledge integration.

choice item KM5, for example, was a difficult one for students, and the results closely matched what was learned from the explanation portion of the question, KE5. In the multiple-choice part of the question students were given a choice of three graphical representations of a situation involving rates of motion. To answer correctly, students had to understand the concept of rate and how to

TABLE 7.1   Percent Frequency Distribution of Knowledge Integration Levels Assessed with Explanations*

Level	KE1	KE2	KE3	KE4	KE5	KE6	KE7
Complex Link	0.2		2.8	1.4	0.4	5.5	0.3
Full Link	35.2	2.3	19.7	21.0	7.5	11.3	2.04
Partial Link	20.5	25.8	33.6	16.9	32.3	23.7	10.4
No Link	38.3	54.3	29.9	50.5	27.4	40.7	59.6
Irrelevant	1.9	6.3	2.9	2.6	10.2	4.1	7.3
Blank	4.1	11.3	11.2	7.6	22.1	14.9	20.5

* KE1–KE7 are the explanation items in the TELS physical science test summarized in the Wright map in Figure 7.8. $N = 1,129$ students.

represent it graphically. Students who answered this item correctly scored between "3" and "4" on the knowledge integration scale based on their answer to the explanation portion of the question, indicating that a fairly sophisticated understanding of the idea being tested was needed in order to get the multiple-choice item correct.

Wright maps also can be used to indicate whether individual items provide the opportunity for students to demonstrate their proficiency along the continuum of the construct being measured. For this set of items, estimates of a student's knowledge integration ability tend to fall in the middle and lower ranges (irrelevant, no link, partial link), with a smaller number of students in the upper range (full link, complex link). For item KE2, for example, which tests students on the difference between heat and temperature, a very small percentage of students scored at the full link level and no students at the complex link level of knowledge integration, making this explanation item a difficult one on which students could demonstrate an integrated understanding, compared with some of the other items. (See Table 7.1 for the percentage of students at each knowledge integration level for each explanation item in the TELS physical science test.)

For an item to elicit the higher levels of knowledge integration, the item must describe a situation that is complex enough to make use of multiple ideas. When an item does not elicit the desired level of knowledge integration compared with what other items elicit, the item can be eliminated or modified. Of course, failure of students to score at a high level probably also indicates that the students had not achieved the goal of knowledge integration, which points to how important it is to develop and implement curriculum and instruction materials that can help students develop a more integrated understanding of science.

USING ASSESSMENT RESULTS TO MODIFY CURRICULUM MATERIALS

In this section we describe how assessment is used at TELS and CCMS to inform the revision of curriculum materials. First we show how TELS researchers use assessment results to modify their online modules, and then how researchers at CCMS use assessment results to make modifications in the IQWST units. Descriptions of the design principles that led to the development of these materials and the learning environments in which they are used appear in Chapter 3 and Chapter 8 (Kali, Fortus, & Ronen-Fuhrmann).

TELS Curriculum Modification Examples

TELS modules focus on particular content that teachers had identified as being difficult for students to learn with typical instructional methods (Chapters 2 and 3). Using the design principles described in Chapter 8, instructional modules were developed to support student learning of this science content. The modules went through a number of development, implementation, assessment, and revision cycles. Changes to the TELS modules were made following a review of the assessment data, observations of student use of the modules, and teacher input regarding their first-hand experience with the modules' effectiveness (for more details about the TELS review process, see Chapter 2). The effectiveness of each TELS module was examined based on the results of tests administered before and after implementation of the module. The test items were designed following knowledge integration design patterns (Linn & Eylon, 2006) and design principles (Kali, 2006) and were scored according to the knowledge integration construct map (Lee, Liu, & Linn, 2008) shown in Figure 7.6.

For instance, in the TELS "Airbags" module (see detailed description in Chapter 3), students learn about graphical representations and interpretations of velocity, force, and acceleration concepts in an airbag deployment situation. Based on the assessment results of the first version of the "Airbags" module, two modifications were made (McElhaney, 2007a). First, the pretest and posttest results for the original version of the module indicated that these mechanical concepts were too easy for most grade 11 and 12 students. Based on this observation, the "Airbags" module was revised to increase content complexity, for example, by adding velocity–time graphs to the position–time graphs that were already in the module. These additions were made both to the simulation activities in the module and to the embedded assessments. Second, analyses of pretest and posttest data, and the logging of data collected during students' simulation experiments in the original module, demonstrated a significant positive relationship between students' sophistication with simulation experimentation strategies and their posttest achievement. Based on this finding, steps were added to scaffold student reflection on the activities.

Another example is the "Recycling" module, in which students learn about different types of chemical bonds (e.g., covalent, ionic, metallic, and van der Waals interactions) present in the materials of real-world objects. After the first run of the "Recycling" module, students demonstrated difficulties distinguishing among different types of bonds. As a result, in the revised "Recycling" module, reflection prompts were modified to elicit more connections and contrasts between materials with these different types of bonds so that students could better link the microscopic-level visualizations to their macroscopic-level observations (McElhaney, 2007b).

The "Asthma" module described in Chapter 4 includes physiological explanations of breathing, asthma attacks, and asthma as an allergic immune response. Results of pretests and posttests indicated that students had improved their understanding of the physiology of asthma related to breathing processes and asthma attack mechanisms after completing the module (Tate, 2007). However, it was also observed that only a few students wrote explanations that meaningfully connected the various components of the allergic immune system. For example, most students described the allergic immune response as an isolated irritant response rather than a physiologically triggered chain reaction. This finding indicated that the original version of the "Asthma" module did not adequately support students in distinguishing between allergens and other irritants in terms of their effects on the body and its immune system. In the next stage of development, the design team modified the module to focus more on that distinction. An ensuing evaluation suggested that the modified module improved students' ability to develop criteria for distinguishing the physiological effects of allergens to a greater degree than did the original module.

CCMS Curriculum Modification Examples

At CCMS, a similar approach is taken in the modification of curriculum units. CCMS researchers working on the development of the IQWST materials use a multi-stage process of enactment and revision (Krajcik et al., 2008). In the example that follows, we illustrate the modifications that were made between the first and second enactments of an IQWST chemistry unit dealing with chemical reactions (see Chapter 3). After the first enactment of the unit, it was observed that students did not make the same pretest to posttest gains on the chemical reactions learning goal that they had made on an earlier learning goal on substances and their properties. It was also observed that students did not gain as much as expected in their use of the claim-evidence-reasoning form of scientific explanation. For example, although students knew that a chemical reaction had occurred when new substances had different properties relative to the old substances, their reasoning lacked precision and rarely used an underlying scientific principle to explain why the evidence supported their claims. For example, a typical student's reasoning stated, "This evidence supports that a chemical reaction occurred because you can follow the evidence and determine that it changed" (Harris et al., 2006).

The learning goals–driven design model described in Chapter 3 relies on unpacking learning goals into their constituent aspects so that instruction can support each one of them. Unpacking the learning goals also allows assessment to be more precise. The feedback obtained by the researchers revealed that important aspects of the targeted claim-evidence-reasoning science practice had not been made clear to teachers or to students. To address this issue, IQWST researchers revised the learning performances to state more explicitly what they wanted students to include in their scientific explanations. They also added a lesson in which teachers introduced the idea of scientific explanations to the students and provided a rationale for using that form of explanation (McNeill & Krajcik, 2008b). In addition, the researchers developed written materials to support students' learning of each of the components (McNeill et al., 2006).

IQWST researchers also found that students were not clear about the difference between chemical reactions and dissolving. When asked, "Which change will produce a new substance?" the majority of students responded that dissolving lemonade powder in water would produce a new substance. Another item presented a situation in which a clear liquid, a white powder, and a red powder were mixed together, and asked students to "describe three pieces of evidence you would look for to determine if a chemical reaction occurred." Here again students wrote that "powder dissolving" would be evidence for a chemical reaction. This idea was actually held by more students after instruction than before (67.4% vs. 55.1%).

The first step the IQWST researchers took in addressing this misconception was to clarify the learning goal by including an expectation that students would know both what did and what did not count as a chemical reaction (by providing both examples and counterexamples), especially the idea that phase change and dissolving were not chemical reactions. They also added a lesson to the unit specifically focused on creating mixtures and comparing the properties before and after to determine if a new substance had been made, and they provided opportunities for students to analyze particle models of chemical reactions, phase changes, and mixtures and to discuss the similarities and differences between these processes. The lessons the researchers learned about the importance of providing counterexamples were then applied more generally to the clarification of other content standards.

After the second enactment of the chemistry unit, the learning gains were considerably larger than after the first enactment, both for the chemistry content and for the use of the claim-evidence-reasoning model of scientific explanation. Regarding the specific problem students had with dissolving as an example of a chemical reaction, in the second enactment the percentage of students who thought that dissolving lemonade was an example of a chemical reaction dropped from 47.4% to 39.0%. This was an improvement over the first enactment, and probably attributable in part to adding the lesson on mixtures, but it demonstrated that the concept continued to be difficult for students to grasp. Thus, in the next round of revision, this section of the curriculum materials will be revised again to further address the area of concern. During each cycle of revision, assessment results inform the researchers' understanding of the strengths and challenges of the materials and guide them in making the materials more successful in classrooms with teachers and students.

SUMMARY AND CONCLUSIONS

In this chapter we defined three types of learning outcomes that are related to the development of an integrated understanding of science. We also demonstrated how qualitative and quantitative approaches can be used to make judgments about item validity, and we gave examples of how CCMS and TELS use assessment in improving curriculum materials. We also showed the limitations of commonly used multiple-choice items in measuring high levels of knowledge integration and how those items can be improved.

Assessment plays an important role in promoting consistency throughout the science education system by offering clear expectations to all participants and by providing feedback on how well those expectations are being met. For assessment to serve these functions well, the design of assessment instruments, as well as the collection, analysis, and interpretation of assessment data, should be aligned with well-articulated and justifiable learning goals. Furthermore, assessment should be aligned with the same learning goals that the curriculum is organized to teach, so that the entire system can function together to achieve the same goal.

For assessment to contribute to the integrated understanding of science envisioned in this volume, assessment developers need to be aware of the limitations of many of the assessment items currently in use and prepared to construct more effective and informative items and tests. The following design principles emerge from a synthesis of the assessment work of the two centers.

Design Principles

First, assessment development should begin with a clear statement of what students are expected to know and be able to do. These expectations should be written in terms of specific knowledge and skills students should have, but they should also be consistent with broader learning goals, such as linking multiple ideas together, connecting science content to science practices, or developing mental models of abstract ideas that will allow students to predict and explain events in the world.

Second, the validity of assessments should be examined both qualitatively and quantitatively to take advantage of the strengths of both approaches and to ensure that assessments are measuring what they are supposed to measure. Quantitative analyses are useful for demonstrating what each item adds to a set of items designed to measure a construct, the comparative difficulty of items, how well items discriminate among students along an ability continuum, and whether or not items function similarly for different subpopulations. However, although quantitative data can point to areas of potential concern, qualitative analysis is needed to pinpoint the nature of the problems that need to be resolved. Qualitative review of items is particularly useful for determining alignment of items with the learning goals, threats to validity due to poor item construction, and appropriateness of task contexts for students from different subgroups. Together, qualitative and quantitative analyses provide powerful tools for the development and evaluation of assessment items and instruments.

Finally, it is clear from the work of TELS and CCMS that data from high-quality assessments can be used to improve the quality of curriculum materials and classroom instruction by determining at various times during instruction what students are thinking and then using that information to modify instruction (Casperson & Linn, 2006; Krajcik et al., 2008).

Policy Implications

A number of policy implications emerge from the assessment work of TELS and CCMS. First, for assessment to be a positive force in science education, especially given the extent to which assessments are used as part of high-stakes accountability, learning goals at the local, state, and national levels need to present a coherent account of the natural world, and they need to be well integrated from grade band to grade band and across related topics at the same grade band. Otherwise assessment, and also instruction, will be based on fragmented and disconnected sets of ideas. The learning goals should form a logically consistent whole, and each idea should build one upon another. For these learning goals to be useful as guides to instruction and assessment, they should also be elaborated so that it is clear what the expectations are for students and what boundaries exist at each grade band. This is consistent with the recommendation of the Commission on Instructionally Supportive Assessment (2001): "A state's high priority content standards must be clearly and thoroughly described so that the knowledge and skills students need to demonstrate competence are evident." These descriptions "should result in relatively brief, educator-friendly descriptions of each high priority standard's meaning" (McColskey & McMunn, 2002, p. 5).

Second, school administrators at all levels, key personnel in funding agencies, education policy makers, and the general public should be aware of the limitations of the assessment instruments currently being used in standardized testing. Most people who make decisions about assessments and use results from the assessments may not be aware of how poorly existing assessments in science measure what students know. This is because most of the users of science assessments do not have the detailed knowledge of science content, the familiarity with research on student learning, or the expertise in item construction needed to make informed judgments about assessments in science.

Finally, given the current lack of high-quality assessment instruments in science, increased funding is necessary for facilitating the development and implementation of more cognitively sensitive and meaningful assessments that can assist teaching and learning at the classroom level and that can be used to conduct high-quality educational research. There is currently a lack of research tools to effectively measure learning outcomes, and without these tools, little progress can be made.

PART III

Synthesis
and
Policy Implications

Synthesizing Design Knowledge

Yael Kali, David Fortus, and
Tamar Ronen-Fuhrmann

THIS CHAPTER PULLS TOGETHER the design principles identified throughout the book. As discussed in the Preface (Kali, Koppal, Linn, & Roseman), design principles are rules of thumb and guidelines for designers. As illustrated in other chapters, design principles support conversations about design decisions. This volume features design principles as well as other forms of synthesis of design knowledge, including more general guiding principles and textbook criteria (see Chapter 2, Roseman, Linn, & Koppal), that impact the design of science curriculum materials to foster students' integrated understanding.

Focusing on a coherent set of important science ideas and thinking through the kinds of connections that must be made explicit and sensible to students are essential first steps. However, as discussed in Chapter 2, addressing only these two concerns is not sufficient to help students achieve the knowledge integration needed for lifelong science learning. Other considerations—such as how to design learning environments to make them relevant and interesting (Chapter 3, Krajcik, Slotta, McNeill, & Reiser), how to address the needs of diverse learners (Chapter 4, Tate, Clark, Gallagher, & McLaughlin), how to support teachers (Chapter 5, Davis & Varma) and principals (Chapter 6, Bowyer, Gerard, & Marx) in adopting and adapting these environments, and finally, how to use assessment so that it supports learning (Chapter 7, DeBoer, Lee, & Husic)—must also be factored in when designing science curricula.

Several researchers have developed guidelines in the form of design principles or design patterns to translate research findings (such as those described in the preceding chapters) into pragmatic design strategies that can assist curriculum designers and developers in this complex process (Fortus, Dershimer, Krajcik, Marx, & Mamlok-Naaman, 2004; Herrington, 2006; Kali, 2006; Kali & Linn, 2007; Linn, Bell, & Davis, 2004; Linn & Eylon, 2006; McNeill et al., 2006; Merrill, 2002; Mor & Winters, 2007; Quintana et al., 2004; Reiser, Krajcik, Moje, & Marx, 2003; Retalis, Georgiakakis, & Dimitriadis, 2006; van den Akker, 1999).

In this chapter we draw from ideas and examples presented in the earlier chapters to describe seven design principles that are representative of the design knowledge gathered by the Delineating and Evaluating Coherent Instructional Designs for Education (DECIDE) project about ways in which coherent curriculum materials and integrated understanding can be promoted. These design principles cut across many of the chapters and are common to both of our centers (TELS and CCMS). We conclude by discussing how these design principles can be used by expert and novice curriculum designers, teachers, and administrators.

FORMULATING DESIGN PRINCIPLES

As described in Part II, TELS and CCMS have developed different approaches for designing curricula and have gained, by extensive research and practice, a considerable body of design knowledge, some of which is unique to one center or the other and some of which is common to both centers. In this section, we synthesize some of this knowledge by identifying commonalities and negotiating terms and assumptions. The value of such negotiation is to overcome communication issues that arise from the existence of "intra-center jargons" in which a great deal of design knowledge is implicitly embedded. These intra-center jargons are useful to each center and facilitate communication regarding the development of coherent materials and research, but they can impede others' access to this design knowledge. By negotiating both centers' design knowledge, we sought to become more aware of intra-center knowledge and to create a more explicit and communicative body of design knowledge. We chose to use design principles as the unit of synthesis in this chapter, and to use the Design Principles Database (http://www.edu-design-principles.org; Kali, 2006) as a means for making this knowledge public and accessible.

The Design Principles Database was developed to collect and synthesize emerging design knowledge about curricular innovations and their effect on learning (Kali, 2006, 2008; Kali & Linn, 2007). The structure of the database, as well as the preliminary set of design principles, was based on the Scaffolded Knowledge Integration framework (Linn, Bell, & Davis, 2004; Linn & Hsi, 2000). The database includes principles contributed by curriculum developers, researchers, and workshop and course participants. It is a collaborative knowledge-building tool for communities who design and explore curricular innovations (Kali, 2006). In relation to this chapter, the Design Principles Database serves not only as a means for making public the findings of the current synthesis but also as a vehicle for connecting the findings reported in this volume with findings that have already been described and formalized as design principles by other researchers.

To synthesize the seven design principles described in this chapter, we first identified design knowledge (such as curricular elements or tools that were designed to address a specific challenge) that was common to several chapters in this book. We then articulated these elements in the form of *features,* as applied in the Design Principles Database (where *feature* is defined as "any effort to use technology to advance learning" [http://www.edu-design-principles.org/dp/aboutDPD.php]). Next we connected these features either to principles that have already been described in the database or to new principles, which we formulated based on the rationales described in the chapters. In all of the cases in which features were connected to principles already existing in the database, we refined the principles so that they would integrate new ideas contributed by the newly connected features. Finally, we invited the chapter authors to review and revise the features and principles enunciated based on their work. (All of the principles described in this chapter and many others, along with descriptions of connected features and additional information, can be found in the Design Principles Database: http://www.edu-design-principles.org.)

SYNTHESIZED DESIGN PRINCIPLES

Seven common design principles were articulated or refined. In the sections that follow, we describe these common principles and provide two examples for each, one from TELS and one from CCMS, that show how they are employed. To illustrate the scope as well as the limits of the design principles, we sought to choose examples that would demonstrate features that are different in their nature. For instance, to illustrate a design principle, one feature might be text-based and the other technology-based, one feature might address teachers as audience and the other students, and so forth. Table 8.1 summarizes the design principles and example features that will be discussed.

Design Principle I:
Connect to Personally Relevant Contexts

Too often, students find academic science lacking in personal relevance. This sense of irrelevance leads to lack of personal interest and low engagement levels (Duschl et al., 2007). Personally relevant problems drawn from students' everyday lives, such as determining how to keep a drink cold or how to minimize the potential radiation danger associated with cellular phone use, can make science accessible and authentic. Such problems can elicit intuitive ideas to fuel inquiry

TABLE 8.1 DECIDE Project Design Principles and Example Features

Design Principle	Example Feature (TELS)	Example Feature (CCMS)
I. Connect to personally relevant contexts	Contextualized definitions in "Hanging with Friends—Velocity Style!"	Using the nature of smell to provide evidence of particles
II. Scaffold the process of generating explanations	Principle Maker	Claim-evidence-reasoning framework
III. Enable just-in-time guidance	Amanda the Panda hint provider	Prompts for reflection-on-action
IV. Provide teachers with supports for adaptation	WISE authoring environment	Alternative curricular paths
V. Engage learners in complex science problems	Introducing the topic of respiration in the context of asthma in the students' community	Introducing physical and chemical changes in the context of making soap
VI. Embed assessment-for-learning within instruction	Providing immediate feedback via the Teacher Manager tool	Guidance for real-time assessment
VII. Promote productive interactions	Engaging principals in multiple levels of interaction	Guiding whole-class discussions

(Fortus, Dershimer, Krajcik, Marx, & Mamlok-Naaman, 2004; Linn & Hsi, 2000; Songer & Linn, 1991) because students have had prior experiences related to the problem scenarios. Linn, Davis, and Bell (2004) show that eliciting the broad range of student ideas about science and supporting students to negotiate and explore these ideas enables them to build more coherent, durable scientific knowledge. The "Connect to personally relevant contexts" principle is described in several chapters of this book, and it is viewed by DECIDE members as one of the most important design principles. Chapter 3 states one aspect of the principle as "Contextualize the learning of key ideas in real-world problems." The chapter focuses on the role of driving questions to anchor instruction in a way that engages learners in the science content, defining a driving question as "an open-ended question that connects with authentic interests and curiosities all students have about the world" (p. 48). Chapter 4 focuses on developing "connections to students' communities, interests, and prior knowledge"—another aspect of this principle, which is especially important when diverse students are involved. The chapter shows how this aspect of the principle is realized in the TELS "Asthma" unit. Designing curriculum materials that use relevant contexts in a nonartificial way is not easy. To illustrate how this can be done, we refer to two additional examples.

Example: Contextualized Definitions in "Hanging with Friends, Velocity Style!" The TELS unit "Hanging with Friends, Velocity Style!" (Tate, 2005) embeds scientific terms in the context of an interview with a teenager. Students' purpose in the interview is to find the teenager's velocity as she traveled from Lake Park to the movie theatre to meet friends. The interviewee speaks in everyday language while communicating the information needed to determine her velocity, saying, "I was running a bit late and almost didn't get a seat. I arrived at the Movie Theatre at 5:05 pm. This is referred to as my *final time*." The discourse blends familiar language and events (being late to a movie) with scientific terminology and the data needed to determine velocity. By bringing a common information-gathering technique (a conversation or interview) into play, the feature draws students into the activity and helps them place it in a familiar context. The real-world relevance is heightened as students compute the velocity of each friend to see if all will arrive in time. The feature motivates students to understand the specific terms and data needed to compute velocity for an everyday event.

Example: Using the Nature of Smell to Provide Evidence of Particles. Almost everyone has had the experience of smelling something good while it is cooking on the stove even though they are not standing near the stove. What is smell and how can you smell a substance across a room? Something that your nose can identify must be coming from the stove and traveling across the room to you. What is it that comes from the stove and how does it move? The sixth-grade CCMS "Investigating and Questioning Our World Through Science and Technology" (IQWST) chemistry unit uses the nature of smell, around which the entire unit is organized, to discuss the particle nature of matter, particle motion, phase change, and scientific modeling.

Design Principle II:
Scaffold the Process of Generating Explanations

Students often view science as knowing the "right" answers—something only "smart" kids can do. This is because science education has often been reduced to rote memorization rather than approached as a process of making sense of situations (Duschl et al., 2007). Generating explanations, raising conjectures, and asking questions are the essence of scientific sense making and are basic processes that identify and reinforce connections that are critical for an integrated

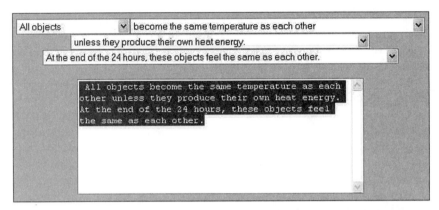

FIGURE 8.1 Example feature for Design Principle II: Scaffold the Process of Generating Explanations. The Principle Maker tool supports students in constructing principles that summarize their understanding of science content. Illustrated here is the TELS "Thermodynamics: Probing Your Surroundings" project.

understanding of science. Chapter 3 identifies "constructing scientific explanations and arguments" as one of six scientific practices that should be considered when designing curricula in science. One approach to supporting this practice that is advocated in Chapter 3 involves breaking it down into three components based on Toulmin's (1958) model: (a) *claim:* a testable statement about some state of the world, (b) *evidence:* data or information that supports the claim, and (c) *reasoning:* justification that employs scientific principles to describe why the evidence provided supports the claim (McNeill et al., 2006; Moje et al., 2004). Such scaffolding can enrich the explanations considered by learners and help groups of learners develop shared criteria and standards for their explanations (McNeill et al., 2006). The examples below focus on scaffolds that elicit learners' explanations and seek to expose a large variety of views held by learners to stimulate discussion. The second example employs the claim-evidence-reasoning framework.

Example: Principle Maker. The "Principle Maker" tool is used in the TELS "Thermodynamics: Probing Your Surroundings" project (Clark & Sampson, 2007) to support students in expressing general principles that summarize their understanding of collected data and simulations from previous stages in the project. Students use a series of pull-down menus—each providing a list of predefined phrases—to construct a principle (Figure 8.1). These phrases represent components of explanations students typically employ to describe heat flow and thermal equilibrium, as identified through the conceptual change literature.

Research conducted by Clark and Sampson suggests that scaffolding students in the creation of principles helps them make their ideas explicit. By taking advantage of the principles students have built, discussions can be set up among groups of students with opposing ideas—a process that promotes dialogical argumentation, according to Clark and Sampson. By making thinking visible, the Principle Maker enables a more sophisticated form of argumentation than is found in typical science classrooms. As a result, students have a good sense of the views of their peers and can spend their time evaluating, supporting, and critiquing ideas.

Example: Claim-Evidence-Reasoning Framework. The CCMS IQWST curriculum supports students in constructing scientific explanations through two strategies. The first strategy involves giving students formal instruction in the claim-evidence-reasoning framework to prepare them for constructing explanations of their own. The second strategy focuses on the characteristics of claims, evidence, and reasoning as students construct and evaluate explanations in terms of each of these components (e.g., asking themselves, Is this evidence sufficient?). In addition, argumentation is used as a context for motivating students to engage in constructing, critiquing, and arguing about scientific explanations, thereby helping them experience a need for explanations and the components therein. Explanations are introduced in sixth grade with an emphasis on evidence. In seventh grade, the focus is on the characteristics of reasoning. Students work through what makes a good scientific principle, and develop an understanding that their explanations must both state the principle and connect that principle to their evidence and claim. In eighth grade, the students' explanations become increasingly complex, and the curriculum places greater focus on alternative and competing explanations.

Design Principle III:
Enable Just-in-Time Guidance

Many learning environments either burden learners with too much information at the beginning of a learning process (when they are still not fully oriented or engaged) or do not provide sufficient guidance when it is needed. The design principle "Enable just-in-time guidance" calls for situating and organizing guidance so that students and teachers are able to access it when they need it. Guidance is best provided when learners know where to find it at any time but are not required to use it when it is not needed (a "pull" instead of a "push" process). Guidance in the form of instructions, tips, hints, metacognitive prompts (Davis, 2006a), links to information, as well as discussions with mentors or peers, can contribute to the development of integrated understanding. Chapter 5 refers to one aspect of this principle, involving teachers, as "Guidance on demand," and states that "new teachers should be allowed the opportunity to request contextualized guidance

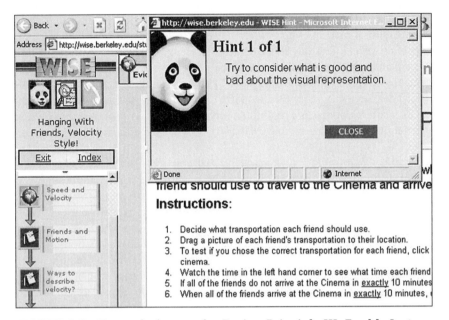

FIGURE 8.2   Example feature for Design Principle III: Enable Just-in-Time Guidance. The Amanda the Panda Hint Provider provides on-demand support in the WISE environment. Illustrated here is the TELS "Hanging with Friends, Velocity Style!" project.

when they need it" (p. 102). The chapter shows how educative hints in CASES (Curriculum Access System for Elementary Science) provide teachers with ideas, for example, about how to enact instructional recommendations. The examples that follow show how this design principle is used to support two audiences: students in the first case, and teachers in the second.

Example: Amanda the Panda Hint Provider.   One of the features in the Web-Based Inquiry Science Environment (WISE) is "Amanda the Panda," an electronic tool for providing students with hints at any stage of a project. The designer or teacher who wishes to adapt a TELS project can insert information or suggestions that might assist students in developing a more integrated understanding at a specific step in the learning process. After the hint has been inserted, Amanda the Panda becomes available to deliver it (Figure 8.2). As students work on the project, they can decide whether they want to "pull" the information or continue without it. Further, they always have the option of going back to steps they have already completed and using Amanda the Panda even if they skipped the use of hints earlier.

Example: Prompts for Reflection-on-Action. CASES (Davis, 2006b) is an online learning environment employed in CCMS curriculum materials to support preservice and inservice elementary and middle school science teachers (see Chapter 5). An important feature in the CASES environment is called "Prompts for Reflection." These prompts appear as sentence starters or questions listed on the left side of the teacher's online journal tool. Building on Loughran and Gunstone's (1997) notion of anticipatory and retrospective reflection, two to six prompts are listed under each of three different categories: (a) thinking about today, (b) planning ahead, and (c) general thoughts. For example, a teacher can select a prompt "How will I know if my objectives are met?" under the category "planning ahead." This prompt appears in her journal, and she can begin thinking and writing about the question.

Design Principle IV:
Provide Teachers with Supports for Adaptation

As described in Chapter 5, curriculum designers cannot predict the actual conditions in which their curricula will be enacted. Class size, students' cultural background, language skills, reading capabilities, prior knowledge and experiences, and access to resources are just a few of the many parameters that influence the way a curriculum can and should be implemented. To maximize the effectiveness of curriculum materials, teachers need to adapt them so that they will meet local requirements and foster knowledge integration among learners. We distinguish between changes to curriculum materials that are made *prior to* instruction and those that are made *during* instruction. Some authors refer to the first type of change as customization (Slotta, 2004; Spitulnik & Linn, 2007), and other authors refer to the second type as adaptation (Remillard, 1999). Following the definition used in Chapter 5, we use the term *adaptation* to refer to all changes made by teachers to curriculum materials. Designers can support teachers in making adaptations by offering multiple paths in the curriculum that teachers can choose from, using feedback from embedded assessments as their guide.

However, adaptation can lead to lethal mutations that may make the curriculum unable to support the original learning goals (Brown & Campione, 1996) or cause it to lack coherence (Chapter 2). To guard against such undesirable consequences, designers should make their design rationales clear and visible to teachers, as we discuss in the final section of this chapter. Technology can support beneficial changes by offering tools and references for adaptation. Another way to support adaptation is by designing learning materials in such a way that they play the dual roles of supporting both students and teachers. Davis and Krajcik (2005) describe such materials as having "educative curriculum features" (see Chapters 3 and 5). The role of educative curriculum materials is discussed also in Chapter 4, in the context of assisting teachers in supporting diverse learners. To illustrate this design principle, we provide two examples of supporting adaptation, one designed for making changes prior to instruction and the other for making changes during instruction.

Example: WISE Authoring Environment. The WISE authoring environment, or "Project Manager," is a complete environment for designing and publishing curricula in WISE. A designer can create new project steps, access WISE curricular tools, and link to evidence and content available on the Internet (Slotta, 2004). There is evidence that a technology-enhanced curriculum can scaffold student learning as well as introduce constructivist reform pedagogy into a teacher's classroom (Linn & Hsi, 2000). However, a curriculum designed for implementation across a diverse range of teachers and students is often limited in its ability to address local content issues and student learning needs. Project Manager allows teachers and curriculum designers to customize existing WISE projects to local conditions, as well as create original projects.

Example: Alternative Curricular Paths. Although the designers of a curriculum cannot foresee exactly how it will be enacted, they can, based on research, predict situations that may arise during enactment. In these cases, the designers can suggest alternative paths the teacher can take, according to the particular circumstances of the enactment. For example, the IQWST "Seeing the Light" unit uses diffraction gratings rather than prisms to separate light into its color components. However, it is entirely possible that some students may be familiar with prisms and ask why they are not being used. The unit offers teachers several ways of dealing with this situation, describing the advantages and disadvantages of each, and providing guidance for choosing between options. For example, a teacher may decide to include an activity with prisms, provide a reading on prisms to those students who had prior knowledge of them, provide the same reading to the entire class, or make a few comments about prisms and continue with the diffraction grating activity. Such guidance can be provided via educative elements within the curriculum materials.

Design Principle V:
Engage Learners in Complex Science Problems

Too often, inquiry-based learning environments introduce science ideas as isolated and oversimplified topics. In many cases, these topics are disconnected from one another, leading to the construction of superficial knowledge that lacks integration. When students are introduced to real-world science problems, they have the opportunity to struggle with the complexity of science and to engage in scientific debates. In this manner, students can make connections between various ideas of central topics in science, develop integrated understanding, and become prepared for future learning.

The complex science problems principle is elaborated primarily in Chapter 2. Chapter 3 focuses in particular on the role scientific practices play in (a) sustaining engagement in complex projects, (b) making connections between different ideas, and (c) combining large and small questions. Participating in scientific practices highlights the importance of knowledge in use. Examples of engaging students in complex science problems are also found in Chapter 4, which shows how the social aspects of science add a layer of complexity and can help engage a diversity of learners. In this section we illustrate application of the complex science problems design principle with two examples described in previous chapters. The first example comes from the "Improving Your Community's Asthma Problem" TELS module. In Chapter 4, this module is described to illustrate how curricula can be designed to connect to personally relevant contexts (Design Principle I). Here, we illustrate how it also realizes the "Engage learners in complex science problems" design principle. The second example comes from the "How Can I Make New Stuff from Old Stuff?" unit of IQWST. In Chapter 3, this unit is used to exemplify how teachers are supported in making adaptations (Design Principle IV), and how students are supported in generating scientific explanations (Design Principle II). Here we use the "Stuff" unit to exemplify how complex science problems can foster an integrated understanding of science. The added value of having a feature employ more than one design principle is discussed in the final section of this chapter.

Example: Introducing the Topic of Respiration in the Context of Asthma in the Students' Community. The "Asthma" module is a TELS high school biology unit that deals with the respiratory, circulatory, and immune systems. To introduce this science content in a real-life context, the unit provides students the opportunity to investigate the systems through an exploration of asthma. The unit assists students in recognizing the asthma epidemic and similar problems as complex, multifactorial science problems relevant to their personal lives. Also, it supports students in understanding that this complexity allows for multiple solutions, as they consider the tradeoffs in pursuing environmental and medical solutions. The topic of asthma was chosen, in addition, to provide a context for students to learn about the relationship between science and social justice issues. A more detailed description of the unit can be found in Chapter 4.

Example: Introducing Physical and Chemical Change in the Context of Making Soap. "How Can I Make New Stuff from Old Stuff?" is a 7-week CCMS unit designed for seventh-grade students that focuses on making new substances from old substances, beginning with making soap from fat (lard) and sodium hydroxide. The nature of chemical reactions is instrumental to understanding and answering the driving question, which is the unit's title. Students complete a number of investigations, each successive one more elaborate and complex, each time cycling back to soap and fat. Each cycle helps the students delve deeper into the science content to develop an integrated understanding of substances, their properties, their interactions to form new substances, and finally conservation of mass. Each cycle begins with an exploration of a macroscopic phenomenon and then molecular models that help explain that phenomenon.

Design Principle VI: Embed Assessment-for-Learning Within Instruction

Any construction process that is not accompanied by ongoing feedback is in danger of proceeding in undesired directions and skipping over crucial steps. The same is true of learning, which involves the construction of knowledge. Ongoing feedback in education is typically called embedded assessment (Treagust, Jacobowitz, Gallagher, & Parker, 2001). Embedded assessment involves the use of teaching and learning activities that reveal students' thinking while they are learning, blurring the line between teaching and assessment. Treagust et al. (2001) define embedded assessment as also including teachers' use of newly gained knowledge of students' understanding to guide subsequent instructional decisions. Thus, they describe embedded assessment as a cyclical, ongoing process whereby teachers gather data about students' understanding as they teach, analyze the data formally or informally, and use the analysis to plan or adjust their teaching. Chapter 5 describes how embedded assessment can support teachers in curriculum adaptation, and illustrates how teachers who have immediate access to students' responses in WISE modules can adapt their teaching practices in real time to address emerging issues in student understanding. Chapter 4 illustrates how embedded assessment can be specifically designed to support diverse learners. By prompting students to link the science content they are learning with their own communities, teachers are able to better relate their teaching to students' specific social contexts. The examples below demonstrate how embedded assessment can be used to promote learning.

Example: Providing Immediate Feedback via the Teacher Manager Tool. The TELS WISE learning environment includes tools for teachers that show the work of students as they participate in any WISE project. The Teacher Manager tool enables teachers get a good sense of their students' understanding, and appropriately adapt their teaching (see Design Principle IV). The tool also allows teachers to send students messages, which are immediately available to them, about their progress and to provide advice as to appropriate next steps. This system of ongoing assessment and feedback is described at greater length in Chapter 5.

Example: Guidance for Real-Time Assessment. IQWST units incorporate significant guidance for teachers on how to assess their students' understanding in real time, without needing to wait for formal assessment activities. For example, many lessons begin by reviewing a reading assignment that was done at home. An example of typical guidance for teachers, regarding how to embed assessment in their teaching, follows:

> *The questions in the reading should be followed up in class. The idea is that students understand: a) that they actually use what they know about solubility in their everyday lives, and b) that solubility is a property of substances. A possible assessment question might be: "According to your reading, does it make sense to say that 'Sugar is soluble.' Why or why not?" The point will be to stress that solubility must be expressed as whether substance A is soluble in substance B. Substances are not simply "soluble."*

The curriculum includes "checkpoints" at which the designers feel the teacher should assess whether the students have reached a prespecified level of understanding. For example:

> *At this time students should understand the concept of chemical reactions both in terms of what is occurring at the macroscopic level and at the particulate level. Students should also understand that phase changes and mixtures are not chemical reactions and why they are not chemical reactions. You may want to use the concept maps they create for homework to check students' understanding.*

Design Principle VII:
Promote Productive Interactions

This principle calls for designing activities to promote productive and respectful interactions among learners, and between learners and teachers. Properly designed interactions, with or without computer support, can encourage learners to participate in individual and group knowledge-building processes, which can foster integrated understanding. Interactions with peers and teachers provide opportunities for individuals to learn about each other and to develop an appreciation of the knowledge and experience of other participants; this assists in generating a productive climate for peer learning. Chapter 3 describes three strategies for promoting productive interactions: (a) encourage scientific patterns of discourse in the classroom, (b) scaffold student interactions with peers and instructors, and (c) improve scientific discourse in the classroom. Promoting productive interactions is important at various levels of in an educational system. The examples that follow illustrate features designed to promote productive interactions among two different audiences: principals in the first case, and students in the second.

Example: Engaging Principals in Multiple Levels of Interaction. Principals are also learners, and productive interactions play a crucial role in the context of professional development programs for them. Chapter 6 shows that successful professional development for principals occurs when they are provided with multiple ways to engage with students, teachers, and peer principals on issues related to the enactment of reform-based curricula.

Example: Guiding Whole-Class Discussions. Teachers must provide support for students in learning what it means to participate in a discussion, and in developing new ways of interacting in science class. IQWST designers have identified three primary types of discussion employed across IQWST units. Any particular discussion is likely to be composed of several of these types. Part of the job of moderating/facilitating discussion is to recognize what type of discussion is in play, and to be aware of the rules of exchange for each. The three types are (a) *brainstorming,* which involves sharing ideas without evaluating their validity; (b) *synthesizing,* which involves putting ideas together, or assembling multiple activities into a coherent whole, and may also include generalizing from specific activities to a more general conclusion; and (c) *pressing for understanding,* which involves figuring things out or making sense of readings or activities, and may involve debate and challenge.

The IQWST *Teacher's Guide* provides teachers with the following tools that can assist them in supporting class discussions: (a) support for the teacher in recognizing the structure of particular discussions; (b) specific questions and prompts, which are intended as possibilities, not as a script; (c) possible student responses and ways a teacher might respond to them; (d) ways to use student responses to assess understanding (formative assessment); and (e) ways to support all students in learning their role in discussion, such as listening and responding to each other instead of only to the teacher.

IMPLEMENTING DECIDE'S DESIGN PRINCIPLES

Design principles can be useful for researchers. They serve as a productive means for synthesizing existing research findings, they support design-based original research (Kali, 2008), and they help researchers participate in knowledge-building communities (Kali, 2006). The process of analyzing how features that are very different in their nature realize the same design principles has certainly expanded our own perspectives about the seven DECIDE design principles described in this chapter (and summarized in Table 8.1). In this final section we explore ways in which these principles and examples can be useful for educators outside the DECIDE community. We start by discussing the possible uses of the DECIDE design principles for the community of expert curriculum designers and developers, we then continue by describing how novice designers can use the principles, and finally we discuss how teachers and administrators can make productive use of design principles in general, and the DECIDE design principles in particular.

The utility of design principles for guiding curriculum developers in a design process is to some extent limited. For instance, Kali, Levin-Peled, and Dori (in press) provide empirical evidence showing that a Web-based course for higher education students that was designed according to a set of principles from the Design Principles Database failed to sufficiently promote the specific type of knowledge sought. Only after a process of trial and refinement of the course, in which features were revised to better employ the design principles, were the desired learning outcomes achieved. Kali et al. assert that two approaches should simultaneously guide a design process: (a) a top-down approach in which design is guided by well-defined rationales in the form of design principles, and (b) a bottom-up approach in which solutions for emerging challenges are sought by a successive trial-and-refinement process. The design principles described in this book, and highlighted in this chapter, can serve as a basic framework for applying a top-down approach in curriculum design.

Moreover, Kali et al. (in press) show that designing curriculum materials according to certain design principles can be enhanced when other principles are addressed. They maintain that certain *clusters* of design principles are more powerful than the individual principles forming the cluster. We believe that the set of design principles identified in this chapter as the DECIDE design principles constitutes such a cluster. Due to proximity of the principles enumerated here, some features discussed in this chapter employ more than one principle in the cluster. For instance, the "Asthma" module employs the design principle "Connect to personally relevant contexts" (Design Principle I) through its use of the asthma context to teach life science topics. At the same time, it adds a layer of real-world complexity by connecting the biology content to social and environmental issues, thus employing the design principle "Engage learners in complex science problems" (Design Principle V). It is this interconnectedness that marks the DECIDE design principles as more than a simple collection of individual principles. Rather, the DECIDE design principles function as a cluster that together more effectively promotes integrated understanding of science than any individual principle can on its own.

The challenges of using design principles, per se, to guide a design process have also been demonstrated in a study that explored the use of the Design Principles Database by novice designers (Ronen-Fuhrmann et al., 2008). These novices—graduate students in education who specifically focused on designing technology-enhanced curriculum materials—were able to take full advantage of the database only when it was used as part of a course, and not when it was approached as a detached unit. However, when embedded in a course, the graduate students were able to use design principles to (a) review and analyze state-of-the-art educational technologies, (b) review and discuss relevant literature, and (c) critique each others' work at various stages of a project in which they were required to design their own educational technology. We assume that the set of DECIDE design principles would serve as a good starting point for novice curriculum designers who participate in science education design courses or workshops.

Finally, design principles can serve as important tools for teachers and administrators. As described earlier in this chapter, and discussed in detail in Chapter 5, teachers adapt curriculum materials according to their specific needs. Whether they customize the materials prior to instruction (Slotta, 2004) or adapt them while they teach (Remillard, 1999), teachers need to be aware of the rationales that guided those who designed the features they are changing. The set of design principles identified in this chapter, together with national and state standards, can help designers communicate their rationales to teachers so that the teachers will be able to make thoughtful adaptations that do not work against the original goals built into the materials. The DECIDE design principles can also serve administrators in making sound decisions in selecting and supporting coherent curriculum materials that can advance their students in acquiring an integrated understanding of science.

Policies to Promote Coherence

Marcia C. Linn, Yael Kali,
Elizabeth A. Davis, and Paul Horwitz

TO ACHIEVE THE PROMISE for science education reflected in the chapters of this book, we need local, state, and federal policies that value the process of achieving integrated understanding. As the research discussed herein demonstrates, we can design textbooks, activities, technologies, assessments, and professional development programs that make it possible for students to learn coherent science ideas and at the same time become responsible for gaining more and more integrated understanding throughout their lives. We call on educational decision makers to take advantage of this research to improve science teaching and learning.

Coherent curriculum materials combined with assessments that measure integrated understanding contribute an important element to effective science teaching and learning. But science education occurs in a complex, multifaceted system that is easily disrupted. As the chapters of this volume document, successful science education programs need goals that are feasible for every learner, assessments that can guide teachers and help students evaluate their own progress, ongoing professional development programs for teachers and school leaders, as well as learning environments with up-to-date resources, including powerful technologies and effective curriculum materials. In this chapter, we offer recommendations for education policies that could improve the science literacy of all learners.

DESIGN CURRICULUM MATERIALS TO
PROMOTE INTEGRATED UNDERSTANDING

Recommendation: Ensure that science textbook designers, curriculum publishers, and technological innovators create materials that promote coherent and generative understanding among students.

Most current textbooks fail to articulate a coherent account of science and fail to motivate learners to develop personal criteria for integrated ideas. It appears that science textbook authors, activity designers, publishers, and technology innovators are often unaware of the research findings reported in this volume. For example, many involved in science materials design are unaware that students are comfortable holding ideas that contradict each other. Effective materials should not only illustrate how ideas fit together but also help students test their ideas to be sure they are coherent.

Few schools select proven, innovative materials, in part because they lack professional development programs that can support changes in practice or infrastructure for effective materials such as computer or science laboratories. The major reason, however, is that such materials are not supported by current policy.

Curriculum materials need to target essential learning goals consistent with available instructional time. Today, the materials available in most classrooms reflect many different state science standards and have not been tested to determine their efficacy, especially given the amount of instructional time available for science learning. Time allotted for science instruction continues to shrink in response to the increasing emphasis on reading and mathematics in the current era of No Child Left Behind. Typical students in the United States study science infrequently in the early grades, for 4 years from fifth through eighth grades, and for only 2 years in high school. During this time they need to learn biology, physics, chemistry, and earth science, along with modern topics that bridge these disciplines, such as biochemistry, geophysics, and biophysics. Rapid advances in scientific knowledge creating an increasing array of complex issues—from cloning to identity theft—compound the problem.

Compared with the approaches in other countries, science teaching in the United States covers many more topics in each class and spends little time making conceptual links. The science curriculum materials themselves fail to model integrated understanding, leaving out important information as well as including incomprehensible content. Current pacing guides and activities neglect the forms of reasoning essential for students to develop the ability to make their own connections, apply ideas to new situations, and evaluate the coherence of their own ideas. Designing instruction that challenges students to explore the role of key science concepts (such as thermodynamics) in personally relevant situations (such as keeping food safe for a picnic) can help students gain more integrated understanding of science and instill the practice of lifelong science learning. State and local policies need to emphasize coherent understanding, not fleeting coverage of far too many topics.

Policy makers can improve science learning by requiring an emphasis on coherence. Review criteria could require materials that illustrate how science ideas are connected, encourage learners to make their own connections, and enable teachers to help students distinguish connected from contradictory ideas. Policy bodies could insist that materials developers provide evidence that their materials succeed, just as other industries are required to test the safety, efficacy, or impact of their products.

CREATE INSTRUCTIONALLY REALISTIC SCIENCE BENCHMARKS AND STANDARDS

Recommendation: National and state policy groups should revise standards for science learning to target essential science ideas and enable students to integrate their understanding of these ideas in the available instructional time.

Recent documents such as *Rising Above the Gathering Storm: Energizing and Employing America for a Brighter Economic Future* (Committee on Prospering in the Global Economy of the 21st Century, 2006) and *Taking Science to School* (Duschl et al., 2007) argue for the importance of moving away from traditional science curricula that focus on unconnected and trivial topics and toward curricula that engage all students in complex scientific practices and big ideas. Learning goals at the local, state, and national levels need to present a coherent account of the natural world. In addition, they need to be well integrated from grade band to grade band and across related topics at the same grade band.

Standards for curriculum materials that enable students to connect science to their everyday life and to make connections across science topics in the available time will increase the chance that students spontaneously continue this process throughout their lives. Content standards should guide teachers and districts to promote deep connections between students' personal and school science experiences rather than provide a barrage of disconnected ideas.

A national framework for science based on evidence from classroom research could improve the situation. Schools need well-designed science standards that are both coherent and feasible for students to achieve and for teachers to communicate in the time available. Teachers need guidance so they can customize instruction to their local context while meeting national goals. Empirical evidence about instructional approaches that enable students to learn important science ideas should inform this framework.

State and national groups need to establish policies that support teachers and schools in identifying local science dilemmas—such as asthma treatment, oil spill cleanup, or career opportunities—and incorporate these issues into science curricula. Schools need to devote resources to professional development for teachers that allows and encourages them to form partnerships with fellow teachers, university research groups, and community organizations to make connections in their local context.

DESIGN SCIENCE MATERIALS THAT SUCCEED FOR ALL STUDENTS

Recommendation: Require that science materials designers provide evidence that their materials can lead to gains in coherent understanding for each of the varied populations used for accountability.

Current science instructional materials often look very different from those shown to improve student outcomes by the Center for Curriculum Materials in Science (CCMS) and the Technology Enhanced Learning in Science (TELS) Center. The instructional materials from both centers include a greater focus on scientific inquiry practices, valuable visualizations of complex scientific phenomena, embedded assessments to guide students and their teachers, and cumulative understanding accomplished over years of instruction. These materials have been refined through classroom research studies and shown to improve integrated understanding for the varied groups studying science.

Publishers need to field test materials in school contexts comprised of students with multiple levels of language abilities and wide-ranging ideas about science topics. Studies should include typical teachers from a representative set of communities and should document the challenges they face. Researchers should investigate the accomplishments of exemplary teachers—such as those who have developed methods for supporting a diverse student body—and find ways to disseminate best practices. These studies will not only inform researchers about the effectiveness of learning materials but can also serve as compelling evidence for educators and policy makers selecting materials for adoption.

CREATE ASSESSMENTS THAT HELP STUDENTS AND TEACHERS IMPROVE PERFORMANCE

Recommendation: Implement assessments that require students to connect ideas and demonstrate integrated understanding and that inform teachers and learners about their progress.

Most current assessments emphasize asking students to recall facts rather than enabling learners to integrate their ideas. Rather than taking time away from the curriculum, tests can serve as both learning events and outcome measures.

Currently, teachers face intense pressure to meet the demands of the No Child Left Behind legislation. They are stymied in their efforts to educate their students by numerous state and local policies, including untested pacing guides, ineffective textbooks, and standardized assessments that are insensitive to instruction. In such a political environment, teachers and administrators resort to teaching to the test. Because standardized tests rarely require respondents to display integrated understanding, such accomplishments are not valued. The result is fleeting coverage of numerous facts followed by rapid forgetting. Innovative teachers often realize that teaching for integrated understanding actually enables their students to perform well on standardized tests, but most fear reprisals if they fail to follow prescribed practices.

Instead, policies should require ongoing assessments that are embedded in curriculum materials and that provide information to guide students, teachers, and designers. Logged data can be used to provide feedback to students that helps them evaluate their own learning. Teachers can use reports generated from student responses to adjust instructional activities. Designers can use embedded assessments to refine and improve instruction. Researchers can combine findings from multiple contexts to determine how materials can be tailored to diverse students.

Policy makers need to change evaluative external assessments, such as standardized tests, to make them sensitive to learning goals and instructional approaches that emphasize coherence. Currently, many textbooks include multiple-choice test items that require recall of facts from the printed page. Today's diverse population of students instead requires innovative assessments that capture the various ways students understand and participate in science. New technologies make tests that emphasize integrated understanding feasible and effective.

Policy makers should be aware of the limitations of the assessment instruments currently being used in standardized testing. Decision makers need to review the test items that are regarded as most indicative of student learning success—the items where the most gains occur after instruction—and determine whether these items measure integrated understanding or simple recall of facts. Policy makers need evidence that tests measure what students know in science and that they are sensitive to available instruction.

DESIGN FLEXIBLE, EVIDENCE-BASED SCIENCE MATERIALS ADOPTION PRACTICES

Recommendation: Set up practices for states and school districts to select materials based on evidence of their impact and to continuously evaluate their effectiveness.

States and school districts need to offer more flexibility in textbook and technology adoption policies and assessment practices so that schools can take advantage of the innovative, research-based curriculum materials now being developed. For example, educative materials that promote teacher learning along with student learning are commercially available but tend to be less widely adopted than are more traditional textbooks. Placing educative curriculum materials on state adoption lists might play an important role in promoting teacher learning on a wide scale.

Allowing schools to test textbooks and technologies that are aligned with relevant standards and accumulate evidence for integrated understanding could empower schools and teachers to take charge of student learning rather than simply react to mandates. Today, most state assessments are insensitive to instruction intended to promote integrated understanding because they fail to ask students to connect their ideas. Decision makers need the opportunity to evaluate available materials using consequential outcome measures—not just in one course or one year but cumulatively across science courses.

REQUIRE SCHOOLS TO DEDICATE TIME TO PRACTICE-BASED PROFESSIONAL DEVELOPMENT

Recommendation: *Allocate professional development resources to educative materials and dedicate time to practice-based, materials-centered professional development.*

Effective professional development allows teachers to learn new instructional practices, test them in their classes, and use evidence from the tests to adapt the practices to local conditions. Schools should allocate resources so that teachers can adopt innovative science teaching practices, recognizing that introducing new practices (such as inquiry learning) might initially disrupt students who expect to memorize rather than understand. School policies might even allow for a dip in student scores while teachers become adept at using the new materials.

ENSURE CONTINUITY IN PROFESSIONAL DEVELOPMENT ACROSS INSTITUTIONS

Recommendation: *Increase return on investment by aligning preservice, inservice, and continuing education programs for teachers to support development of effective practices.*

States could mandate continuity between preservice and inservice preparation of teachers, thereby dramatically increasing the return on investment in professional development. By shifting emphasis away from the primarily content-focused expectations in current preservice and many inservice programs, professional development could guide teachers in developing science teaching practices that lead to integrated understanding. Schools of education can play an important role by integrating subject matter knowledge with effective science teaching practices. Preservice teachers need to learn how to productively adapt curriculum materials to their local situation and to guide individual students to become independent, self-motivated science learners.

A major policy concern and economic drag on education is the high level of attrition among beginning teachers. Increased continuity and support for induction teachers could sustain participation of promising teachers and reduce costs. To succeed, such a policy must reward excellence and innovation among induction teachers and ensure that cooperating teachers who mentor preservice teachers have the resources necessary to provide high-quality support.

ENABLE EXPERIENCED TEACHERS TO CONTINUOUSLY IMPROVE THEIR PRACTICE

Recommendation: *Reward experienced teachers who take the risk of trying new practices, and gather evidence about the impact of their teaching.*

Districts should reward excellence and innovation in experienced teachers by offering leadership and financial incentives. Most teachers are willing to try new curriculum materials and learn about new teaching strategies in their classrooms but fear they will be chastised if their experiments fail. All teachers need incentives to change, as well as sufficient time to adapt their curricula and teaching practices to best meet their students' needs. Policies should require districts to provide high-quality professional development, allow teachers to monitor their progress over several years, and provide support from local mentors. Successful teachers should be rewarded with mentoring roles.

PROVIDE MODERN TECHNOLOGIES AND APPROPRIATE TECHNICAL SUPPORT

Recommendation: *Set funding priorities to enable schools to improve science learning by using modern technologies and tested curriculum materials shown to improve understanding.*

Schools fail to benefit from many effective instructional solutions because they neglect modern technologies. Scientists use modern technologies to examine phenomena that are too small to see and to study processes that happen too rapidly to be observed. Innovative science materials offer these same opportunities to students, helping them visualize complex phenomena such as chemical reactions or mechanical processes.

Few schools have both the computers and the infrastructure to implement proven technologies. Policy makers can help by funding technology programs that include the same support for users that is found in typical government and industry settings.

EMPOWER SCHOOL LEADERS TO CREATE SYNERGISTIC ENVIRONMENTS FOR SCIENCE LEARNING

Recommendation: School leaders need the authority and resources to select curriculum materials, assessments, and professional development opportunities that build on students' natural linguistic practices and afford students multiple opportunities to develop integrated understanding of science.

Policies related to curriculum, testing, instruction, and the allocation of resources must work synergistically to enable leaders at the national, state, and school level to meet the diverse needs of all learners.

To take advantage of students' linguistic resources, school leaders need the ability to support multilingual education. Policies requiring monolingual instruction deprive many English language learners of critical resources needed to develop their science understanding. Schools must build on students' home language and enable connections across linguistic contexts. In this way, students will be allowed to marshal their linguistic resources as they work to acquire the complex and highly technical language of science. In addition, teachers need access to innovations—such as multimodal, multilingual technology and related professional development—that can support these processes.

To take advantage of the curricular context, teachers and students need ways to connect instruction to their career and life goals. Students have opportunities to use reading and mathematics regularly in their lives, yet they are rarely supported in seeing any way to use the information they learn in science class. Unless policies strengthen the connections among science ideas and highlight the implications of science for everyday life, most learners will conclude that science is irrelevant.

Policy makers can help by requiring curriculum materials that build critical educational sequences around topics with obvious real-world implications, such as energy, ecology, and states of matter. Such materials should emphasize the connections from one science topic to another and promote involvement of local leaders in connecting science to community issues.

SUPPORT THE PROCESS OF SYNTHESIZING DESIGN KNOWLEDGE

Recommendation: Support multiple approaches to synthesis of design knowledge to support refinement of innovations, design of new materials, and conduct of educational research.

Research shows that design principles can provide a useful framework for those refining or adapting innovations, for designers creating new materials, and for researchers testing the effectiveness of innovations. Because science education takes place in a complex, contextualized system, research findings are often dependent on factors that cannot be completely controlled. And even the most promising practices generally need fine tuning when they are implemented in a new context. To facilitate development, refinement, adaptation, and evaluation of innovative new materials, researchers need to engage in ongoing synthesis of design knowledge into pragmatic design principles that can guide all stages of the process.

Design principles can serve as important tools for those adapting curriculum materials, assessments, or professional development programs. For example, professional development programs are more and more likely to support the process of adapting innovations. Whether users customize materials prior to implementation or adapt them during implementation, they need to be aware of the rationales that guided those who designed the materials they are changing. The set of design principles identified in this volume can help designers communicate their rationales to users so that users can make thoughtful adaptations.

Designers of new materials often neglect findings from prior research because they find the available reports too detailed and specific for their needs. However, once diverse and detailed research findings have been synthesized and expressed in the form of design principles and design patterns, such as those described in this book, they can serve as the foundation for a top-down approach to curriculum design. These principles and patterns can also serve as a good starting point for novice curriculum designers who participate in science education design courses or workshops.

Design principles can also serve as criteria for decision makers in selecting curriculum materials and professional development programs, because they point to critical elements of programs that lead to integrated understanding of science.

PROVIDE SUSTAINED, REALISTIC FUNDING FOR RESEARCH ON EFFECTIVE SCIENCE MATERIALS

Recommendation: Support research that includes design, testing, and refinement of instructional materials based on the best knowledge available about how students learn and about what instructional strategies work. Ensure that this research is cumulative and sustained.

Little improvement in science learning can be accomplished without better and more uniform data on what works, why, and with whom. Such research takes place in the complex system of science education and requires careful design. Those involved in designing and carrying out research on the effectiveness of curriculum know the enormous complexities involved in conducting the kinds of research that are needed and in interpreting the results. It is essential that we have high-quality data to inform the many decisions in which curriculum plays a role.

Effective professional development programs also require careful design and study. When teachers engage in sustained, coherent efforts to improve their practice and tailor materials to the needs of their students, the outcomes are impressive. This research requires a commitment of time and support from districts and from research funding to yield general recommendations.

Given the current lack of high-quality assessment instruments in science, increased funding is necessary for facilitating the development and implementation of more cognitively sensitive and meaningful assessments. Such measures are needed to conduct high-quality educational research.

To improve science learning we need consistent funding over the long term from federal government agencies such as the National Science Foundation and the Department of Education, from private foundations and professional organizations, and from state agencies. Creating high-quality materials and outcome measures requires time and resources to produce, test, refine, and study effectiveness. Materials need to be tested in diverse learning contexts under authentic conditions, ideally in partnership with state and local decision makers. Research on the effectiveness of curriculum materials should be viewed as an essential step in the development of standards, assessments, and curricula. Budgets and timelines for development projects should reflect this reality.

FINAL THOUGHTS

This volume draws national attention to remediable weaknesses in current science instruction. Research demonstrates that coherent curriculum materials, instruction that leads to integrated understanding, and assessments that allow teachers and students to monitor their progress and adjust their practices can dramatically improve science outcomes for all learners. Yet, this knowledge is of no value without policies that allow schools, teachers, and students to act responsibly.

The recommendations made in this chapter reflect the synergy of work conducted at TELS and CCMS. Participants in the Delineating and Evaluating Coherent Instructional Designs for Education (DECIDE) project negotiated new design knowledge and gained deeper insights into how coherent science instruction can promote integrated understanding. The recommendations represent the cumulative wisdom in the chapters of this volume and guide the actions that must be taken so that these insights can be widely disseminated. The policy recommendations call for major reallocations of resources and substantial rethinking of educational practices. They reflect the impact of new technologies in all aspects of society. We call on policy makers to make productive use of these recommendations, and we pledge to continue to support a dialogue between research and policy.

References

Abedi, J. (2003). The No Child Left Behind Act and English language learners: Assessment and accountability issues. *Educational Researcher, 33,* 4–14.

Ainsworth, S., & Burcham, S. (2007). The impact of text coherence on learning by self-explanation. *Learning and Instruction, 17,* 286–303.

American Association for the Advancement of Science (AAAS). (1989). *Science for all Americans.* New York: Oxford University Press.

American Association for the Advancement of Science (AAAS). (1993). *Benchmarks for science literacy.* New York: Oxford University Press.

American Association for the Advancement of Science (AAAS). (2001). *Atlas of science literacy: Project 2061.* Washington, DC: American Association for the Advancement of Science and the National Science Teachers Association.

American Association for the Advancement of Science (AAAS). (2005). *High school biology textbooks: A benchmarks-based evaluation.* Retrieved May 24, 2007, from http://www.project2061.org/publications/textbook/hsbio/report/default.htm

American Association for the Advancement of Science (AAAS). (2007). *Atlas of science literacy: Project 2061* (Vol. 2). Washington, DC: American Association for the Advancement of Science and the National Science Teachers Association.

American Federation of Teachers. (2006). *Smart testing: Let's get it right* (Policy Brief No. 19). Washington, DC: Author.

Anderson, C. W., & Smith, E. L. (1987). Teaching science. In V. Richardson-Koehler (Ed.), *The educator's handbook: A research perspective* (pp. 84–111). New York: Longman.

Anderson, R. C., Nguyen-Jahiel, K., McNurlen, B., Archodidou, A., Kim, S.-Y., Reznitskaya, A., et al. (2001). The snowball phenomenon: Spread of ways of talking and ways of thinking across groups of children. *Cognition and Instruction, 19*(1), 1–46.

Anderson, R. E., & Dexter, S. L. (2005). School technology leadership: An empirical investigation of prevalence and effect. *Education Administration Quarterly, 41*(1), 49–82.

Atchinstein, B. (2002). Conflict amid community: Micropolitics of teacher collaboration. *Teachers College Record, 104*(3), 421–455.

Atwater, M. M. (1996). Social constructivism: Infusion into the multicultural science education research agenda. *Journal of Research in Science Teaching, 33*, 821–837.

Atwater, M. M., & Wiggins, J. (1995). A study of urban middle school students with high and low attitudes toward science. *Journal of Research in Science Teaching, 32*(6), 665–677.

August, D., & Hakuta, K. (Eds.). (1997). *Improving schooling for language-minority children: A research agenda.* Washington, DC: National Academy Press.

August, D., & Hakuta, K. (Eds.). (1998). *Educating language minority children.* Washington, DC: National Academy Press.

Bagno, E., Eylon, B.-S., & Ganiel, U. (2000). From fragmented knowledge to a knowledge structure: Linking the domains of mechanics and electromagnetism. *The American Journal of Physics, 68*(7), S16–S26.

Ball, D. L., & Bass, H. (2000). Interweaving content and pedagogy in teaching and learning to teach: Knowing and using mathematics. In J. Boaler (Ed.), *Multiple perspectives on teaching and learning* (pp. 83–104). Westport, CT: Ablex Publishing.

Ball, D. L., & Cohen, D. K. (1996). Reform by the book: What is—or might be—the role of curriculum materials in teacher learning and instructional reform? *Educational Researcher, 25*(9), 6–8.

Banks, J., Au, K., Ball, A., Bell, P., Gordon, E., Gutierrez, K., et al. (2007). *Learning in and out of school in diverse environments: Life-long, life-wide, life-deep.* Seattle: The LIFE (Learning in Informal and Formal Learning Environments) Center and the Center for Multicultural Education, University of Washington. Retrieved June 1, 2007, from http://life-slc.org/wp-content/up/2007/05/Banks-et-al-LIFE-Diversity-Report.pdf

Barab, S., & Luehmann, A. (2003). Building sustainable science curriculum: Acknowledging and accommodating local adaptation. *Science Education, 87*(4), 454–467.

Baumgartner, E. (2004). Synergy research and knowledge integration: Customizing activities around stream ecology. In M. C. Linn, E. A. Davis, & P. Bell (Eds.), *Internet environments for science education* (pp. 261–287). Mahwah, NJ: Erlbaum.

Becker, H. J., & Riel, M. M. (2000). *Teacher professional engagement and constructive-compatible computer use.* Teaching, Learning and Computing Report No. 7. Center for Research on Information Technology and Organizations. Retrieved February 28, 2002, from http://www.crito.uci.edu/tlc/findings/report_7/

Bell, P. (2004). The educational opportunities of contemporary controversies in science. In M. C. Linn, E. A. Davis, & P. Bell (Eds.), *Internet environments for science education* (pp. 233–260). Mahwah, NJ: Erlbaum.

Bell, P., & Davis, E. A. (2000). Designing Mildred: Scaffolding students' reflection and argumentation using a cognitive software guide. In B. Fishman & S. O'Connor-Divelbiss (Eds.), *Proceedings of the International Conference for the Learning Sciences 2000* (pp. 142–149). Mahwah, NJ: Erlbaum.

Bell, P., Davis, E. A., & Linn, M. C. (1995). The Knowledge Integration Environment: Theory and design. In J. L. Schnase & E. L. Cunnius (Eds.), *Proceedings of the Computer Supported Collaborative Learning Conference, CSCL '95* (pp. 14–21). Mahwah, NJ: Erlbaum.

Bell, P., & Linn, M. C. (2000). Scientific arguments as learning artifacts: Designing for learning from the Web with KIE. *International Journal of Science Education, 22*(8), 797–817.

Bell, P., & Linn, M. C. (2002). Beliefs about science: How does science instruction contribute? In B. K. Hofer & P. R. Pintrich (Eds.), *Personal epistemology: The psychology of beliefs about knowledge and knowing* (pp. 321–346). Mahwah, NJ: Erlbaum.

Ben-Peretz, M. (1990). *The teacher–curriculum encounter: Freeing teachers from the tyranny of texts*. Albany: State University of New York Press.

Berliner, D. C. (2006). Our impoverished view of educational reform. *Teachers College Record, 108*(6), 949–995.

Beyer, C., & Davis, E. A. (in press). Fostering second-graders' scientific explanations: A beginning elementary teacher's knowledge, beliefs, and practice. *Journal of the Learning Sciences.*

Beyer, C. J., Delgado, C., Davis, E. A., & Krajcik, J. S. (2006). *Investigating high school biology texts as educative curriculum materials: Curriculum review process*. Ann Arbor: University of Michigan.

Bielaczyc, K. (2006). Designing social infrastructure: Critical issues in creating learning environments with technology. *The Journal of the Learning Sciences, 15*(3), 301–329.

Bielaczyc, K., Pirolli, P., & Brown, A. L. (1995). Training in self-explanation and self-regulation strategies: Investigating the effects of knowledge acquisition activities on problem solving. *Cognition and Instruction, 13*(2), 221–252.

Bishop, B. A., & Anderson, C. W. (1990). Student conceptions of natural selection and its role in evolution. *Journal of Research in Science Teaching, 27,* 415–427.

Bjork, R. A. (1994). Memory and metamemory considerations in the training of human beings. In J. Metcalfe & A. Shimamura (Eds.), *Metacognition: Knowing about knowing* (pp. 185–205). Cambridge, MA: MIT Press.

Blumenfeld, P., Fishman, B., Krajcik, J. S., Marx, R., & Soloway, E. (2000). Creating usable innovations in systemic reform: Scaling up technology-embedded project-based science in urban schools. *Educational Psychologist, 35*(3), 149–164.

Blumenfeld, P. C., Soloway, E., Marx, R. W., Krajcik, J. S., Guzdial, M., & Palincsar, A. (1991). Motivating project-based learning: Sustaining the doing, supporting the learning. *Educational Psychologist, 26*(3&4), 369–398.

Borko, H., Wolf, S., Simone, G., & Uchiyama, K. (2003). Schools in transition: Reform efforts and school capacity in Washington state. *Educational Evaluation and Policy Analysis, 25*(2), 171–201.

Bouillion, L. M., & Gomez, L. M. (2001). Connecting school and community with science learning: Real world problems and school–community partnerships as contextual scaffolds. *Journal of Research in Science Teaching, 38*(8), 878–898.

Bransford, J. D., Barron, B., Pea, R., Meltzoff, A., Kuhl, P., Bell, P., et al. (2006). Foundations and opportunities for an interdisciplinary science of learning. In K. Sawyer (Ed.), *The Cambridge handbook of the learning sciences* (pp. 19–34). New York: Cambridge University Press.

Bransford, J. D., Brown, A. L., & Cocking, R. R. (Eds.). (1999). *How people learn: Brain, mind, experience, and school.* Washington, DC: National Academy Press.

Bransford, J. D., Brown, A. L., & Cocking, R. R. (Eds.). (2000). *How people learn: Brain, mind, experience, and school* (Expanded ed.). Washington, DC: National Academy Press.

Bridgham, K. (1971). Comments on some thoughts on science curriculum development. In E. Eisner (Ed.), *Confronting curriculum reform* (pp. 61–67). Boston: Little Brown.

Britton, B. K., & Gulgoz, S. (1991). Using Kintsch's computational model to improve instructional text: Effects of repairing inference calls on recall and cognitive structures. *Journal of Educational Psychology, 83*(3), 329–345.

Brown, A. L., & Campione, J. C. (1994). Guided discovery in a community of learners. In K. McGilly (Ed.), *Classroom lessons: Integrating cognitive theory and classroom practice* (pp. 229–270). Cambridge, MA: MIT Press/Bradford Books.

Brown, A. L., & Campione, J. C. (1996). Psychological learning theory and the design of innovative environments: On procedures, principles and systems. In L. Shauble & R. Glaser (Eds.), *Contributions of instructional innovation to understanding learning.* Mahwah, NJ: Erlbaum.

Brown, J. S., Collins, A., & Duguid, P. (1989). Situated cognition and the culture of learning. *Educational Researcher, 18*(1), 32–41.

Brown, M. (in press). Toward a theory of curriculum design and use: Understanding the teacher–tool relationship. In J. T. Remillard, B. Herbel-Eisenman, & G. Lloyd (Eds.), *Mathematics teachers at work: Connecting curriculum materials and classroom instruction.* New York: Routledge.

Brown, M., & Edelson, D. (2003). *Teaching as design: Can we better understand the ways in which teachers use materials so we can better design materials to support their changes in practice?* (Design Brief). Evanston, IL: The Center for Learning Technologies in Urban Schools.

Bruer, J. T. (1994). *Schools for thought: A science of learning in the classroom.* Cambridge, MA: MIT Press.

Bruner, J. S. (1960). *The process of education.* Cambridge, MA: Harvard University Press.

Bruner, J. S. (1995). Seventy-fifth anniversary retrospective: On learning mathematics. *Mathematics Teacher, 8*(4), 330–335. (Reprinted from *Mathematics Teacher, 53,* 610–619, December 1960)

Bryan, L. A., & Atwater, M. M. (2002). Teacher beliefs and cultural models: A challenge for science teacher preparation programs. *Science Education, 86*(6), 821–839.

Buckley, B., Gobert, J. D., Kindfield, A. C. H., Horwitz, P., Tinker, R., Gerlits, B., et al. (2004). Model-based teaching and learning with BioLogica: What do they learn? How do they learn? How do we know? *Journal of Science Education and Technology, 13*(1), 23–41.

Bullough, R. (1992). Beginning teacher curriculum decision making, personal teaching metaphors, and teacher education. *Teaching and Teacher Education, 8*(3), 239–252.

Burch, P., & Spillane, J. (2003). Elementary school leadership strategies and subject matter: Reforming mathematics and literacy instruction. *Elementary School Journal, 103*(5), 519–535.

Burkhart, H., & Schoenfeld, A. (2003). Improving educational research: Toward a more useful, more influential, and better-funded enterprise. *Educational Researcher, 32*(9), 3–14.

Bybee, R. (1997). *Achieving science literacy: From purposes to practice.* Portsmouth, NH: Heinemann Books.

Calabrese Barton, A. (1998). *Feminist science education.* New York: Teachers College Press.

Carey, S. (1985). *Conceptual change in childhood.* Cambridge, MA: MIT Press.

Casperson, J. M., & Linn, M. C. (2006). Using visualizations to teach electrostatics. *American Journal of Physics, 74*(4), 316–323.

Castania, K. (1992). Cultural diversity in rural communities. *Innovations in Community and Rural Development.* Ithaca, NY: Community and Rural Development Institute (CaRDI), Cornell University.

CEO Forum on Education and Technology. (2000). *The CEO Forum School Technology and Readiness Report, Year 3.* Retrieved October 1, 2006, from http://www.ceoforum.org/downloads/report3.pdf

Champagne, A., Gunstone, R., & Klopfer, L. (1985). Effecting changes in cognitive structures among physics students. In L. West & A. Pines (Eds.), *Cognitive structure and conceptual change* (pp. 61–90). Orlando, FL: Academic Press.

Chi, M. T. H., Bassok, M., Lewis, M. W., Reimann, P., & Glaser, R. (1989). Self-explanations: How students study and use examples in learning to solve problems. *Cognitive Science, 13*, 145–182.

Chi, M. T. H., Feltovich, P. J., & Glaser, R. (1981). Categorization and representation of physics problems by experts and novices. *Cognitive Science, 5*, 121–152.

Chun, D. M., & Plass, J. L. (1996). Effects of multimedia annotations on vocabulary acquisition: Using CyberBuch. *Modern Language Journal*, 183–198.

Clark, D. B., & Linn, M. C. (2003). Scaffolding knowledge integration through curricular depth. *Journal of Learning Sciences, 12*(4), 451–494.

Clark, D. B., Nelson, B., Atkinson, R., Ramirez, F., & Medina, W. (in press). Integrating flexible language supports within online science learning environments. In R. Bloymeyer, T. Ganesh, & H. Waxman (Eds.), *Research on technology use in multicultural settings*.

Clark, D. B., & Sampson, V. (2007). Personally-seeded discussions to scaffold online argumentation. *International Journal of Science Education, 29*, 253–277.

Clement, J. (1993). Using bridging analogies and anchoring intuitions to deal with students' preconceptions in physics. *Journal of Research in Science Teaching, 30*(10), 1241–1257.

Clough, E. E., & Driver, R. (1985). Secondary students' conceptions of the conduction of heat: Bringing together scientific and personal views. *The Physical Educator, 20*, 176–182.

Cobb, P., Confrey, J., diSessa, A., Lehrer, R., & Schauble, L. (2003). Design experiments in educational research. *Educational Researcher, 32*(1), 9–13.

Cobb, T. (1997). Is there any measurable learning from hands-on concordancing? *System, 25*(3), 301–315.

Coburn, C. (2003). Rethinking scale: Moving beyond numbers to deep and lasting change. *Educational Researcher, 32*(6), 3–12.

Coffey, J., Douglas, R., & Stearns, C. (Eds.). (2008). *Assessing Science Learning: Perspectives from Research and Practice*. Arlington, VA: NSTA Press.

Coffland, A., & Strickland, A. (2004). Factors related to teacher usage of technology in secondary geometry instruction. *Journal of Computers in Math and Science Teaching, 23*(4), 347–365.

Cognition and Technology Group at Vanderbilt. (1990). Anchored instruction and its relationship to situated cognition. *Educational Researcher, 19*(5), 2–10.

Colella, V. S., Klopfer, E., & Resnick, M. (2001). *Adventures in modeling: Exploring complex, dynamic systems with StarLogo*. New York: Teachers College Press.

Collins, A. (1998). *National Science Education Standards*: A political document. *Journal of Research in Science Teaching, 35*(7), 711–727.

Collins, A., Brown, J. S., & Holum, A. (1988). The computer as a tool for learning through reflection. In H. Mandl & A. M. Lesgold (Eds.), *Learning issues for intelligent tutoring systems* (pp. 1–18). Chicago: Springer-Verlag.

Collins, A., & Gentner, D. (1987). How people construct mental models. In D. Holland & N. Quinn (Eds.), *Cultural models in thought and language* (pp. 243–265). Cambridge, UK: Cambridge University Press.

Collopy, R. (2003). Curriculum materials as a professional development tool: How a mathematics textbook affected two teachers' learning. *The Elementary School Journal, 103*(3), 227–311.

Commission on Instructionally Supportive Assessment. (2001). *Building tests to support instruction and accountability: A guide for policymakers*. Washington, DC: National Education Association. Retrieved October 30, 2007, from http://www.nea.org/accountability/buildingtests.html

Committee on Prospering in the Global Economy of the 21st Century. (2006). *Rising above the gathering storm: Energizing and employing America for a brighter economic future.* Washington, DC: National Academies Press.

Cuban, L. (2001). *Overused and undersold: Computers in the classroom.* Cambridge, MA: Harvard University Press.

Cullin, M. J., & Crawford, B. A. (2004, March–April). *The interplay between prospective science teachers' modeling strategies and understandings.* Paper presented at the annual meeting of the National Association for Research in Science Teaching, Vancouver, Canada.

Cuthbert, A., & Slotta, J. D. (2004). Designing a Web-based design curriculum for middle school science: The WISE Houses in the Desert project. *International Journal of Science Education, 24*(7), 821–844.

Davidson, J. (2003). A new role in facilitating school reform: The case of the educational technologist. *Teachers College Record, 105*(5), 729–752.

Davis, E. A. (2003). Prompting middle school science students for productive reflection: Generic and directed prompts. *The Journal of the Learning Sciences, 12*(1), 91–142.

Davis, E. A. (2004). Knowledge integration in science teaching: Analyzing teachers' knowledge development. *Research in Science Education, 34*(1), 21–53.

Davis, E. A. (2006a). Characterizing productive reflection among preservice elementary teachers: Seeing what matters. *Teaching and Teacher Education, 22*(3), 281–301.

Davis, E. A. (2006b). Preservice elementary teachers' critique of instructional materials for science. *Science Education, 90*(2), 3–14.

Davis, E. A., Beyer, C., Forbes, C., & Stevens, S. (2007, April). *Promoting pedagogical design capacity through teachers' narratives.* Paper presented at the annual meeting of the National Association for Research in Science Teaching, New Orleans, LA.

Davis, E. A., & Krajcik, J. S. (2005). Designing educative curriculum materials to promote teacher learning. *Educational Researcher, 34*(3), 3–14.

Davis, E. A., Petish, D., & Smithey, J. (2006). Challenges new science teachers face. *Review of Educational Research, 76*(4), 607–651.

Davis, E. A., Smithey, J., & Petish, D. (2004). Designing an online learning environment for new elementary science teachers: Supports for learning to teach. In W. Y. B. Kafai, A. Sandoval, N. Enyedy, A. S. Nixon, & F. Herrera (Eds.), *Proceedings of the 6th International Conference of the Learning Sciences, ICLS2004* (p. 594). Mahwah, NJ: Erlbaum.

DeBoer, G. E. (1991). *A history of ideas in science education: Implications for practice.* New York: Teachers College Press.

DeBoer, G. E. (2000). Scientific literacy: Another look at its historical and contemporary meanings and its relationship to science education reform. *Journal of Research in Science Teaching, 37*(6), 582–601.

DeBoer, G. E. (2005). Standard-izing test items. *Science Scope, 28*(4), 10–11.

DeBoer, G. E., & Ache, P. (2005, April). *Aligning assessment to content standards: Applying the Project 2061 analysis procedure to assessment items in school mathematics.* Paper presented at the annual meeting of the American Educational Research Association, Montreal, Canada. Retrieved September 29, 2006, from http://www.project2061.org/research/assessment/aera2005.htm

DeBoer, G. E., Herrmann Abell, C., & Gogos, A. (2007, April). *Assessment linked to science learning goals: Probing student thinking during item development.* Paper presented at the annual meeting of the National Association for Research in Science Teaching, New Orleans, LA.

Diamond, J., & Spillane, J. (2004). High stakes accountability in urban elementary schools: Challenging or reproducing inequality? *Teachers College Record, 106*(6), 1145–1176.

Dietz, C., & Davis, E. A. (in press). Preservice elementary teachers' reflection on narrative images of inquiry. *Journal of Science Teacher Education.*

diSessa, A. A. (1988). Knowledge in pieces. In G. Forman & P. Pufall (Eds.), *Constructivism in the computer age* (pp. 49–70). Mahwah, NJ: Erlbaum.

diSessa, A. A. (2000). *Changing minds: Computers, learning and literacy.* Cambridge, MA: MIT Press.

diSessa, A. A., & Minstrell, J. (1998). Cultivating conceptual change with benchmark lessons. In J. G. Greeno & S. Goldman (Eds.), *Thinking practices* (pp. 155–187). Mahwah, NJ: Erlbaum.

Dow, P. (1991). *Schoolhouse politics: Lessons from the Sputnik era.* Cambridge, MA: Harvard University Press.

Driver, R., Newton, P., & Osborne, J. (2000). Establishing the norms of scientific argumentation in classrooms. *Science Education, 84,* 287–312.

Duke, D. (1993). Removing barriers to professional growth. *Phi Delta Kappan, 74*(9), 702–704.

Duschl, R., & Gitomer, D. (1997). Strategies and challenges to changing the focus of assessment in science classrooms. *Educational Assessment, 4,* 37–73.

Duschl, R. A., Schweingruber, H. A., & Shouse, A. W. (Eds.). (2007). *Taking science to school: Learning and teaching science in grades K–8.* Washington, DC: National Academies Press.

Eaton, J. F., Anderson, C. W., & Smith, E. L. (1984). Student preconceptions interfere with learning: Case studies of fifth-grade students. *Elementary School Journal, 64,* 365–379.

Edelson, D. C. (2001). Learning-for-use: A framework for the design of technology-supported inquiry activities. *Journal of Research in Science Teaching, 38*(3), 355–385.

Edelson, D. C. (Ed.). (2005). *Investigations in environmental science: A case-based approach to the study of environmental systems.* Armonk, NY: It's About Time.

Edelson, D. C., Gordin, D. N., & Pea, R. D. (1999). Addressing the challenges of inquiry-based learning through technology and curriculum design. *Journal of the Learning Sciences, 8*(3/4), 391–450.

Edelson, D. C., & Reiser, B. J. (2006). Making authentic practices accessible to learners: Design challenges and strategies. In R. K. Sawyer (Ed.), *Cambridge handbook of the learning sciences* (pp. 335–354). New York: Cambridge University Press.

Eisenhart, M., Cuthbert, A., Shrum, J., & Harding, J. (1988). Teacher beliefs about work activities: Policy implications. *Theory into Practice, 27*(2), 137–144.

Eisenhart, M., Finkel, E., Behm, L., Lawrence, N., & Tonso, K. L. (1996). *Learning from the margins: Gender, power, and change in scientific and engineering practice.* Chicago: University of Chicago Press.

Elmore, R. F. (1996). Getting to scale with good educational practice. *Harvard Educational Review, 66*(1), 1–26.

Elmore, R. F. (2000). *Building a new structure for school leadership.* Washington, DC: Albert Shanker Institute.

Erickson, G. L. (1979). Children's conceptions of heat and temperature. *Science Education, 63*(2), 221–230.

Feiman-Nemser, S. (2001). From preparation to practice: Designing a continuum to strengthen and sustain teaching. *Teachers College Record, 103*(6), 1013–1055.

Fink, E., & Resnick, L. (2001). Developing principals as instructional leaders. *Phi Delta Kappan, 82*(8), 598–606.

Finlay, G. C. (1962). The physical science study committee. *The School Review, 70,* 63–81.

Fishman, B. (2003). Linking on-line video and curriculum to leverage community knowledge. In J. Brophy (Ed.), *Advances in research on teaching: Using video in teacher education* (Vol. 10, pp. 201–234). New York: Elsevier.

Fishman, B., & Gomez, L. (2000). New technologies and the challenge for school leadership. In M. Honey & C. Shookhoff (Eds.), *The Wingspread Conference on Technology's Role in Urban School Reform: Achieving Equity and Quality* (pp. 13–21). Racine, WI: The Joyce Foundation, The Johnson Foundation, and the EDC Center for Children and Technology.

Fishman, B., Gomez, L., & Soloway, E. (2002). *New technologies and the challenges for school leadership.* Evanston, IL: Northwestern University and University of Michigan, Center for Learning Technologies in Urban Schools.

Fishman, B., Marx, R., Blumenfeld, P., Krajcik, J. S., & Soloway, E. (2004). Creating a framework for research on systemic technology innovations. *Journal of the Learning Sciences, 13*(1), 43–76.

Fogleman, J., Fishman, B., & Krajcik, J. S. (2006). Sustaining innovations through lead teacher learning: A learning sciences perspective on supporting professional development. *Teaching Education, 17*(2), 181–194.

Forbes, C. T., & Davis, E. A. (2007, April). *Beginning elementary teachers' learning through the use of science curriculum materials: A longitudinal study.* Paper presented at the annual meeting of the National Association for Research in Science Teaching, New Orleans, LA.

Forbes, C. T., & Davis, E. A. (in press-a). Exploring preservice elementary teachers' critique and adaptation of science curriculum materials in respect to socioscientific issues. *Science and Education.* ("Online First" version available at http://www.springerlink.com/content/l55722g13693640u/?p=46fbf936ef374495b6ebdb1527ae7140&pi=59)

Forbes, C., & Davis, E. A. (in press-b). The development of preservice elementary teachers' curricular role identity for science teaching. *Science Education.* ("Early View" version available at http://www3.interscience.wiley.com/journal/117915022/abstract)

Fortus, D., Dershimer, R. C., Krajcik, J. S., Marx, R. W., & Mamlok-Naaman, R. (2004). Design-based science (DBS) and student learning. *Journal of Research in Science Teaching, 41*(10), 1081–1110.

Fortus, D., Grueber, D., Nordine, J., Rozelle, J., Schwarz, C., & Weizman, A. (in press). Seeing the Light: Can I Believe My Eyes? In J. Krajcik, B. Reiser, D. Fortus, & L. Sutherland (Eds.), *Investigating and Questioning Our World Through Science and Technology (IQWST).* Columbus, OH: Glencoe.

Fortus, D., & Kanter, D. (2005, January). *Curriculum driven practice-based professional development.* Paper presented at the annual meeting of the Association for the Education of Teachers in Science (AETS), Colorado Springs.

Fradd, S. H., Lee, O., Sutman, F. X., & Saxton, M. K. (2001). Promoting science literacy with English language learners through instructional materials development: A case study. *Bilingual Research Journal, 25*(4), 479–501.

Franke, M. L., Carpenter, T., Levi, L., & Fennema, E. (2001). Capturing teachers' generative change: A follow-up study of professional development in mathematics. *American Educational Research Journal, 38,* 653–690.

Fullan, M., & Stiegelbauer, S. (1991). *The new meaning of educational change.* New York: Teachers College Press.

Fusco, D., & Calabrese Barton, A. (2001). Representing student achievements in science. *Journal of Research in Science Teaching, 38*(3), 337–354.

Galambos, S., & Hakuta, K. (1988). Subject-specific and task-specific characteristics of metalinguistic awareness in bilingual children. *Applied Psycholinguistics, 9,* 141–162.

Gallagher, J. J. (2000). Teaching for understanding and application of science knowledge. *School Science and Mathematics, 100*(6), 310–318.

Gallagher, J. J. (2007). *Teaching science for understanding: A practical guide for secondary teachers.* Columbus, OH: Merrill.

Gallagher, J. J., & McLaughlin, D. (2007). *Addressing issues of diversity in curriculum materials and teacher education.* East Lansing: Michigan State University.

García, E. (2001). *Student cultural diversity: Understanding and meeting the challenge.* Boston: Houghton Mifflin.

García, E. (2002). Bilingualism and schooling in the United States. *International Journal of the Sociology of Language, 134*(1), 1–123.

García, E. E., & Lee, O. (2008). Science instruction for all: Creating a responsive learning community. In A. S. Rosebery & B. Warren (Eds.), *Teaching science to English language learners.* Arlington, VA: National Science Teachers Association.

Gay, G. (2000). *Culturally responsive teaching: Theory, research, and practice.* New York: Teachers College Press.

Gerard, L. F., Bowyer, J. B., & Linn, M. C. (2008a). A community of principals: Effects on leadership and scaling in technology-enhanced science. In V. Jonker & A. Lazonder (Eds.), *Proceedings of the 8th International Conference of the Learning Sciences: Cre8ing a Learning World.* Utrecht: International Society of the Learning Sciences.

Gerard, L. F., Bowyer, J. B., & Linn, M. C. (2008b). Principal leadership for technology-enhanced science. *Journal of Science Education and Technology, 17*(1), 1–18.

Gerard, L. F., Bowyer, J. B., & Marx, R. W. (2008, March). *Scaling technology-enhanced science curriculum reform: Professional development for principals.* Paper presented at the annual meeting of the American Educational Research Association, New York.

Gettys, S., Imhof, L. A., & Kautz, J. O. (2001). Computer-assisted reading: The effects of glossing format on comprehension and vocabulary retention. *Foreign Language Annals, 34*(2), 91–106.

Gilbert, J. K., & Boulter, C. J. (2000). *Developing models in science education.* Dordrecht: Kluwer.

Glass, B. (1962). Renascent biology: A report on the AIBS Biological Sciences Curriculum Study. *The School Review, 70,* 16–43.

Glenn, J. (2000). *Before it's too late: A report to the nation from the National Commission on Mathematics and Science Teaching for the 21st Century.* Washington, DC: U.S. Department of Education.

Goldring, E., Spillane, J. P., Barnes, C., & Supovitz, J. (2006, April). *Measuring the instructional leadership competence of school principals.* Paper presented at the annual meeting of the American Educational Research Association, San Francisco.

Gomez, L., & Fishman, B. (2001). *The administrators' reform community: Phase II.* Proposal to the Joyce Foundation, Chicago.

Goncz, B., & Kodzepeljic, D. (1991). Cognition and bilingualism revisited. *Journal of Multicultural Development, 12,* 137–163.

Greene, J. (1998). *A meta-analysis of the effectiveness of bilingual education*. Claremont, CA: Tomas Rivera Policy Institute.

Greeno, J. G. (1980). Psychology of learning, 1960–1980: One participant's observations. *American Psychologist, 35*(8), 713–728.

Grigg, W., Lauko, M., & Brockway, D. (2006). *The nation's report card: Science 2005* (NCES 2006-466). Washington, DC: U.S. Government Printing Office.

Grossman, P., Wineburg, S., & Woolworth, S. (2001). Toward a theory of teacher community. *Teachers College Record, 103*(6), 942–1012.

Halberstam, D. (1993). *The best and the brightest*. New York: Ballantine Books.

Hallinger, P. (2003). Leading educational change: Reflections on the practice of instructional and transformative leadership. *Cambridge Journal of Education, 33*(3), 329–351.

Hammerness, K., Darling-Hammond, L., & Bransford, J. (2005). How teachers learn and develop. In L. Darling-Hammond & J. Bransford (Eds.), *Preparing teachers for a changing world: What teachers should learn and be able to do* (pp. 358–389). San Francisco: John Wiley & Sons.

Harris, C., McNeill, K. L., Lizotte, D. L., Marx, R. W., & Krajcik, J. S. (2006). Usable assessments for teaching science content and inquiry standards. In M. McMahon, P. Simmons, R. Sommers, D. Debaets, & F. Crowley (Eds.), *Assessment in science: Practical experiences and education research* (pp. 67–88). Arlington, VA: National Science Teachers Association.

Harrison, A. G., Grayson, D. J., & Treagust, D. F. (1999). Investigating a grade 11 student's evolving conceptions of heat and temperature. *Journal of Research in Science Teaching, 36*(1), 55–87.

Hatano, G., & Inagaki, K. (Eds.). (1991). *Sharing cognition through collective comprehension activity*. Washington DC: American Psychological Association.

Hatton, N., & Smith, D. (1995). Reflection in teacher education: Towards definition and implementation. *Teaching and Teacher Education, 11*(1), 33–49.

Heller, P. (2001, February–March). *Lessons learned in the CIPS curriculum project*. Paper presented at the AAAS Conference on Developing Textbooks That Promote Science Literacy, Washington, DC. Retrieved October 17, 2006, from http://www.project2061.org/events/meetings/textbook/literacy/default.htm

Herrington, J. A. (2006). Authentic e-learning in higher education: Design principles for authentic learning environments and tasks. In T. C. Reeves & S. Yamashita (Eds.), *Proceedings of World Conference on E-Learning in Corporate, Government, Healthcare, and Higher Education 2006* (pp. 3164–3173). Chesapeake, VA: AACE.

Hew, K., & Brush, T. (2007). Integrating technology into K–12 teaching and learning: Current knowledge gaps and recommendations for future research. *Educational Technology Research and Development, 55*(3), 223–252.

Hickey, D. T., Kindfeld, A. C., Horwitz, P., & Christie, M. A. (2003). Integrating instruction assessment, and evaluation in a technology-supported genetics environment. *American Educational Research Journal, 40*(2), 495–538.

Hiebert, J., Carpenter, T. P., Fuson, J., Human, P., & Wearne, D. (1996). Problem solving as a basis for reform in curriculum and instruction: The case of mathematics. *Educational Researcher, 25*(4), 12–21.

Holland, L., & Moore-Steward, T. (2000). A different divide: Preparing tech-savvy leaders. *Leadership, 30*(1), 37–38.

Horwitz, P., & Christie, M. (1999). Hypermodels: Embedding curriculum and assessment in computer-based manipulatives. *Journal of Education, 181*(2), 1–23.

Hubisz, J. L. (n.d.). *Review of middle school physical science texts.* North Carolina State University, Middle School Physical Science Resource Center. Retrieved May 31, 2008, from http://www.science-house.org/middleschool/reviews/index.html

Hug, H., Krajcik, J. S., & Marx, R. W. (2005). Using innovative learning technologies to promote learning and engagement in an urban science classroom. *Urban Education, 40,* 446–472.

Hurd, P. (1970). *New directions in teaching secondary school science.* Chicago: Rand McNally.

Ingersoll, R. (2001). Teacher turnover and teacher shortage: An organizational analysis. *American Educational Research Journal, 38*(3), 499–534.

Isserman, A. (2001). Competitive advantages of rural America in the next century. *International Regional Science Review, 24*(1), 38–58.

Jackson, S. L., Stratford, S. J., Krajcik, J., & Soloway, E. (1994). Making dynamic modeling accessible to precollege science students. *Interactive Learning Environments, 4*(3), 233–257.

Kali, Y. (2002). CILT2000: Visualization and modeling. *Journal of Science Education and Technology, 11*(3), 305–310.

Kali, Y. (2006). Collaborative knowledge building using the Design Principles Database. *International Journal of Computer Support for Collaborative Learning, 1*(2), 187–201.

Kali, Y. (2008). The Design Principles Database as means for promoting design-based research. In A. E. Kelly, R. A. Lesh, & J. Y. Baek (Eds.), *Handbook of design research methods in education: Innovations in science, technology, engineering, and mathematics learning and teaching.* Mahwah, NJ: Erlbaum.

Kali, Y., Levin-Peled, R., & Dori, Y. J. (in press). The role of design-principles in designing courses that promote collaborative learning in higher-education. *Computers in Human Behavior.*

Kali, Y., & Linn, M. C. (2007). Technology-enhanced support strategies for inquiry learning. In J. M. Spector, M. D. Merrill, J. J. G. V. Merriënboer, & M. P. Driscoll (Eds.), *Handbook of research on educational communications and technology* (3rd ed., pp. 445–490). Mahwah, NJ: Erlbaum.

Kali, Y., & Linn, M. C. (in press). Curriculum design—as subject matter: Science. In B. McGraw, E. Baker, & P. Peterson (Eds.), *International encyclopedia of education* (3rd ed.). Philadelphia: Elsevier.

Kali, Y., Spitulnik, M., & Linn, M. C. (2004). Building community using the Design Principles Database. In P. Gerjets, P. A. Kirschner, P. A. Allen, J. Elen, & R. Joiner (Eds.), *Instructional design for effective and enjoyable computer-supported learning. Proceedings of the first joint meeting of the EARLI SIGs: 'Instructional Design' and 'Learning and Instruction with Computers'* (pp. 294–305). Tübingen: Knowledge Media Research Center.

Kanter, D., & Schreck, M. (2006). Learning content using complex data in project-based science: An example from high school biology in urban classrooms. *New Directions in Teaching and Learning, 108,* 77–91.

Keller, E. F. (1983). Gender and science. In S. Harding & M. Hintikka (Eds.), *Discovering reality: Feminist perspectives on epistemology, metaphysics, methodology, and philosophy of science* (pp. 187–205). Dordrecht: Reidel.

Kesidou, S., & Roseman, J. E. (2002). How well do middle school science programs measure up? Findings from Project 2061's curriculum review. *Journal of Research in Science Teaching, 39*(6), 522–549.

Kessler, C., & Quinn, M. E. (1987). ESL and science learning. In J. Crandall (Ed.), *ESL through content-area instruction* (pp. 55–87). Englewood Cliffs, NJ: Prentice Hall Regents.

Kirst, M. W., & Bird, R. L. (1997). *The politics of developing and maintaining mathematics and science curriculum content standards.* National Center for Improving Science Education, Research Monograph 2. Madison: University of Wisconsin.

Knapp, M. S. (1997). Between systemic reforms and the mathematics and science classroom: The dynamics of innovation, implementation, and professional learning. *Review of Educational Research, 67*(2), 227–266.

Kozma, R. B., Russell, J., Jones, T., Marx, N., & Davis, J. (1996). The use of multiple, linked representations to facilitate science understanding. In S. Vosniadou, E. DeCorte, & H. Mandel (Eds.), *International perspectives on the psychological foundations of technology-based learning environments* (pp. 41–60). Mahwah, NJ: Erlbaum.

Kozol, J. (2005). Still separate, still unequal. *Harper's Magazine, 311,* 41–54.

Krajcik, J. S., & Blumenfeld, P. (2006). Project-based learning. In R. K. Sawyer (Ed.), *The Cambridge handbook of the learning sciences* (pp. 317–334). New York: Cambridge University Press.

Krajcik, J. S., Blumenfeld, P. C., Marx, R. W., Bass, K. M., Fredricks, J., & Soloway, E. (1998). Inquiry in project-based science classrooms: Initial attempts by middle school students. *The Journal of the Learning Sciences, 7*(3/4), 313–350.

Krajcik, J. S., Blumenfeld, P. C., Marx, R. W., & Soloway, E. (1994). A collaborative model for helping middle grade science teachers learn project-based instruction. *The Elementary School Journal, 94*(5), 483–497.

Krajcik, J., Blumenfeld, P., Marx, R., & Soloway, E. (2000). Instructional, curricular, and technological supports for inquiry in science classrooms. In J. Minstell & E. V. Zee (Eds.), *Inquiry into inquiry: Learning and teaching in science* (pp. 283–316). Washington, DC: American Association for the Advancement of Science Press.

Krajcik, J. S., & Czerniak, C. (2007). *Teaching science in elementary and middle school classrooms: A project-based approach* (3rd ed.). London: Taylor and Francis.

Krajcik, J. S., McNeill, K., & Reiser, B. J. (2008). Learning-goals-driven design model: Curriculum materials that align with national standards and incorporate project-based pedagogy. *Science Education, 92*(1), 1–32.

Krajcik, J. S., & Reiser, B. J. (Eds.). (2006). *IQWST: Investigating and Questioning Our World Through Science and Technology.* Ann Arbor: University of Michigan.

Kuhn, L., & Reiser, B. J. (2006, April). *Structuring activities to foster argumentative discourse.* Paper presented at the annual meeting of the American Educational Research Association, San Francisco.

Kusmin, L. (Ed.). (2006). *Rural America at a glance: 2006 edition.* Economic Information Bulletin No. (EIB-18). Washington, DC: U.S. Department of Agriculture Economic Research Service. Retrieved May 31, 2008, from http://www.ers.usda.gov/Publications/EIB18/

Ladson-Billings, G. (1994). *The Dreamkeepers: Successful teachers of African American children.* San Francisco: Jossey-Bass.

Ladson-Billings, G. (1998). Just what is critical race theory and what's it doing in a nice field like education? *International Journal of Qualitative Studies in Education, 11*(1), 7–24.

Larkin, J., & Reif, F. (1979). Understanding and teaching problem-solving in physics. *European Journal of Science Education, 1*(2), 191–203.

Laufer, B., & Hill, M. (2000). What lexical information do L2 learners select in a CALL dictionary and how does it affect word retention? *Language Learning & Technology, 3*(2), 58–76.

Lave, J., & Wenger, E. (1991). Situated learning: Legitimate peripheral participation. In R. Pea & J. S. Brown (Eds.), *Learning in doing: Social, cognitive, and computational perspectives* (pp. 29–129). Cambridge, UK: Cambridge University Press.

Lee, H.-S., Linn, M. C., & Varma, K. (in press). Impact of visualization-based inquiry science experience on classroom learning. *Journal of Research in Science Teaching*.

Lee, H.-S., Liu, O. L., & Linn, M. C. (2008). *Construct validity of inquiry assessments: The role of multiple-choice and explanation item formats*. Manuscript submitted for publication.

Lee, H.-S., & Songer, N. (2003). Making authentic science accessible to students. *International Journal of Science Education, 25*(8), 923–948.

Lee, O., Eichinger, D. C., Anderson, C. W., Berkheimer, G. D., & Blakeslee, T. S. (1993). Changing middle school students' conceptions of matter and molecules. *Journal of Research in Science Teaching, 30*, 249–270.

Lee, O., & Fradd, S. H. (1998). Science for all, including students from non-English language backgrounds. *Educational Researcher, 27*(3), 12–21.

Leithwood, K., & Montgomery, D. (1982). The role of the elementary school principal in program improvement: A review. *Review of Educational Research, 52*(3), 309–339.

Leithwood, K., & Stager, M. (1989). Expertise in principals' problem solving. *Education Administration Quarterly, 25*(2), 126–161.

Leithwood, K., & Steinbach, R. (1992). Improving the problem-solving expertise of school administrators: Theory and practice. *Education and Urban Society, 24*(3), 317–345.

Lemke, J. L. (1990). *Talking science: Language, learning, and values*. Norwood, NJ: Ablex.

Lewis, C. (1995). *Educating hearts and minds: Reflections on Japanese preschool and elementary education*. New York: Cambridge University Press.

Lewis, C., Perry, R., & Hurd, J. (2004). A deeper look at lesson study. *Educational Leadership, 61*(5), 6–11.

Lewis, C., & Tsuchida, I. (1998). A lesson is like a swiftly flowing river: Research lessons and the improvement of Japanese education. *American Educator, Winter, 12*, 14–17, 50–52.

LIFE Center. (2007). *Learning in and out of school in diverse environment*. Seattle: The LIFE Center (The Learning in Informal and Formal Environments Center) and the Center for Multicultural Education, University of Washington.

Lin, X. D., & Schwartz, D. (2003). Reflection at the crossroad of cultures. *Mind, Culture & Activities, 10*(1), 9–25.

Linn, M. C. (1995). Designing computer learning environments for engineering and computer science: The scaffolded knowledge integration framework. *Journal of Science Education and Technology, 4*(2), 103–126.

Linn, M. C. (1997). Learning and instruction in science education: Taking advantage of technology. In D. Tobin & B. J. Fraser (Eds.), *International handbook of science education*. Dordrecht: Kluwer.

Linn, M. C. (2005). WISE design for lifelong learning—Pivotal cases. In P. Gärdenfors & P. Johansson (Eds.), *Cognition, education and communication technology* (pp. 223–256). Mahwah, NJ: Erlbaum.

Linn, M. C. (2006). The knowledge integration perspective on learning and instruction. In R. K. Sawyer (Ed.), *The Cambridge handbook of the learning sciences* (pp. 243–264). New York: Cambridge University Press.

Linn, M. C., Bell, P., & Davis, E. A. (2004). Specific design principles: Elaborating the scaffolded knowledge integration framework. In M. C. Linn, E. A. Davis, & P. Bell (Eds.), *Internet environments for science education* (pp. 315–340). Mahwah, NJ: Erlbaum.

Linn, M. C., Clark, D., & Slotta, J. D. (2003). WISE design for knowledge integration. *Science Education, 87*, 517–538.

Linn, M. C., Davis, E. A., & Bell, P. (Eds.). (2004). *Internet environments for science education*. Mahwah, NJ: Erlbaum.

Linn, M. C., & Eylon, B.-S. (2006). Science education: Integrating views of learning and instruction. In P. A. Alexander & P. H. Winne (Eds.), *Handbook of educational psychology* (2nd ed., pp. 511–544). Mahwah, NJ: Erlbaum.

Linn, M. C., & Holmes, J. (2006). *Establishing a design process for technology enhanced learning* (TELS Report). Berkeley: University of California.

Linn, M. C., & Hsi, S. (2000). *Computers, teachers, peers: Science learning partners.* Mahwah, NJ: Erlbaum.

Linn, M. C., Husic, F., Slotta, J., & Tinker, R. (2006). Technology Enhanced Learning in Science (TELS): Research programs. *Educational Technology, 46*(3), 54–68.

Linn, M. C., Lee, H.-S., Tinker, R., Husic, F., & Chiu, J. L. (2006). Teaching and assessing knowledge integration in science. *Science, 313,* 1049–1050.

Linn, M. C., & Slotta, J. D. (2006). Enabling participants in online forums to learn from each other. In A. O'Donnell, C. Hemelo-Silver, & G. Erkens (Eds.), *Collaborative learning, reasoning, and technology* (pp. 61–98). Mahwah, NJ: Erlbaum.

Little, J. W. (1999). Organizing schools for teacher learning. In L. Darling-Hammond & G. Sykes (Eds.), *Teaching as the learning profession: Handbook of teaching and policy* (pp. 233–262). San Francisco: Jossey Bass.

Little, J. W. (2003). Inside teacher community: Representations of classroom practice. *Teachers College Record, 105*(6), 913–945.

Liu, O. L., Lee, H. S., Hofstetter, C., & Linn, M. C. (2008). Assessing knowledge integration in science: Construct, measures and evidence. *Educational Assessment, 13*(1), 33–55.

Lomicka, L. (1998). To gloss or not to gloss: An investigation of reading comprehension online. *Language Learning & Technology, 1*(2), 41–50.

Longino, H. (1994). The fate of knowledge in social theories of science. In F. F. Schmitt (Ed.), *Socializing epistemology: The social dimensions of knowledge* (pp. 135–158). Lanham, MD: Rowan and Littlefield.

Loughran, J., & Gunstone, R. (1997). Professional development in residence: Developing reflection on science teaching and learning. *Journal of Education for Teaching, 23*(2), 159–178.

Louis, K. S., & Kruse, S. D. (1995). *Professionalism and community: Perspectives on reforming urban schools.* Thousand Oaks, CA: Corwin Press.

Lynch, S., Kuipers, J., Pyke, C., & Szesze, M. (2005). Examining the effects of a highly rated science curriculum unit on diverse students: Results from a planning grant. *Journal of Research in Science Teaching, 42*(8), 912–946.

Magnusson, S., Krajcik, J. S., & Borko, H. (1999). Nature, sources and development of pedagogical content knowledge for science teaching. In J. Gess-Newsome & N. G. Lederman (Eds.), *Examining pedagogical content knowledge: The construct and its implications for science education* (pp. 95–132). Boston: Kluwer.

Maleki, E. J. (2001). Going digital in rural America. In M. Drabenstott (Ed.), *Exploring policy options for a new rural America* (pp. 49–68). Kansas City, MO: Center for the Study of Rural America, Federal Reserve Bank of Kansas City.

Markham, K., Mintzes, J., & Jones, G. (1994). The concept map as a research and evaluation tool: Further evidence of validity. *Journal of Research in Science Teaching, 31*(1), 91–101.

Martinez-Lage, A. (1997). Hypermedia technology for teaching reading. In M. D. Bush & R. M. Terry (Eds.), *Technology-enhanced language learning.* Lincolnwood, IL: National Textbook.

Marx, R. W., & Harris, C. (2006). No Child Left Behind and science education: Opportunities, challenges and risks. *The Elementary School Journal, 106*(5), 467–477.

Massell, D. (1994). Three challenges for national content standards. *Education and Urban Society, 26*(2), 185–195.

Mawyer, K., Johnson, H., & Edelson, D. (2008). *Professional development for novice curriculum users.* Manuscript in preparation.

McCloskey, M., Caramazza, A., & Green, B. (1980). Curvilinear motion in the absence of external forces: Naive beliefs about the motion of objects. *Science, 210,* 1139–1141.

McColskey, W., & McMunn, N. (2002). Can high-stakes state testing be improved? *The Vision, 1*(2), 4–6.

McDermott, L. C. (1984). Research on conceptual understanding in mechanics. *Physics Today, 37,* 24–32.

McElhaney, K. W. (2007a, April). *Relating students' experimentation with a visualization to their understanding of kinematics.* Poster presented at the annual meeting of American Educational Research Association, Chicago.

McElhaney, K. W. (2007b, April). *Using pivotal cases to help learners understand and integrate chemistry representations.* Paper presented at the annual meeting of American Educational Research Association, Chicago.

McGilly, K. (Ed.). (1994). *Classroom lessons: Integrating cognitive theory and classroom practice.* Cambridge, MA: MIT Press.

McGinn, M. K., & Roth, W.-M. (1998). Assessing students' understandings about levers: Better test instruments are not enough. *International Journal of Science Education, 20,* 813–832.

McGinn, M. K., & Roth, W.-M. (1999). Towards a new science education: Implications of recent research in science and technology studies. *Educational Researcher, 28*(3), 14–24.

McKeown, M. G., Beck, I. L., Sinatra, G. M., & Loxterman, J. A. (1992). The contribution of prior knowledge and coherent text to comprehension. *Reading Research Quarterly, 27*(1), 78–93.

McLaughlin, M. W., & Mitra, D. (2001). Theory-based change and change-based theory: Going deeper, going broader. *Journal of Educational Change, 2,* 301–323.

McNamara, T. P., Kintsch, E., Songer, N. B., & Kintsch, W. (1996). Are good texts always better? Interactions of text coherence, background knowledge, and levels of understanding in learning from text. *Cognition and Instruction, 14,* 1–43.

McNeill, K. L., Harris, C. J., Heitzman, M., Lizotte, D. J., Sutherland, L. M., & Krajcik, J. S. (2004). How can I make new stuff from old stuff? In J. Krajcik & B. J. Reiser (Eds.), *IQWST: Investigating and Questioning Our World Through Science and Technology.* Ann Arbor: University of Michigan.

McNeill, K. L., & Krajcik, J. S. (2008a). Assessing middle school students' content knowledge and reasoning through written scientific explanations. In J. Coffey, R. Douglas, & C. Stearns (Eds.), *Assessing science learning: Perspectives from research and practice* (pp. 101–116). Arlington, VA: National Science Teachers Association Press.

McNeill, K. L., & Krajcik, J. S. (2008b). Inquiry and scientific explanations: Helping students use evidence and reasoning. In J. Luft, R. Bell, & J. Gess-Newsome (Eds.), *Science as inquiry in the secondary setting* (pp. 121–134). Arlington, VA: National Science Teachers Association Press.

McNeill, K. L., & Krajcik, J. S. (2008c). Scientific explanations: Characterizing and evaluating the effects of teachers' instructional practices on student learning. *Journal of Research in Science Teaching, 45*(1), 53–78.

McNeill, K. L., Lizotte, D. J., Krajcik, J. S., & Marx, R. W. (2006). Supporting students' construction of scientific explanations by fading scaffolds in instructional materials. *The Journal of the Learning Sciences, 15*(2), 153–191.

Merrill, M. D. (2002). First principles of instruction. *Educational Technology Research and Development, 50*(3), 43–59.

Merrill, R., & Ridgway, D. (1969). *The CHEM Study story.* San Francisco: Freeman.

Merritt, J., Schwartz, Y., & Krajcik, J. (2007, April). *Middle school students' development of the particle model of matter.* Paper presented at the annual meeting of the National Association for Research in Science Teaching, New Orleans, LA.

Metcalf-Jackson, S. J., Krajcik, J. S., & Soloway, E. (2000). Model-It: A design retrospective. In J. M. Jacobson & R. B. Kozma (Eds.), *Innovations in science and mathematics education: Advanced design for technologies of learning* (pp. 77–115). Mahwah, NJ: Erlbaum.

Meyer, M., & Fienberg, S. (1992). *Assessing evaluation studies: The case of bilingual education strategies.* Washington, DC: National Academy Press.

Minstrell, J. (1991). Facets of students' knowledge and relevant education. In R. Duit, F. Goldberg, & H. Niedderer (Eds.), *Proceedings of an international workshop—Research in Physics Learning: Theoretical Issues and Empirical Studies* (pp. 110–128). Kiel, Germany: The Institute for Science Education (IPN).

Moje, E. B., Peek-Brown, D., Sutherland, L. M., Marx, R. W., Blumenfeld, P., & Krajcik, J. (2004). Explaining explanations: Developing scientific literacy in middle-school project-based science reforms. In D. Strickland & D. E. Alvermann (Eds.), *Bridging the gap: Improving literacy learning for preadolescent and adolescent learners in grades 4–12* (pp. 227–251). New York: Teachers College Press.

Mor, Y., & Winters, N. (2007). Design approaches in technology enhanced learning. *Interactive Learning Environments, 15,* 61–75.

Murphy, J. (2002). Reculturing the profession of educational leadership: New blueprints. *Educational Administration Quarterly, 38*(2), 176–191.

Murray, O., Fishman, B., Gomez, L., Williams, K., & Marx, R. (2001, April). *Building a community of administrators between and within urban school districts in support of systemic reform efforts.* Paper presented at the annual meeting of the American Educational Research Association, Seattle.

Nagel, E. (1961). *The structure of science: Problems in the logic of science education.* New York: Harcourt, Brace, & World.

National Center for Education Statistics. (2003). *Digest of education statistics, 2003.* Retrieved May 31, 2008, from http://nces.ed.gov/pubsearch/pubsinfo.asp?pubid=2005025

National Center for Education Statistics. (2006). *The condition of education 2006* (NCES 2006-071). Washington, DC: U.S. Government Printing Office.

National Commission on Excellence in Education. (1983). *A nation at risk: The imperative for educational reform.* Washington, DC: U.S. Government Printing Office.

National Council of Teachers of Mathematics. (1989). *Curriculum and evaluation standards for school mathematics.* Washington, DC: National Council of Teachers of Mathematics.

National Research Council (NRC). (1996). *National Science Education Standards: 1996.* Washington, DC: National Academy Press.

National Research Council (NRC). (1999). *Improving student learning.* Washington, DC: National Academy Press.

National Research Council (NRC). (2007). *Taking science to school: Learning and teaching science in grades K–8.* Washington, DC: National Academies Press.

National Research Council (NRC). (2000a). *Inquiry and the National Science Education Standards.* Washington, DC: National Academy Press.

National Research Council (NRC). (2000b). *National Science Education Standards.* Washington, DC: National Academy Press.

National Science Foundation (2004). *Science and engineering indicators 2004.* Retrieved December 29, 2004, from http://www.nsf.gov/sbe/srs/seind04/

National Science Foundation Cyberinfrastructure Council. (2007). *Cyberinfrastructure vision for 21st century discovery.* Washington, DC: National Science Foundation.

National Science Teachers Association. (1982). *Science-technology-society: Science education for the 1980s.* Washington, DC: National Science Teachers Association.

National Society for the Study of Education. (1947). *Science education in American schools: Forty-sixth yearbook of the NSSE.* Chicago: University of Chicago Press.

Novak, A., & Krajcik, J. S. (2004). Using learning technologies to support inquiry in middle school science. In L. Flick & N. Lederman (Eds.), *Scientific inquiry and nature of science: Implications for teaching, learning, and teacher education* (Vol. 75-102). Dordrecht: Kluwer.

Office of Technology Assessment, U.S. Congress. (1988). *Power On! New tools for teaching and learning* (No. OTA-SET-379). Washington, DC: U.S. Government Printing Office.

Ogborn, J. (1999). Modeling clay for thinking and learning. In W. Feurzeig & N. Roberts (Eds.), *Modeling and simulation in science and mathematics education* (pp. 5–37). New York: Springer.

Olson, L., & Hoff, D. J. (2006). Framing the debate. *Education Week, 26*(15), 22, 24, 26–27.

O'Sullivan, C. Y., Reese, C. M., & Mazzeo, J. (1997). *NAEP 1996 science report card for the nation and the states.* Washington, DC: National Center for Education Statistics.

Overbaugh, R. (2002). Undergraduate education majors' discourse on an electronic mailing list. *Journal of Research on Technology in Education, 35*(1), 117–138.

Palincsar, A. S., & Brown, A. L. (1984). Reciprocal teaching of comprehension-fostering and comprehension-monitoring activities. *Cognition and Instruction, 1,* 117–175.

Pea, R. D. (2004). The social and technological dimensions of scaffolding and related theoretical concepts for learning, education, and human activity. *The Journal of the Learning Sciences, 13,* 423–451.

Pea, R. D., Gomez, L. M., Edelson, D. C., Fishman, B. J., Gordin, D. N., & O'Neill, D. K. (1997). Science education as a driver of cyberspace technology development. In K. C. Cohen (Ed.), *Internet links for science education* (pp. 189–220). New York: Plenum Press.

Pea, R. D., Wulf, W., Elliot, S. W., & Darling, M. (2003). *Planning for two transformations in education and learning technology* (Committee on Improving Learning with Information Technology). Washington, DC: National Academies Press.

Peal, E., & Lambert, W. E. (1962). The relation of bilingualism to intelligence. *Psychological Monographs, 76*(27, 546), 1–23.

Peers, C., Diezmann, C., & Watters, J. J. (2003). Supports and concerns for teacher professional growth during the implementation of a science curriculum innovation. *Research in Science Education, 33,* 89–110.

Pellegrino, J. W., Chudowsky, N., & Glaser, R. (Eds.). (2001). *Knowing what students know: The science and design of educational assessment.* Washington, DC: National Academy Press.

Perkins, D. N., Crismond, D., Simmons, R., & Unger, C. (1995). Inside understanding. In D. N. Perkins, J. L. Schwartz, M. M. West, & M. S. Wiske (Eds.), *Software goes to school: Teaching for understanding with new technologies* (pp. 70–87). New York: Oxford University Press.

Peterson, K. (2000). The professional development of principals: Innovations and opportunities. *Education Administration Quarterly, 38*(2), 213–232.

Peterson, P. L., & Barnes, C. (1996). Learning together: The challenge of mathematics, equity, and leadership. *Phi Delta Kappan, 77*(7), 485–491.

Pintó, R. (2005). Introducing curriculum innovations in science: Identifying teachers' trans-formations and the design of related teacher education. *Science Education, 89*(1), 1–12.

Polakow, V. (2000). Savage policies: Systematic violence and the lives of children. In V. Polakow (Ed.), *The public assault on America's children: Poverty, violence, and juvenile injustice* (pp. 1–20). New York: Teachers College Press.

Prawat, R., & Peterson, P. L. (1999). Social constructivist views of learning. In J. Murphy & K. S. Lewis (Eds.), *Handbook of research in educational administration* (pp. 203–226). New York: Macmillan.

President's Committee of Advisors on Science and Technology (PCAST). (1997, March). *Report to the President on the use of technology to strengthen K–12 education in the United States.* Washington, DC: White House Office of Science and Technology Policy. Retrieved December 29, 2007, from http://tinyurl.com/2u3mqa

Prestine, N., & Nelson, B. (2005). How can educational leaders support and promote teaching and learning? New conceptions of learning and leading in schools. In W. Firestone & C. Riehl (Eds.), *A new agenda for educational leadership* (pp. 46–61). New York: Teachers College Press.

Putnam, R., & Borko, H. (2000). What do new views of knowledge and thinking have to say about research on teacher learning? *Educational Researcher, 29*(1), 4–15.

Quintana, C., Reiser, B. J., Davis, E. A., Krajcik, J. S., Fretz, E., Golan, R. D., et al. (2004). A scaffolding design framework for software to support science inquiry. *Journal of the Learning Sciences, 13*(3), 337–386.

Reiser, B., Krajcik, J., Moje, E., & Marx, R. (2003, March). *Design strategies for developing science instructional materials.* Paper presented at the annual meeting of the National Association for Research in Science Teaching (NARST), Philadelphia.

Reiser, B. J., Tabak, I., Sandoval, W. A., Smith, B. K., Steinmuller, F., & Leone, A. J. (2001). BGuILE: Strategic and conceptual scaffolds for scientific inquiry in biology classrooms. In S. M. Carver & D. Klahr (Eds.), *Cognition and instruction: Twenty five years of progress* (pp. 263–305). Mahwah, NJ: Erlbaum.

Remillard, J. T. (1999). Curriculum materials in mathematics education reform: A framework for examining teachers' curriculum development. *Curriculum Inquiry, 19*(3), 315–342.

Remillard, J. T. (2000). Can curriculum materials support teachers' learning? Two fourth-grade teachers' use of a new mathematics text. *The Elementary School Journal, 100*(4), 331–350.

Repenning, A., & Sumner, T. (1995). Agentsheets: A medium for creating domain-oriented visual languages. *IEEE Computer, 28,* 17–25.

Resnick, M., & Wilensky, U. (1998). Diving into complexity: Developing probabilistic decentralized thinking through role-playing activities. *The Journal of the Learning Sciences, 7*(2), 153–172.

Retalis, S., Georgiakakis, P., & Dimitriadis, Y. (2006). Eliciting design patterns for e-learning systems. *Computer Science Education, 16*(2), 105–118.

Roby, W. B. (1999). "What's in a gloss?" A response to Lara L. Lomicka's "To Gloss or Not to Gloss: An Investigation of Reading Comprehension Online." *Language Learning & Technology, 2*(2), 94–101.

Rodriguez, A. (1998). Busting open the meritocracy myth: Rethinking equity and student achievement in science education. *Journal of Women and Minorities in Science and Engineering, 4,* 195–216.

Ronen-Fuhrmann, T., Kali, Y., & Hoadley, C. M. (2008). Helping education students understand learning through designing. *Educational Technology, 48*(2), 26–33.

Roseman, J. E., Caldwell, A., Gogos, A., & Kurth, L. (2006, April). *Mapping a coherent learning progression for the molecular basis of heredity.* Paper presented at the annual meeting of the National Association for Research in Science Teaching, San Francisco.

Roseman, J., Kesidou, S., & Stern, L. (1996, November). *Identifying curriculum materials for science literacy: A Project 2061 evaluation tool.* Paper presented at the National Research Council Colloquium: Using the *National Science Education Standards* to Guide the Evaluation, Selection, and Adaptation of Instructional Materials, Washington, DC.

Roseman, J., Stern, L., & Koppal, M. (2008). *A method for analyzing the coherence of textbooks and its application to high school biology textbooks.* Manuscript submitted for publication.

Roth, K. J., Anderson, C. W., & Smith, E. L. (1987). Curriculum materials, teacher talk and student learning: Case studies in fifth grade science teaching. *Journal of Curriculum Studies, 19*(6), 527–548.

Roth, W.-M., & Lee, S. (2004). Science education as/for participation in the community. *Science Education, 88,* 263–291.

Ruiz-Primo, M., & Furtak, E. (2006). Informal formative assessment and scientific inquiry: Exploring teachers' practices and student learning. *Educational Assessment, 11*(3&4), 205–235.

Rutherford, F. J., & Ahlgren, A. (1991). *Science for all Americans.* New York: Oxford University Press.

Sadler, P. M. (1987). Misconceptions in astronomy. In J. Novak (Ed.), *Misconceptions and educational strategies in science and mathematics* (pp. 422–437). Ithaca, NY: Cornell University Press.

Salomon, G., Perkins, D. N., & Globerson, T. (1991). Partners in cognition: Extending human intelligence with intelligent technologies. *Educational Researcher, 20*(3), 2–9.

Sarason, S. B. (1971). *The culture of the school and the problem of change.* Boston: Allyn & Bacon.

Sarason, S. B. (1996). *Revisiting "The culture of the school and the problem of change."* New York: Teachers College Press.

Scardamalia, M., & Bereiter, C. (1994). Computer support for knowledge-building communities. *The Journal of the Learning Sciences, 3*(3), 265–283.

Scardamalia, M., & Bereiter, C. (1999). Schools as knowledge-building organizations. In D. Keating & C. Hertzman (Eds.), *Today's children tomorrow's society: The developmental health and wealth of nations* (pp. 274–289). New York: Guildford.

Schmidt, W. H., McKnight, C. C., & Raizen, S. A. (1997). *A splintered vision: An investigation of U.S. science and mathematics education.* Dordrecht, Boston: Kluwer.

Schneider, R., & Krajcik, J. S. (2002). Supporting science teacher learning: The role of educative curriculum materials. *Journal of Science Teacher Education, 13*(3), 221–245.

Schneider, R., Krajcik, J. S., & Marx, R. W. (2000, April). *The role of educative curriculum materials in reforming science education.* Paper presented at the annual meeting of the American Educational Research Association, New Orleans, LA.

Schoenfeld, A. H. (1985). *Mathematical problem solving.* Orlando, FL: Academic Press.

Schwarz, C., Gunckel, K., Smith, E., Covitt, B., Bae, M., Enfield, M., et al. (2008). Helping elementary preservice teachers learn to use curriculum materials for effective science teaching. *Science Education, 92*(2), 345–377.

Shen, J., Gerard, L. F., & Bowyer, J. B. (2008). *Getting from here to there: The roles of policy makers and principals in increasing science teacher quality.* Manuscript submitted for publication.

Shternberg, B., & Yerushalmy, M. (2003). Models of functions and models of situations: On the design of modeling-based learning environments. In R. A. Lesh & H. M. Doerr (Eds.), *Beyond constructivism: Models and modeling perspectives on mathematics problem solving, learning, and teaching* (pp. 479–500). Mahwah, NJ: Erlbaum.

Shulman, L. S. (1986). Those who understand: Knowledge growth in teaching. *Educational Researcher, 15*(2), 4–14.

Shwartz, Y., Weizman, A., Fortus, D., Krajcik, J., & Reiser, B. (in press). The IQWST experience: Coherence as a design principle. *The Elementary School Journal.*

Shymansky, J. A., Kyle, W. C., & Alport, J. M. (1983). The effects of new science curricula on student performance. *Journal of Research in Science Teaching, 20,* 387–404.

Singer, J., Marx, R. W., Krajcik, J., & Chambers, J. C. (2000). Constructing extended inquiry projects: Curriculum materials for science education reform. *Educational Psychologist, 35*(3), 165–178.

Slotta, J. D. (2004). The Web-based Inquiry Science Environment (WISE): Scaffolding knowledge integration in the science classroom. In M. C. Linn, E. A. Davis, & P. Bell (Eds.), *Internet environments for science education* (pp. 203–232). Mahwah, NJ: Erlbaum.

Slotta, J. D., & Linn, M. C. (2000). How do students make sense of Internet resources in the science classroom? In M. J. Jacobson & R. Kozma (Eds.), *Learning the sciences of the 21st century* (pp. 193–226). Hillsdale, NJ: Erlbaum.

Smith, J. P., diSessa, A. A., & Roschelle, J. (1993/1994). Misconceptions reconceived: A constructivist analysis of knowledge in transition. *The Journal of the Learning Sciences, 3*(2), 115–163.

Smith, T., & Ingersoll, R. (2004). What are the effects of induction and mentoring on beginning teacher turnover? *American Educational Research Journal, 41*(3), 681–714.

Smithey, J., & Davis, E. A. (2004). Preservice elementary science teachers' identity development: Identifying with particular images of inquiry. In Y. B. Kafai, W. A. Sandoval, N. Enyedy, A. S. Nixon, & F. Herrera (Eds.), *Proceedings of the 6th International Conference of the Learning Sciences, ICLS2004.* Mahwah, NJ: Erlbaum.

Smylie, M., Bennet, A., Konkol, P., & Fendt, C. (2002). What do we know about developing school leaders? A look at existing research and next steps for new study. In W. Firestone & C. Riehl (Eds.), *A new agenda for educational leadership* (pp. 138–156). New York: Teachers College Press.

Soloway, E., Grant, W., Tinker, R., Roschelle, J., Mills, M., Resnick, M., et al. (1999). Science in the palm of their hands. *Communications of the ACM, 42*(8), 21–26.

Songer, N. B. (1996). Exploring learning opportunities in coordinated network-enhanced classrooms—A case of kids as global scientists. *Journal of the Learning Sciences, 5*(4), 297–327.

Songer, N. B., Lee, H. S., & Kam, R. (2002). Technology-rich inquiry science in urban classrooms: What are the barriers to inquiry pedagogy? *Journal of Research in Science Teaching, 39*(2), 128–150.

Songer, N. B., & Linn, M. C. (1991). How do students' views of science influence knowledge integration? *Journal of Research in Science Teaching, 28*(9), 761–784.

Songer, N. B., & Linn, M. C. (1992). How do students' views of science influence knowledge integration? In M. K. Pearsall (Ed.), *Scope, sequence and coordination of secondary school science, Volume I: Relevant research* (pp. 197–219). Washington, DC: The National Science Teachers Association.

Spillane, J. P. (2001). All students: Policy, practitioners, and practice. In S. Fuhrman (Ed.), *From the capitol to the classroom: Standards-based reform in the states.* National Society for the Study of Education Yearbook. Chicago: University of Chicago Press.

Spillane, J. P., Diamond, J., Walker, L., Halverson, R., & Loyisa, J. (2001). Urban school leadership for elementary science instruction: Identifying and activating resources in an undervalued school subject. *Journal of Research in Science Teaching, 38*(8), 918–940.

Spillane, J. P., Reiser, B., & Reimer, T. (2002). Policy implementation and cognition: Reframing and refocusing implementation research. *Review of Educational Research, 72*(3), 387–431.

Spiro, R., Feltovich, P., Jackson, M., & Coulson, R. (1991). Cognitive flexibility, constructivism, and hypertext: Random access instruction for advanced knowledge acquisition in ill-structured domains. *Educational Technology, 31*(5), 24–33.

Spitulnik, M., Corliss, S., & Kirkpatrick, D. (2008, April). *Developing school-based mentors to support technology-enhanced science reform.* Paper presented at the annual meeting of the American Educational Research Association, New York.

Spitulnik, M. W., & Linn, M. C. (2006, April). *Professional development and teachers' curriculum customizations: Supporting science in diverse middle schools.* Paper presented at the annual meeting of the National Association for Research in Science Teaching, San Francisco.

Spitulnik, M. W., & Linn, M. C. (2007). *Professional development and teachers' curriculum customizations: Supporting science in diverse middle schools.* MODELS Report. Berkeley: University of California.

Squire, K., MaKinster, J., Barnett, M., Luehmann, A., & Barab, S. (2003). Designed curriculum and local culture: Acknowledging the primacy of classroom culture. *Science Education, 87*(4), 468–489.

Standard & Poor's. (2005). *Fact of fiction: Data tell the true story behind America's urban school districts.* Retrieved November 21, 2005, from http://admin.schoolmatters.com/SMResourceHandler/resourcehandler.res?rtype=file&rpid=20354327&flnm=Data%20Tell%20the%20True%20Story%20Behind%20America's%20Urban%20School%20Districts.pdf

Stein, M. K., Hubbard, L., & Mehan, H. (2004). Reform ideas that travel far afield: The two cultures of reform in New York's District #2 and San Diego. *Journal of Educational Change, 5*(2), 161–197.

Stein, M. K., & Nelson, B. S. (2003). Leadership content knowledge. *Educational Evaluation and Policy Analysis, 25*(4), 423–448.

Stern, L., & Ahlgren, A. (2002). Analysis of students' assessments in middle school curriculum materials: Aiming precisely at benchmarks and standards. *Journal of Research in Science Teaching, 39*(9), 889–910.

Stern, L., & Roseman, J. (2004). Can middle school science textbooks help students learn important ideas? *Journal of Research in Science Teaching, 41*(6), 538–568.

Stevens, S., & Davis, E. A. (2007, April). *New elementary teachers' knowledge and beliefs about instructional representations: A longitudinal study.* Paper presented at the annual meeting of the National Association for Research in Science Teaching, New Orleans, LA.

Stewart, J. (1983). Student problem solving in high school genetics. *Science Education, 67,* 523–540.

Stine, D. D. (2007). *Congressional Research Service report for Congress: U.S. civilian space policy priorities: Reflections 50 years after Sputnik* (No. RL34263). Washington, DC: Congressional Research Service.

Strike, K. A., & Posner, G. J. (1985). A conceptual change view of learning and understanding. In L. H. West & A. L. Pines (Eds.), *Cognitive structure and conceptual change* (pp. 211–231). Orlando, FL: Academic Press.

Strong, L. (1962). Chemistry as a science in the high school. *The School Review, 70,* 44–50.

Sutherland, L., & Shwartz, Y. (2007). Discussion types. In *IQWST materials* (frontmatter). Ann Arbor: University of Michigan.

Swain, M., & Lapkin, S. (1991). Heritage language children in an English–French bilingual program. *The Canadian Modern Language Review, 47*(4), 635–641.

Tate, E. D. (2005, April). *Hanging with Friends, Velocity Style! Learning from multiple representations of velocity.* Poster presented at the annual meeting of the American Educational Research Association, Montreal, Canada.

Tate, E. D. (2007, April). *Designing community based biology curriculum: How do students learn and make decisions about the asthma problem in their communities?* Poster presented at the annual meeting of the American Educational Research Association, Chicago.

Tate, E. D. (2008, April). *The impact of an asthma curriculum on students' integrated understanding of biology.* Poster presented at the annual meeting of American Educational Research Association, New York.

Teruel, E. (2006). *Examining the effects of a technology-enhanced inquiry-based curriculum on student understanding of evolution.* Unpublished master's thesis, University of California, Berkeley.

Textual Tools Study Group at the University of Michigan. (2006). Developing scientific literacy through the use of literacy teaching strategies. In R. Douglas, M. P. Klentschy, K. Worth, & W. Binder (Eds.), *Linking science and literacy in the K–8 classroom* (pp. 261–285). Arlington, VA: National Science Teachers Association Press.

Thomas, W., & Collier, V. (1995). Language minority achievement and program effectiveness. *California Association for Bilingual Education Newsletter, 17,* 19–24.

Thompson, P. W. (2002). Didactic objects and didactic models in radical constructivism. In K. Gravemeijer, R. Lehrer, B. v. Oers, & L. Verschaffel (Eds.), *Symbolizing and modeling in mathematics education* (pp. 191–212). Dordrecht: Kluwer.

Thorndike, R. L. (1963). *The concepts of over- and under-achievement.* New York: Bureau of Publications, Teachers College, Columbia University.

Tinker, R., & Krajcik, J. (Eds.). (2001). *Portable technologies: Science learning in context.* New York: Kluwer Academic/Plenum.

Tobin, K., Seiler, G., & Walls, E. (1999). Reproduction of social class in the teaching and learning of science in urban high schools. *Research in Science Education, 29,* 171–187.

Toulmin, S. (1958). *The uses of argument.* Cambridge, UK: Cambridge University Press.

Treagust, D. F., Jacobowitz, R., Gallagher, J., & Parker, J. (2001). Using assessment as a guide in teaching for understanding: A case study of a middle school science class learning about sound. *Science Education, 85,* 137–157.

Trends in International Mathematics and Science Study. (1995). *IEA's Third International Mathematics and Science Study. TIMSS science items for the middle school years: Released set for Population 2 (seventh and eighth grades).* Retrieved May 31, 2008, from http://timss.bc.edu/timss1995i/TIMSSPDF/BSItems.pdf

Tversky, B., Morrison, J. B., & Betrancourt, M. (2002). Animation: Can it facilitate? *International Journal of Human–Computer Studies, 57,* 247–262.

Tyack, D., & Cuban, L. (1995). *Tinkering toward utopia: A century of public school reform.* Cambridge, MA: Harvard University Press.

U.S. Department of Education. (2002). *The growing numbers of limited English proficient students 1991/92–2001/02.* Office of English Language Acquisition, Language Enhancement and Academic Achievement for Limited English Proficient Students. Retrieved July 10, 2008, from National Clearinghouse for English Language Acquisition and Language Instruction Educational Programs, http://www.ncela.gwu.edu/policy/states/state poster.pdf

van den Akker, J. (1999). Principles and methods of development research. In J. van den Akker, N. Nieveen, R. M. Branch, K. L. Gustafson, & T. Plomp (Eds.), *Design methodology and developmental research in education and training* (pp. 1–14). Dordrecht: Kluwer.

Varma, K. (2006, April). *Documenting teacher learning in the TELS center research: Examining changes in teacher beliefs and practices.* Paper presented at the annual meeting of the National Association for Research in Science Teaching, San Francisco.

Varma, K., Husic, F., & Linn, M. C. (in press). Targeted support for using technology-enhanced science inquiry modules. *Journal of Science Education and Technology.* ("Online First" version available at http://www.springerlink.com/content/n73rm61414754 267/?p=d73cce3bf9da4649b0f2594b7f111caa&pi=9)

Ven de Ven, A., Polley, D., Garud, R., & Venkataraman, S. (1999). *The innovation journey.* New York: Oxford University Press.

Villegas, A. M., & Lucas, T. (2002). Preparing culturally responsive teachers: Rethinking the curriculum. *Journal of Teacher Education, 53*(1), 20–32.

Vosniadou, S., & Brewer, W. (1992). Mental models of the earth: A study of conceptual change in childhood. *Cognitive Psychology, 24,* 535–558.

Warren, B., Ballenger, C., Ogonowski, M., Rosebery, A. S., & Hudicourt-Barnes, J. (2001). Rethinking diversity in learning science: The logic of everyday sense-making. *Journal of Research in Science Teaching, 38*(5), 529–552.

Weizman, A., & Fortus, D. (2007a, April). *The driving question board: A tool to support inquiry-based learning in diverse classes.* Paper presented at the annual meeting of the National Association for Research in Science Teaching, New Orleans, LA.

Weizman, A., & Fortus, D. (2007b, April). *Using scientific models to learn about shadows.* Paper presented at the annual meeting of the National Association for Research in Science Teaching, New Orleans, LA.

Wellesley College Center for Research on Women. (1992). *How schools shortchange girls* (Executive Summary). Washington, DC: American Association of University Women Educational Foundation.

White, B. Y. (1984). Designing computer activities to help physics students understand Newton's laws of motion. *Cognition and Instruction, 1,* 69–108.

White, B. Y., & Frederiksen, J. R. (1998). Inquiry, modeling, and metacognition: Making science accessible to all students. *Cognition and Instruction, 16*(1), 3–118.

Wilensky, U. (1999). *NetLogo* [Computer Program]. Evanston, IL: Center for Connected Learning and Computer-Based Modeling, Northwestern University. http://ccl.north western.edu/netlogo.

Wilensky, U., & Reisman, K. (2006). Thinking like a wolf, a sheep or a firefly: Learning biology through constructing and testing computational theories—An embodied modeling approach. *Cognition & Instruction, 24*(2), 171–209.

Willig, A. (1985). A meta-analysis of selected studies on the effectiveness of bilingual education. *Review of Educational Research, 55,* 269–317.

Wilson, M. R. (2005). *Constructing measures: An item response modeling approach.* Mahwah, NJ: Erlbaum.

Wilson, M. R., & Berenthal, M. W. (2006). *Systems for state science assessment.* Washington, DC: National Academies Press.

Wilson, S. M., & Berne, J. (1999). Teacher learning and the acquisition of professional knowledge: An examination of research on contemporary professional development. *Review of Research in Education, 24,* 173–209.

Wing, J. Y. (2004). *Closing the racial achievement gap in diverse California schools.* UC/Accord Public Policy Series PB-003-0504. Los Angeles: University of California. Retrieved May 31, 2008, from http://ucaccord.gseis.ucla.edu/publications/pubs/wing.pdf

Wood, D. (2007). Teachers' learning communities: Catalysts for change or a new infrastructure for the status quo? *Teachers College Record, 109*(3), 699–739.

Wood, D., Bruner, J., & Ross, G. (1976). The role of tutoring in problem solving. *Journal of Child Psychology and Psychiatry and Allied Disciplines, 17,* 89–100.

Yager, R. E., & Penick, J. E. (1986). Perceptions of four age groups toward science classes, teachers, and the value of science. *Science Education, 70*(4), 355–363.

Zacharia, Z., & Calabrese Barton, A. (2004). Urban middle-school students' attitudes toward a defined science. *Science Education, 88,* 197–222.

Zhang, B. H., Liu, X., & Krajcik, J. S. (2006). Expert models and modeling processes associated with a computer modeling tool. *Science Education, 90*(4), 579–604.

Zhao, Y., Pugh, K., Sheldon, S., & Byers, J. (2002). Conditions for classroom technology innovations. *Teachers College Record, 104*(3), 482–515.

About the Editors and Contributors

YAEL KALI is a Senior Researcher in the Department of Education in Science and Technology, Technion—Israel Institute of Technology. She studies how technology-enhanced learning environments affect student learning at different age levels (middle school to higher education). Her research focuses on the role of design principles for synthesizing design research and for guiding the design of technology-enhanced learning environments.

MARCIA C. LINN is a Professor of Development and Cognition specializing in education in mathematics, science, and technology in the Graduate School of Education at the University of California, Berkeley. She directs the NSF-funded Technology-Enhanced Learning in Science (TELS) Center. Linn is a member of the National Academy of Education and a Fellow of the American Association for the Advancement of Science. She received the Council of Scientific Society Presidents first award for Excellence in Educational Research.

JO ELLEN ROSEMAN, Director of Project 2061, has been involved in the design, testing, and dissemination of Project 2061's science literacy reform tools since 1989. She directs the NSF-funded Center for Curriculum Materials in Science (CCMS). Roseman participated in the development of *Benchmarks for Science Literacy*, which describes specific K–12 learning goals, and she led Project 2061's evaluative studies of science and mathematics textbooks. She holds a Ph.D. in biochemistry from Johns Hopkins University.

JANE BOWYER is a Professor and Dean of the Mills College School of Education. Her primary interests are the role of educational leadership and professional development in science and technology. Bowyer directs research on educational leadership and professional development in science and technology, with a focus on how educational leaders can best support the use of instructional technology for improving science education.

DOUGLAS B. CLARK is an Associate Professor of Science Education at Arizona State University. He directs the TODOS (Technology Opening Diverse Opportunities for Science) research group, which studies how computer and Internet technology can improve equity in science learning. The TODOS group investigates computer-based supports for scientific discourse, technology-based language supports in online environments, and core issues regarding conceptual change and knowledge structure coherence.

ALLAN COLLINS is a Professor of Education and Social Policy at Northwestern University. He is best known in psychology for his work on semantic memory and mental models; in artificial intelligence for his work on plausible reasoning and intelligent tutoring systems; and in education for his work on inquiry teaching, cognitive apprenticeship, situated learning, epistemic games, and systemic validity in educational testing.

ELIZABETH A. DAVIS, Associate Professor of Science Education at the University of Michigan, studies elementary science teacher education and how educational technologies and curriculum materials can promote teacher learning. Her research integrates aspects of science education, teacher education, and the learning sciences. Davis earned a Ph.D. from the University of California, Berkeley.

GEORGE E. DeBOER, Deputy Director of Project 2061 since 2002, joined the staff from the Division of Elementary, Secondary, and Informal Science Education of the National Science Foundation. He is also Professor of Education Emeritus at Colgate University. DeBoer's primary research interests lie in clarifying the goals of the science curriculum, studying what students know and how they think about science, and analyzing the history of science education, including the many meanings of science literacy. He has written extensively on these topics and holds a Ph.D. in Science Education from Northwestern University.

DAVID FORTUS, Senior Scientist at the Weizmann Institute of Science in Israel, studies ways to support the learning and teaching of scientific practices, in particular modeling and data gathering, organization, and analysis. His dissertation on Design-Based Science from the University of Michigan was awarded the Outstanding Dissertation Award by the National Association for Research in Science Teaching (NARST) and by the Educational Psychology Division of the American Psychological Association.

JAMES J. GALLAGHER served as Professor of Science Education at Michigan State University for 31 years, working with prospective and practicing teachers of science at the middle school and high school levels, in the United States and in several developing nations. He served as a Co-Director of the Center for Curriculum Materials in Science and recently co-directed a national study of leadership development in science and mathematics education. He received his Ed.D. from Harvard University.

LIBBY GERARD is a graduate student at the Mills College School of Education. Her research focuses on professional development in the area of technology and science. Her work examines the design of professional learning communities and their impact on leadership for scaling and sustaining technology-enhanced curricular innovation in middle schools and high schools.

PAUL HORWITZ, Director of the Modeling Center at the Concord Consortium, is interested in the application of information technology to education. Much of his research has focused on the use of computer-based models for teaching students how to use mental models as tools for reasoning and problem solving in various domains of science and mathematics. Recently he has turned his attention to analyzing students' manipulation of these computer models in order to generate reliable inferences concerning their understanding of the underlying domain.

FREDA HUSIC manages Education Solutions at PASCO Scientific, designing and developing inquiry-based laboratory activities for middle school and high school sciences. She was Program Manager for the Technology-Enhanced Learning in Science (TELS) Center at the University of California, Berkeley, where she coordinated implementation of online science units and contributed to TELS research. Husic directed creation and development of all instructional materials, manuals, tutorials, and help systems for Apple products. She has received numerous national and international awards for technical communication.

MARY KOPPAL is the Communications Director for Project 2061 of the American Association for the Advancement of Science. She is responsible for the project's publishing and outreach programs. Previously, Koppal was the publisher for the National Academy of Sciences' *Issues in Science and Technology,* where she began her work as the associate publisher/circulation manager. From 1987 to 1994, she was responsible for the overall business and administrative operation of this award-winning national science and technology policy journal.

JOSEPH S. KRAJCIK, Professor of Science Education and Associate Dean for Research in the School of Education at the University of Michigan, focuses his research on re-engineering science classrooms so that all students can engage in finding solutions to complex problems through inquiry and the use of technologies. He is an author of numerous papers on project-based science, inquiry learning, and the use of technology in science classrooms. Krajcik received his Ph.D. in Science Education from the University of Iowa.

HEE-SUN LEE is an Assistant Professor of Science Education at Tufts University. She conceptualized, implemented, and analyzed assessments that measure inquiry-based learning of subjects that students have explored using information technology. Lee's work combines knowledge integration theory as a cognitive foundation, cutting-edge psychometric techniques, and inquiry-promoting pedagogy. She has generated information that TELS researchers and teachers are using to modify instruction and revise curricular materials.

RONALD W. MARX is a Professor of Educational Psychology and Dean of Education at the University of Arizona. His research focuses on how classrooms can be sites for learning that is highly motivated and cognitively engaging. Since 1994, Marx has been engaged in large-scale urban school reform in Detroit and Chicago. With his appointment as Dean of the University of Arizona College of Education in 2003, he has been working to link the College's research, teaching, and outreach activities closely to P–12 schools and school districts.

DAVID McLAUGHLIN is a graduate student in the College of Education at Michigan State University. His research interests include preservice science education and access to basic educational opportunities in international settings.

KATHERINE L. McNEILL is an Assistant Professor of Science Education at Boston College. She is interested in helping students with diverse backgrounds become interested in science and learn both science content and scientific inquiry practices. Specifically, she has focused on how curricular scaffolds, activity structures, and teacher instructional strategies can support students in engaging in scientific explanation and argumentation. McNeill earned her Ph.D. in Science Education at the University of Michigan.

ROY D. PEA is Professor of Education and the Learning Sciences at Stanford University, Co-Director of the Stanford Center for Innovations in Learning, and Director of a new Ph.D. Program in Learning Sciences and Technology Design. Since 1981, Pea has been active in exploring, defining, and researching new issues in how information technologies can fundamentally support and advance learning and teaching, with particular focus on topics in science, mathematics, and technology education.

BRIAN J. REISER, Professor of Education and Social Policy, focuses on the design and study of investigation environments that support reflective inquiry, and on the teaching practices that support inquiry. He heads the BGuILE Project, developing inquiry support tools for students investigating biological phenomena, including topics in ecosystems and selection, behavioral ecology, and cell structure and function. Reiser, who previously served as Chair of the Learning Sciences Ph.D. program, holds a Ph.D. in Psychology from Yale University.

TAMAR RONEN-FUHRMANN is a graduate student in the Department of Education in Science and Technology, Technion—Israel Institute of Technology. Her research focuses on investigating how people learn to design educational technologies, and on the role of the Design Principles Database in supporting the design processes.

JAMES D. SLOTTA builds on a background in physics and cognitive psychology to design and investigate Web-based learning environments. He studies how these environments can add inquiry activities to the K–12 curriculum and improve student learning. Slotta guides partnerships with curriculum developers, technology designers, educational researchers, and school districts. He works with the Concord Consortium to design and implement open source learning environments.

ERIKA D. TATE is a graduate student at the Graduate School of Education at the University of California, Berkeley. Her research focuses on the impact of community-based science curriculum on students' science learning and decision making. She explores students' understanding of asthma-related physiology and how to determine what counts as evidence in community advocacy.

ROBERT TINKER is the President of The Concord Consortium, a nonprofit organization dedicated to improving learning opportunities for all students in science and mathematics. He is internationally recognized as a pioneer in using educational technology for scientific inquiry. He developed the MBL and Network Science concepts and has directed numerous educational research projects. Tinker founded the Concord Consortium and pioneered its INTEC and Virtual High School projects.

KEISHA VARMA is a Researcher at the University of California, Berkeley. She studies teacher learning and development, focusing on how technology-enhanced inquiry instruction impacts teachers' formative assessment practices. She also studies how teachers' knowledge about inquiry instruction and student learning develops as they use technology in their classrooms. Varma designs teacher professional development experiences to encourage an integrated understanding of assessment, student learning, and teaching practices.

Credits

Grateful acknowledgment is made for permission to reprint the following:

Figures 2.1, 3.1, 4.1, 4.2, 4.3, 5.1, 5.2, 5.3, 8.1, and 8.2 from Technology Enhanced Learning in Science (TELS) Center online curricula.

Figures 2.2, 2.3, and 2.4 from American Association for the Advancement of Science (AAAS) Project 2061.

Figure 4.4 from Fortus, David, *Teacher's Guide*, IQWST "Seeing the Light: Can I Believe My Eyes?" unit.

Figures 4.5 and 4.6 from Anderson, C. W., & Smith, E. L. (1983). *Transparencies on Light: Teacher's Manual* (Research Series No. 130). East Lansing: Michigan State University, Institute for Research on Teaching.

Figures 5.4 and 5.5 from Curriculum Access System for Elementary Science (CASES) online learning environment for teachers. Copyright 2002 by the CASES Research Group, University of Michigan.

Figure 7.1 from American Association for the Advancement of Science (AAAS). (2007). *Atlas of Science Literacy: Project 2061* (Vol. 2). Washington, DC: American Association for the Advancement of Science and the National Science Teachers Association.

Figure 7.2 from American Association for the Advancement of Science (AAAS) Project 2061.

Figures 7.3 and 7.4 from Coffey, J., Douglas, R., & Stearns, C. (Eds.). (2008). *Assessing Science Learning: Perspectives from Research and Practice.* Arlington, VA: NSTA Press.

Figure 7.5 from *IQWST Materials* (frontmatter). Ann Arbor: University of Michigan.

Figure 7.7A from TIMSS Science Items for the Middle School Years. Released Set for Population 2 (Seventh and Eighth Grade). http://timss.bc.edu/timss1995i/TIMSSPDF/BSItems.pdf.

Table 3.3 from Sutherland, L., & Shwartz, Y. (2007). Discussion Types. In *IQWST Materials* (frontmatter). Ann Arbor: University of Michigan.

Table 4.3 from Weizman, A., & Fortus, D. (2007, April). *The Driving Question Board: A Tool to Support Inquiry-Based Learning.* Paper presented at the annual meeting of the National Association for Research in Science Teaching, New Orleans, LA.

Table 4.4 from Weizman, A., & Fortus, D. (2007, April). *Using Scientific Models to Learn About Shadows.* Paper presented at the annual meeting of the National Association for Research in Science Teaching, New Orleans, LA.

Index

SUBJECTS

CITED AUTHORS